The Magic Prism

The Magic Prism

*An Essay in the
Philosophy of Language*

Howard Wettstein

OXFORD
UNIVERSITY PRESS

2004

OXFORD
UNIVERSITY PRESS

Oxford New York
Auckland Bangkok Buenos Aires Cape Town Chennai
Dar es Salaam Delhi Hong Kong Istanbul Karachi Kolkata
Kuala Lumpur Madrid Melbourne Mexico City Mumbai Nairobi
São Paulo Shanghai Taipei Tokyo Toronto

Copyright © 2004 by Oxford University Press, Inc.

Published by Oxford University Press, Inc.,
198 Madison Avenue, New York, New York 10016
www.oup.com

Oxford is a registered trademark of Oxford University Press

Library of Congress Cataloging-in-Publication Data
Wettstein, Howard K.
The magic prism : an essay in the philosophy of language / Howard Wettstein.
p. cm.
Includes bibliographical references and index.
ISBN 0-19-516052-5
1. Language and languages—Philosophy. 2. Wittgenstein, Ludwig.
1889–1951—Contributions in philosophy of language. I. Title

P107.W48 2004
121'.68—dc21   2003042986

4/23/04

2 4 6 8 9 7 5 3 1
Printed in the United States of America
on acid-free paper

For
Barbara Wettstein

אֱמֹר לַחָכְמָה אֲחֹתִי אָתְּ
Say to Wisdom, "You are my Sister"
(Proverbs 7.4)

The truth is that man's capacity for symbol mongering in general and language in particular is so intimately part and parcel of his being human, of man's perceiving and knowing, of his very consciousness itself, that it is all but impossible for him to focus on the magic prism through which he sees everything else.

In order to see it, one must either be a Martian, or, if an earthling, sufficiently detached, marooned, bemused, wounded, crazy, one eyed and lucky enough to become a Martian for a second and catch a glimpse of it.

From "The Delta Factor," in A Message in the Bottle, *by Walker Percy*

In philosophy one is constantly tempted to invent a mythology of symbolism or of psychology, instead of simply saying what we all know.

From Philosophical Grammar, *by Ludwig Wittgenstein*

Acknowledgments

I wish to thank many people: teachers, students, colleagues, APA and colloquium lecturers, and those present at many talks I have given on these matters. A complete list is out of the question, but I do wish to offer special thanks to a number of people. My way of developing direct reference owes much to the ideas, criticisms, stimulation, and tremendous generosity of David Kaplan and John Perry. Joseph Almog and I spent years in which it seemed that we were constantly wrestling with these questions, and his influence is present in all sorts of ways and places in this book. Genoveva Marti, beginning when she was a graduate student and I was halfway across the country, engaged in an endless and endlessly helpful discussion.

My study of Wittgenstein began in the early 1980s; many of my direct reference colleagues probably thought I went off the deep end. By 1989, I was well into it and when I moved from Notre Dame to University of California, Riverside, I was fortunate to have a colleague, Larry Wright, who had been dwelling in Wittgenstein's thought for many years. Our discussions since then have been tremendously helpful, as have many others with my Riverside colleagues.

Jumping back many years, beginning in the 1960s, I have learned an enormous amount from the work in the philosophy of mind of my former teacher Arthur Collins. I see his influence here, not only but perhaps especially in the last two chapters, perhaps in ways he does not. Also beginning in those early days, I have learned much from discussions with Richard Mendelsohn, and more recently with David Braun, Paul Hoffman, and Martha Burns. Many thanks to Rodrigo de Castro, Orsolya Schreiner, and especially to Dillon Emerick for editorial assistance.

I am grateful beyond words to my wife, Barbara Wettstein. That this book took so long is a tribute to the lice comb that sits on my desk, something she gave me many years ago for just such a purpose. My children, Jonathan and Eve Wettstein, grew up with various drafts of this book as virtual siblings, without any trace of sibling rivalry. I thank them for their support and encouragement, and for so much more.

Contents

The Magic Prism

Introduction

The late twentieth century witnessed a revolution in the philosophy of language, the *direct reference* revolution. One of the magical things about this revolution is its relative invisibility; it is easy to miss. For many, both players and observers, something considerably less dramatic is at issue. They see direct reference as something more like an elaboration—albeit with considerable revision—of the insights of our teachers, Gottlob Frege and Bertrand Russell.

These players and observers are not wrong: direct reference, as it has been developed by advocates[1] and criticized by neo-Fregeans

---

[1] Leading advocates include Keith Donnellan, "Reference and Definite Descriptions," *The Philosophical Review* 75 (1966): 281–304, and "Proper Names and Identifying Descriptions," in D. Davidson and G. Harman, eds., *Semantics of Natural Language* (Dordecht, The Netherlands: Reidel, 1972); Saul Kripke, *Naming and Necessity* (Cambridge, Mass.: Harvard University Press, 1972); David Kaplan, "Dthat," in P. Cole, ed., *Pragmatics, Syntax and Semantics*, no. 9 (New York: Academic Press, 1978), and "Demonstratives: An Essay on Semantics, Logic, Metaphysics, and Epistemology of Demonstratives and Other Indexicals," in J. Almog, J. Perry, and H. Wettstein, eds., *Themes from Kaplan* (Oxford: Oxford University Press, 1989); John Perry, "Frege on Demonstratives," *The Philosophical Review* 86 (1977): 474–97, and "The Problem of the Essential Indexical," *Noûs* 13 (1979): 3–21; Ruth Barcan Marcus, "Modalities and Intensional Languages," *Boston Studies in the Philosophy of Science*, vol. 1 (New York: Humanities Press, 1963).

In general these works are informed by the outlooks of Frege and Russell, but this varies from author to author.

and neo-Russellians,[2] shares much of the fathers' fundamental outlook on language and its philosophical study. Nevertheless, there
is subversion humming beneath the surface. The direct reference
literature, conservative as it has been, repeatedly verges on questions that are genuinely fundamental; it edges up to disagreements
about the basics.

My aim in this book is to engage the Frege–Russell tradition[3]
at such a fundamental level. To make things manageable I'll focus
on Frege; Russell will appear when his differences with Frege make
a difference. The perspective on language that I will develop here
radically rejects the tradition's[4] individualism as well as its "thought
orientation," its prioritizing thought over language. In place of
these tendencies, I will emphasize linguistic practice, a social phenomenon. The reference of words—focal in late twentieth-century
philosophy of language and in this book—is not to be grounded in
the mind's grasp of the things it thinks about. Quite the contrary,
one of the ways we become equipped to think about things is by
having words that, as our practices go, stand for things. Linguistic
practice, a social phenomenon, thus becomes pivotal. And the philosophy of language takes on an anthropological bent; its quarry is
our linguistic practice.

This book has been many years in the making. Early in the

[2] The taxonomy here is to some extent arbitrary, but one might well count the
following as neo-Fregean although there are Russellian elements sometimes represented in their work: John McDowell, "On Sense and Reference of a Proper Name,"
Mind 86 (1977): 159–85; Diana Ackerman, "Proper Names, Propositional Attitudes,
and Non-Descriptive Connotations," *Philosophical Studies* 35 (1979): 55–69; Gareth
Evans, *Varieties of Reference* (Oxford: Oxford University Press, 1982), and "Understanding Demonstratives," in H. Parret and J. Bouveresse, eds., *Meaning and Understanding* (Berlin: W. de Gruyter, 1981); Christopher Peacocke, *Sense and Content*
(Oxford: Oxford University Press, 1983); Graeme Forbes, "Indexicals and Intension-
ality: A Fregean Perspective," *The Philosophical Review* 96 (1987): 3–31, and "The
Indispensability of Sinn," *The Philosophical Review* 99 (1990): 535–63.

The following may be counted as neo-Russellian, but one could also count
some or all as representing developments within direct reference: Nathan Salmon,
Frege's Puzzle (Cambridge, Mass.: MIT Press, 1986); Scott Soames, "Direct Reference, Propositional Attitudes, and Semantic Content," *Philosophical Topics* 15
(1987): 44–87; Mark Richard, *Propositional Attitudes*((Cambridge: Cambridge University Press, 1990); also various articles in N. Salmon and S. Soames, eds., *Propositions and Attitudes* (Oxford: Oxford University Press, 1988).

[3] In chapter 2 I argue that Frege and Russell propound versions of the same
fundamental idea, an idea with which my version of direct reference takes strong
issue. This is the "cognitive fix requirement" which I will discuss directly.

[4] I see the Frege-Russell tradition in the philosophy of language as in many ways
reflecting the broader tradition of modern philosophy. See chapter 3 for more on this
matter.

1980s it became apparent to me that I was thinking about these matters very differently from the way my direct reference colleagues were, not to mention the neo-traditionalists. I had already written a dissertation[5] and published a number of essays on the subject,[6] but I wished to develop and elaborate my overall conception further, in a book-length treatment. I believed, moreover, that my approach had something different to say about a number of crucial questions that seemed at once overworked and inadequately understood, for example, about belief and the other "propositional attitudes." My outlook also had implications for more general, less explored questions, for example, that of the explanatory adequacy of direct reference as opposed to the Fregean approach.

Much in my current outlook reflects the profound influence of Wittgenstein. For years I avoided Wittgenstein's work almost entirely. I was systemically allergic to the jargon and the idiosyncratic, perhaps indulgent, style of exposition; I couldn't bear talk of language games, forms of life, meaning as use, and the rest. But as I explain in chapter 5, I eventually made contact with Wittgenstein, and the experience was transforming. Wittgenstein helped me to understand more deeply what it was that I found troubling about traditional ways in philosophy and specifically in the philosophy of language. And Wittgenstein's thought suggested ways forward.

Given these remarks, it is important that I explain Wittgenstein's ideas as I make use of them. This I promise to do. Wittgenstein does not show up *in propria persona* until chapter 5, but there I will express as clearly as I can what I want to take from his work. And why I think Wittgenstein's insights ought to be focal in our reflections on language and thought, and even, surprisingly, in the development of direct reference.

This introduction provides a way into my project through the notion of a proposition. The contrast with Frege will loom large, and since my Frege may not be yours, I'll also remark on the topic of interpretation in the history of philosophy. I'll conclude with a sketch of what's to come.

1. Propositions

Since my undergraduate days, I've been taken with the notion of a proposition. What are propositions? Many writers in the early twen-

---

[5] "What Propositions Could Not Be," City University of New York, 1976.
[6] Collected in *Has Semantics Rested on a Mistake? and Other Essays* (Palo Alto, Cal.: Stanford University Press, 1995).

tieth century and before use the term synonymously with "declarative sentence": Frege, Russell, and Wittgenstein all employ this usage at least part of the time. But occasionally for some of those same writers—and increasingly this has become the practice—propositions are not the sentences themselves but nonlinguistic abstract things that sentences express, or that we express by uttering sentences. And it has become common to speak of propositions as the *contents* of our sentences.[7]

The metaphor of containment—content is what is contained—is worth keeping one's eye on. The metaphor has often hardened, or deadened, to the point that philosophers are not conscious of anything metaphorical here. (Or, if it's really hardened, there is nothing metaphorical left.) It's a fact, they assume, that sentences have contents, the crucial question being what sort of theory of content one adopts. It seems important to me, on the contrary, to keep before our minds that content-talk is metaphorical; or at least that it begins in metaphor. I will return to this at various points throughout the book.

Focusing on propositions will allow me to provide a preliminary contrast between direct reference and traditional philosophy of language. In my 1976 dissertation, I was moving away from Frege—my candidate for the foremost advocate of the tradition[8]—specifically away from Frege's conception of *thoughts*, his own terminology for propositions. My sense that something very different was needed was reinforced when shortly thereafter I began to read David Kaplan's work. His work was particularly exciting because where I had a rough sense of a new conception of proposition, Kaplan appeared to elaborate a theoretical idea, the *singular proposition,*[9] a radically non-Fregean take on propositions, one that quickly became direct reference orthodoxy.

Attention to propositions will also allow me to underscore what is distinctive about my outlook. For by the end of this book—

---

[7] Propositions are also said to be the objects of the propositional attitudes. More on this in the first chapter, and especially in chapters 8 and 9, where I elaborate my own view of the attitudes.

[8] I am with Wittgenstein here. In the *Philosophical Investigations,* and earlier in the *Blue and Brown Books,* Frege is both respected and criticized in just such terms.

[9] More correctly, Kaplan's explication of propositional content makes a distinction between singular and general propositions. Both can have objects and properties as constituents. For most of my purposes I will restrict my attention to singular propositions.

contrary to what I would have guessed early in the project—propositions turn out to have no significant role in my story. Indeed, I am probably further from those who theorize in terms of propositions, even those of direct reference stripe, than the latter are from their Fregean antagonists.

To start at the beginning, early along, as an undergraduate and then a graduate student, I was of two minds about propositions. On one hand, it seemed that talk of what we assert, the thoughts we express, the contents of our sentences, ought to be unproblematic. After all, we say things, express our thoughts.

At the same time, propositions seemed problematic. The most forceful problem early along concerned the fact that propositions—like numbers, sets, and the like—are abstract entities. It seemed innocent enough to speak about *what someone said*. But it was troubling that such plain talk seemed to involve commitment to a realm other than the natural world, if such an additional realm is indeed the home of abstracta. This didn't seem quite a good enough reason to stop speaking of things asserted. But it certainly gave pause.

Some of the literature's best-known problems about propositions were difficult for me to appreciate; they had little force for me. Here's an example: Quine frowned upon propositions for, as he liked to say, their identity conditions are unclear: in many cases, it's hard to say whether two sentences express precisely the same thing or not. This sounds right;[10] but how exactly does it lead to denying propositions? Lots of other, relatively uncontroversial, sorts of things suffer from the same malady—ships, people, mountains, and the like. Quine's point, I supposed, was somehow a consequence of something more deeply buried in his overall outlook. But I didn't quite see what that was. And certainly I didn't see why it went without saying.

My interest in propositions led me in graduate school to Richard Cartwright's classic essay "Propositions."[11] I had been told that Cartwright advanced a theory of propositions. I had no idea what such a theory might look like, but the promise of this virtual pot of gold was enough to keep me going for quite a while. In the end,

---

[10] Though note that the problem mentioned seems not merely about criteria of identity but about something arguably more serious: our inability to make discriminating judgments. Even if in practice we could make such judgments with confidence, it's still another thing to sort out the criteria to which we appeal.

[11] In R. Butler, ed., *Analytical Philosophy* (First Series) (Oxford: Blackwell, 1966).

Cartwright's essay was indeed a gold mine, but the advertised theory failed to materialize. Not that Cartwright himself advertised any such thing. Pondering Cartwright's incisive thought on the matter was helpful in all sorts of ways and led me to Frege.

I called my dissertation "What Propositions Could Not Be"; it was largely a series of applications of Benacerraf's central form of argument in "What Numbers Could Not Be."[12] I advanced nothing like a theory of propositions, but I did argue that various contenders would not do, most notably Frege's candidate for propositions—his *thoughts*, the senses of sentences.[13] And there was a positive side— what I earlier called a rough sense—one that, as I was happily to learn, found resonance in the work of people like Keith Donnellan, David Kaplan, Saul Kripke, Ruth Marcus, and John Perry.

At the time of my dissertation writing, however, most of their work was either not yet widely available or formulated in an idiom that made it difficult for me to appreciate. Kripke's *Naming and Necessity*, for example, was circulating when I began my dissertation, and I knew people who with considerable excitement heard the original lectures. But I couldn't for the life of me see what *rigid designation*, Kripke's notion concerning referential stability across possible worlds, had to do with the issues of concern to me.[14]

Donnellan's work was different. I had studied it with great interest. It seemed immediately relevant, even motivated by concerns with which I felt considerable sympathy. That was no trivial matter. Among the philosophers with whom I had contact, Quine exerted something of a dominating influence. And so Donnellan's taking seriously many of the very things for which Quineans had little use was like fresh air.

My interest in propositions and my developing conviction that Frege's sense-reference picture was inadequate led me in my disser-

---

[12] The stimulation was provided by Cartwright. He dismisses a related kind of argument, and it seemed to me that he did so prematurely. This led to Benacerraf, who develops the form of argument with great care. Benacerraf's essay is widely anthologized. It appeared originally in *Philosophical Review*, (JA) 74, 1965: 47–73.

[13] Frege's view is that thoughts were the senses of sentences that were "complete in every respect." See Frege's essay, "The Thought," trans. M. Quinton, in P. F. Strawson, ed., *Philosophical Logic* (Oxford: Oxford University Press, 1967).

[14] I was wrong. Kripke's notion of rigidity was certainly relevant to my concerns. But making rigidity the central notion still seems to me to divert attention from the issues at the core. Arguing, as Kripke does, that proper names are rigid does not seem like a frontal assault on the tradition, which is Kripke's apparent aim. Indeed, neo-traditionalists subsequently embraced the idea that names are rigid and sought to accommodate it within their own framework. This is not to endorse those

tation to what we now call, following David Kaplan, *direct reference*. Indexical expressions—unambiguous words like 'I', 'she', 'that', 'here', 'now',[15] the references of which vary with context—were, I argued, devices of reference but did not fit Frege's model. We do not associate them with anything like Fregean senses;[16] they are instead like pointing devices.

And just as indexicals had no associated Fregean senses, the propositions that we assert by the use of such expressions fail to contain such senses. When I say, "She is a famous novelist," it is not the *sense* of 'she' but the *reference* that figures in what I assert.[17] Nor is it only indexicals that violate Frege's strictures. If Donnellan is correct, even definite descriptions, at least when they function "referentially," do so as well. This idea was exciting: Definite descriptions, Frege's own paradigm referring expression, don't fit his model.

There is a famous dispute between Frege and Russell on the nature of propositions about which I will say more in the first two chapters. Frege—his is the classical idea—saw propositions as thoroughly conceptual entities, constituted by senses. Russell, no friend of senses, saw propositional constituents as the references of linguistic expressions: particulars or universals. I was moving in Russell's direction. And, as I came to see, Kaplan had reintroduced Russell's conception, now dubbed *singular propositions*.[18]

Kaplan's idea was theoretically refined: A singular proposition is an abstract entity with ordered constituents. My idea was more impressionistic: The referent, and not any sort of concept or sense, "figures in" what is asserted. At first and for a long while, I saw Kaplan's idea as representing a major step forward. For reasons I'll

---

accommodations; the moves often seem strained. But it is to say that insensitivity to rigidity does not seem like the most powerful indictment of the tradition.

[15] Throughout this book, I use single quotes to mention single words and expressions, double quotes for just about everything else including mentioning sentences, quoting utterances, and referring to concepts, meanings, and the like.

[16] I argue in chapter 5 that views like Kaplan's and John Perry's share too much of Frege's picture. To anticipate my discussion, Kaplan's *characters*, while they admittedly differ in some respects from Fregean senses, function in many ways just like senses.

[17] This compresses a discussion from my essay "Indexical Reference and Propositional Content," in *Has Semantics Rested on a Mistake? and Other Essays*.

[18] In simple cases of subject-predicate or relational sentences the propositions expressed are *singular*. Other object/property containing sentences, for example, quantified sentences, are called by Kaplan *general propositions*. But as I said above, I won't be careful to mention the general ones.

discuss later,[19] I no longer think so. For one thing, my formulation
has a certain virtue: It accommodates views, like my present one,
in which propositions play no role. For to say that the referent is
what figures in what was asserted may come to no more than saying that the predicate is applied directly to the referent.[20]

As I've said, by the end of this book propositions no longer figure in my way of explaining or developing direct reference. This
development is very gradual. The book begins with the perspectives
of Frege and Russell, for whom propositions— the contents of our
utterances and thoughts—are philosophically central. By the mid-
dle of the book, however, we find ourselves increasingly aware of
the metaphorical character of "content" talk. This fact should not
by itself make one skeptical about *content*. But it may—and here
it will—prompt the question of precisely what work *content* is doing in the philosophy of language (and mind). Even in the end, I
don't want to deny the utility of the metaphor—no doubt it's con-
venient to speak, for example, of the single thing that speakers of
different languages can assert. The question, though, is whether the
metaphor, or its remains in a philosophical theory of content, does
any serious and needed explanatory work.[21]

2. My Frege and Yours

Here is a story from David Kaplan: In the course of his lecturing in
Oxford on direct reference and Frege, he was told that Frege held

---

[19] See my discussion in chapter 10, section 3.2, where I suggest that Kaplan's
ordered pair conception fails to provide more than a model, a representation, or singular proposition.

[20] I don't claim theoretical refinement for this formulation either. But it does
get at a fundamental intuition, and it does so without talk of content or the like.

[21] Perhaps the first chink in the armor—see chapter 6—is my dispensing with
the idea of cognitive content that figures prominently in Frege's explanation of the
classical puzzle about informative identities. Direct reference advocates, under
Frege's influence, tried to refashion the idea of cognitive content so as to make it
kosher. All manner of Frege-style explanations of informativeness ensue. But there
is, or so I argue, a much simpler way, one that involves no idea of cognitive content.

But cognitive content is one thing, semantic content—propositions—is quite
another. Frege, as I read him, identified the two, but as you will see in chapter 6,
the direct reference work of Kaplan and Perry makes it seem natural to distinguish
these sorts of contents. Even if one goes along with my rejection of cognitive contents in chapter 6, one has not yet rejected propositions, as I do later in the book.
Perhaps it would be more accurate to say, not that I reject propositions, but that I
do not rely on them in my account of the relevant phenomena. (The distinction
between cognitive and semantic content has worked its way in the literature into
new readings of Frege and new Frege-inspired views. See Tyler Burge, "Sinning
Against Frege," *The Philosophical Review* 86 (1977): 159–85, and Burge's "Frege on

no such views (as the ones Kaplan attributed to him) and further-more that had Frege held such views, he would be right. Kaplan's joke makes oblique reference to a recent trend in historical scholar-ship.

Here's an example of the trend: There are a number of recent thought-provoking interpretations of Kant's ethical outlook that emphasize continuity with Aristotle. These contrast with a more extreme reading of Kant, one arguably based on a naïve reading of some of the relevant texts. The more extreme rendition emphasizes Kant's contention that the moral worth of an action is a function of its motivating intentions and of the extent to which the under-taking involves fighting inclination. Historical scholarship aside, the more extreme reading is philosophically interesting, for it em-bodies a radical alternative to Aristotle. If such a Kant didn't exist, he would be worth inventing, if just for the questions raised and the contrasts provided. In what follows, when I speak of Kant, I mean my hypothetical Kant.

Indeed, to say that Aristotle and Kant are opposed, even dramat-ically so, is to understate their differences. Indeed, they look at things so differently that it's no longer easy to play them off against one another, as we could if they shared a philosophical project and differed merely doctrinally. Their projects display a kind of light incommensurability.[22] Whereas Aristotle conducts a largely empiri-cal study of human flourishing, Kant explores a priori the theoreti-cal underpinnings of those duties incumbent on any rational being. For Aristotle the fundamental ethical question is not that of our obligations qua rational agents but rather that of our living well as intelligent, social organisms. For Kant, duty is the fundamental notion; much of what is involved in living well is not of specifically moral concern.

The trend of seeing historical continuities where others see fun-damental disagreement may result in a more nuanced understand-ing of major figures. Yet one needs to be careful not to lose insight

---

Sense and Linguistic Meaning," in D. Bell and N. Cooper, eds., *The Analytic Tradi-tion* (Oxford: Blackwell, 1990); Gareth Evans, *Varieties of Reference*, ed., J. Mc-Dowell (Oxford: Clarendon Press, 1982); Richard Heck, "The Sense of Communica-tion," *Mind* 104 (1995): 79–106; and Michael Luntley, *Contemporary Philosophy of Thought* (Oxford: Blackwell, 1999).

[22] "Light" by contrast with the sort of incommensurability of which Kuhn ap-peared to speak in *The Structure of Scientific Revolutions* (Chicago: University of Chicago Press, 1962). Kuhn's notion appeared to involve conceptual differences that were so radical as to preclude formulating the theses of one theory in the vocabulary of the other.

while (possibly) gaining accuracy. However one ultimately inter-
prets Kant (or, as we will see, Frege), it is important to explore the
radically divergent conceptions that reflect themselves in the (arguably) naïve interpretations.

To bring the interpretative trend home, the Frege you will meet
here is a more extreme character than often portrayed in recent
literature. Where I see stark contrast with Wittgenstein, others see
continuity. My reading is admittedly selective, especially attentive
to Frege's later, more philosophical essays like "On Sense and Reference" and "The Thought." It is, however, based upon what I hope
is a naïve and plain approach to that material. And, whether or
not I have him right, my Frege can certainly be recognized in later
Fregeans—the view is certainly in the air. Nor is it only a matter
of his later admirers; I would argue that Wittgenstein, in *Philosophical Investigations*, sees Frege as the foremost advocate for traditional philosophy.

Of course there may be much to be said for the recent continu-
ity-emphasizing interpretive work. At the same time, I would be
surprised if my reading fails to represent a strand in the actual
Frege's thought. In any case, my Frege—even if fictional—is a very
useful character to have around. In what follows, I'll refer to him
simply as Frege. Joking aside, for purposes of my project I remain
agnostic on the admittedly important question of the best overall
interpretation of Frege's thought.

My reconstruction of the debate in the philosophy of language
is thus doubly controversial. There is my reading of Frege as well
as my take on direct reference as revolutionary. The latter has a
prescriptive aspect, pushing the direct reference literature in a certain direction. I thus not only highlight the differences between
Frege and his recent critics; I will seek to widen the gap where
doing so is suggested by the natural flow of the ideas. My direct
reference advocate, as you will see, plays Aristotle to Frege's Kant.
The respective philosophical projects are strikingly different.[23]

My prescription aside, direct reference literature has often inti-
mated deep disagreement with the tradition. This disagreement
shares in the magic invisibility mentioned at the beginning of this
introduction: The divergence can be easy to miss, to misidentify as

---

[23] Such focus on larger issues underlying the direct reference critique decreases
the temptation to revert to traditional modes of thought when the going gets rough.
As we will see, it gets rough for the anti-Fregean when one turns to the topics of
chapters 6 through 9, the puzzles that for Frege and Russell were at the heart of this
subject.

being of merely local significance, a matter of detail. There is a clue to disagreement over fundamentals, one that deserves considerably more attention than it is usually afforded: talk at cross-purposes. Such talk is characteristic of certain philosophic debates. It is sometimes positively striking in ethical discussions between Kantians and Aristotelians. It is perhaps even more arresting—or more so to me, at least—in the debate between direct reference advocates and Fregeans, as I will comment on in the following section and more extensively in chapter 6. Instead of minimizing the significance of such failed communication, instead of trying to paraphrase the opponents so as to maximize conceptual contact, we might seize on such talk as revealing clues to possibly gaping underlying differences. When philosophers' projects—and not only their theoretical proposals—differ significantly, one can expect considerable talk at cross-purposes.

3. What's to Come

Chapter 1 introduces the reader—who I do not assume is a specialist in the philosophy of language[24]—to Frege's outlook. Chapter 2 takes one deeper into the traditional picture, in part by playing Russell off Frege, in part by studying what their much noted fellowship consists in. Here I introduce one of the pivotal notions in what is to come—an idea that goes to the heart of traditional thinking— what I call the cognitive fix idea: The reference of a word is grounded in the mind's grasp of the item in question. This idea suggests a requirement that is endorsed, in one way or another, by Frege and Russell as well as their many followers (even, alas, many direct reference brothers and sisters): The use of a linguistic expression to refer requires that the speaker possess a discriminating cognitive fix on the would-be referent; reference requires that something about the speaker's cognitive state must distinguish the relevant item from everything else in the universe.

In chapter 3 I adumbrate two large-scale pictures of language and thought that set the tone for what is to follow. One of the pictures is traditional; I refer to it as Cartesian-inspired. Somewhere near its heart is the idea that thought is prior to language, in any number of respects I set out. The other picture is my own; it emphasizes social practice and in many ways turns the tables on the Cartesian-inspired picture.

---

[24] Specialists may wish to glance at the first chapter and skip to the second.

In chapter 4 my radical anti-Fregean rejects, on roughly empirical grounds, what is at the very heart of the Fregean outlook, the cognitive fix idea. The Fregean is incredulous—not at his opponent's challenge concerning actual practice, about which the Fregean can admit that he owes an answer. He is incredulous at the radical suggestion that there can be reference in the absence of a discriminating cognitive fix, that reference can be "cognitively unmediated." For him, this raises the question of the very intelligibility of the anti-Fregean position. The question of the coherence of what is on my view the core idea of direct reference—cognitively unmediated reference—is the topic of this chapter.[25]

Chapter 5 further explores the fundamental disagreement. Both Fregeans and opponents seek to render intelligible the phenomenon of name reference. As Fregeans sometimes urge, however, only their approach gets so far as to explain the name-referent connection, to get beneath our practices. A tendentious Fregean might say that direct reference fails to articulate a semantic theory, an explanatory account of the connection between words and things.

I'll argue that on the contrary, the Fregean "explanation," like positing a god to explain the existence of the universe, is bogus. Even worse, there is no explanatory space between a name and a referent, no room, or need, for the sort of explanation the Fregean offers. Not only is the Fregean account empirically inadequate, as I'll argue in chapters 3 and 4, its explanatory project is illusory.[26] The proper task for philosophical semantics is a more surface-level characterization of practice: What, as our practices go, links up name and referent?

Thus in chapter 5 the debate gets even more polarized. And views about the character of the semantical project—the task of philosophical work on meaning and reference—are beginning to di-

---

[25] My endorsement of cognitively unmediated reference, so-called, amounts to the denial of a family of cognitive fix requirements, the strong form being the Fregean requirement of a purely qualitative uniquely applying characterization, and an example of a weak form being Kaplan's idea that with indexicals, the agent cognizes the referent by way of what Kaplan calls "the character" of the indexical. (Much more about Kaplan's view later.) But I am certainly not denying that the realm of the cognitive is relevant here. Surely the use of language involves the exercise of all sorts of cognitive capacities. But what isn't required is anything like a discriminating characterization of the referent, or even one that is discriminating in a context.

[26] As I explain in chapter 5, there is a version of anti-Fregeanism that attempts an externalist (e.g., a causal) explanation of reference. From a Fregean point of view, the attempt does not succeed, and from my point of view, elaborated in chapter 5, there is nothing to explain.

verge (as they will further in later chapters), despite a mutual inter-est in the name-referent connection.

I said earlier that talk at cross-purposes was conspicuous in the literature I'm exploring.[27] Here's what I meant: Anti-Fregeans—like Kripke in *Naming and Necessity*—portray the traditionalist as missing the boat on actual linguistic practice, no trivial matter. On the other side—and this will be my emphasis in chapters 6 through 9—traditionalists see the anti-Fregeans as insensitive to what is for them at the very heart of the philosophical study of language, the puzzles concerning the "cognitive significance" of language. The most famous of these is of course Frege's puzzle about informative identity sentences, elaborated in chapter 1.

This difference of focus and emphasis—actual practice versus the puzzles—has sometimes been noted, but I want to underscore it as another great divide, right up there with the cognitive fix re-quirement, and with the question of the propriety of a Frege-style explanation of reference that attempts to get behind or beneath our practices. Indeed, while I emphasize these other great divides in earlier chapters, what gets pride of place in the literature as well as in the oral tradition are the puzzles. The focus of chapter 6 is the informative identity puzzle; chapter 7 will explore empty names, that is, names that lack reference. In chapters 8 and 9 I turn to sentences that report belief and the other "propositional attitudes."

Attention to the puzzles in chapters 6–9 will extend our sense of what is at issue. We will need to see why at least early in the debate, direct reference advocates often seemed to place relatively little weight on the puzzles.[28] Was this just inattention, or avoid-ance, or—as I'll suggest—are there methodological and substan-tive reasons for supposing that the puzzles don't belong at center stage?

---

[27] This fact is striking especially—perhaps only—when one studies early stages of the debate. I've suggested earlier and I'll argue in the book that such cross-talk provides a handle on the fundamental issues at stake. This is a virtue that is lost in later, more "cooperative" discussions. Indeed, these later discussions, I'll argue, tend to share in the sterility of "Gettierology." (I allude to some of the developments in the post-Gettier epistemological literature on the analysis of knowledge.) But more of this later.

[28] Kripke, for example, in *Naming and Necessity*. Early in the First Lecture, Kripke mentions a number of considerations that "seem conclusive in favor of the view of Frege and Russell," prominently including some of the puzzles. But he con-cludes that even though he doesn't have anything like adequate solutions on behalf of the contrary Millian view he prefers, "it's pretty certain that the view of Frege and Russell is false" (pp. 28–29). If as Russell maintained, puzzles play the role of experiments, Kripke's remark is strange indeed.

Given my idea that the roots of the debate go deeper than is often realized, it is natural that I carefully attend to the actual instances of talk at cross-purposes, and so to the famous puzzles. But there is another reason for extended discussion of the puzzles. In chapter 3 I'll make something like a campaign promise:

> To overthrow a paradigm . . . requires more than the presentation of problematic data (from actual practice), even if that data can be seen as pointing to a different fundamental conception. The received view, after all, presumably has its own intuitive motivation, a range of examples or considerations that have made it seem attractive and natural. Before the revolutionary can rest, then, he needs to take seriously the considerations that motivate his opponents' view, data that may well be difficult to accommodate on the new picture. . . . If my preferred account cannot accommodate such phenomena in a natural, organic fashion, if epicyclical sophistication is required (or, what seems just as bad, biting the bullet and settling for relatively unintuitive judgments dictated by theory), this will count heavily against my approach.

The Fregean is able to provide relatively natural solutions to the puzzles. This ability, more than anything else, is what fortifies Frege's picture, what makes it seem attractive, straightforward, unstrained. Whether or not the puzzles deserve the role traditionalists have given them, the phenomena in question surely need accommodation. And as I say in the quotation, the accommodation had better be natural; and it had better be coherent with one's overall picture.

What emerged from my study of the puzzles was not what I expected or sought. Struggling with the puzzles over the years led me to think that if one really effects the sort of gestalt switch that I'm advocating—if one, for example, really begins to think of reference as not requiring cognitive mediation—the phenomena that were formerly seen to be puzzling look very different. They fall into place requiring no special explanation at all. So in the end I want to dispel the sense that there are puzzling phenomena here, things that shouldn't be as they appear to be, the sense that we are faced with several ideas that seem at once correct and incompatible.

To use the jargon, my account does not seek to provide solutions to the classical puzzles. It seeks rather to dissolve them. Talk of dissolving puzzles has Wittgensteinian resonance. I certainly don't mind this. At the same time, it's important to me that I did not set out to dissolve puzzles, to provide Wittgensteinian therapy. Nor are my conclusions a matter of applying some sort of general therapeutic idea or technique. It is best not to come to putative puzzles, here or elsewhere, with the thought that somehow they must be dissolved. The question is how best—most naturally—to think about the phenomena that are alleged to be puzzling. Dissolution, if and when it occurs, amounts to the recognition that the intellectual cramp was not intrinsic to the example but was a product of unnecessary assumptions brought to it.

The tendency in Wittgenstein's thought is to suppose—I like to think of it as a hypothesis or conjecture—that many if not all classical philosophical puzzles are products of inadequate conceptions of the relevant domains, of unnecessary and misleading assumptions brought to the alleged puzzle cases. This supposition, needless to say, does not encourage ignoring the puzzles, taking a dismissive attitude. Puzzles turn out to be crucial, as Russell taught. But contrary to Russell, they do not play the role of experiments. They are rather symptoms that announce an inadequate underlying picture. The idea is not to leave the picture in place and to use theoretical ingenuity to devise a way out. The underlying picture is what needs our attention.[29]

---

[29] Wittgenstein likened the matter to psychotherapy, a useful likeness I think—as long as one does not begin with the assumption that puzzling phenomena need to be dissolved.

1

Two Fundamental Problems: Frege's Classical Approach

A *proposition* may be defined to be anything which can be said to be true or false. But we shall understand this definition more clearly if we also indicate what a proposition is not.

1. A proposition is not the same thing as the sentence which states it. The three sentences, "I think, therefore I am," "*Je pense, donc je suis,*" "*Cogito ergo sum,*" all state the same proposition. A sentence is a group of words, and words, like other symbols, are in themselves physical objects, distinct from that to which they refer or which they symbolize. Sentences when written are thus located on certain surfaces, and when spoken are sound waves passing from one organism to another. But the proposition of which a sentence is the verbal expression is distinct from the visual marks or sound waves of the expression. Sentences, therefore, have a physical existence. They may or may not conform to standards of usage or taste. But they are not true or false. Truth or falsity can be predicated only of the propositions they signify.

4. Propositions are often confounded with the mental acts required to think them. . . . But just as we have distinguished the proposition (as the objective meaning) from the sentence which states it, so we must distinguish it from the act of the mind or the judgment which thinks it.

5. Nor must propositions be identified with any concrete object, thing, or event. . . . When we affirm or deny the proposition *The moon*

is nearer to the earth than the sun, neither the moon, nor the earth, nor the sun, nor the spatial distance between them is the proposition.[1]

I read this passage in my first undergraduate course in philosophy, and I have not yet recovered from the experience. Cohen and Nagel seemed to me then, and still seem to me, to have laid their hands on a problem that is distinctively philosophical. It is distinctively philosophical first because it is intellectually fundamental—the question of what it is that is true or false is certainly very basic—and second, because something very much like common sense seems to push us in conflicting directions on this question.

First, it seems intuitive to suppose that the things that are true or false ought to be distinguished from the symbols we use to express these things, that the mere marks on paper are not the items that are right or wrong in the most fundamental sense. Sentences constitute our means of saying the things we say. What we say, the propositions we express by means of our sentences, are what is true or false in the primary instance. More support is indeed available for this prima facie quite reasonable idea. We can think of many examples, as Cohen and Nagel note, in which you and I can say the same thing using very different words, very different sentences. This would seem to show that the single thing we say cannot be a sentence.[2]

The conflicting dictate of common sense, or perhaps of common sense when its attention is turned to matters abstract, appears when we inquire further about the nature of the things said, the propositions. Cohen and Nagel give us a fairly exhaustive list, partially quoted above, of the things with which we should not confuse propositions. They give us less help, however, on the positive side: What exactly are propositions? Cohen and Nagel tell us that propositions do not have a physical existence and that they do not exist in the mind. Propositions rather are more like "objective meanings." What in the world are objective meanings?

We begin with the problem of propositions. This brings us to Frege, the foremost exponent of the doctrine of propositions to which Cohen and Nagel appeal. Our question about the nature of

---

[1] Morris R. Cohen and Ernest Nagel, *An Introduction to Logic and Scientific Method* (New York: Simon, 1934), pp. 27–28.

[2] See Richard Cartwright, "Propositions," in R. Butler, ed., *Analytical Philosophy* (First Series) (Oxford: Blackwell, 1966), pp. 82–103; and Howard Wettstein, "Can What Is Asserted Be a Sentence?" *Philosophical Review* 85 (1976): 196–207, for analyses of this and related arguments.

propositions, and Frege's treatment of that question, will soon bring us to matters even more fundamental, to the nature of the connection between language and what language is used to speak about—the world.

1. Frege's Sense-Reference Distinction

No discussion of Frege's account of propositions, or, as he prefers, "thoughts,"[3] is possible without a grasp of Frege's notion of the sense of a linguistic expression. This is so for two reasons. First, Frege identifies thoughts with sentential *senses*. Second, the notion of sense, and, more generally, the distinction between sense and reference, lies at the heart of Frege's approach to the philosophy of language. I begin then with a discussion of the sense-reference distinction.

Frege introduces his famous distinction by formulating a crucial puzzle. His contention is that any adequate semantic account must provide a solution to this puzzle and that his account nicely does so. Frege begins by noting an uncontroversial datum: There are many factually correct and *informative* (perhaps better, potentially informative)[4] identity sentences in which proper names flank the identity sign. An example is the factually correct identity sentence "Hesperus = Phosphorus." Like "Hesperus = Hesperus," this first sentence is true, but *unlike the latter, it is nontrivial.*

Frege's puzzle concerns the explanation of this cognitive difference—potentially informative versus trivial—between sentences of the forms "$a = a$" and "$a = b$." In assertions of identity,[5] something is referred to, something (possibly something else) is then referred to, and the relation of *being the same thing* is predicated of the thing(s) referred to. Given this apparently harmless, apparently obvious account of identity statements, it now becomes very difficult

[3] Frege's practice, following that of the German logicians—as he tells us—was to use (the German translation of) the term "proposition" for the sentence that expresses the thought. See Frege's letter to Russell of October 20, 1902, in Brian McGuinness, ed., *Gottlob Frege: Philosophical and Mathematical Correspondence*, Hans Kaal, trans. (Chicago: University of Chicago Press, 1980), p. 149.

[4] Whether an utterance is informative is a matter of what information the listener possesses prior to the utterance. The appropriate notion for Frege's purposes is something like "capable of being informative." Even this requires further refinement. See section 3 of this chapter.

[5] I will not be careful about the fact that, as Strawson says, it is only people and not sentences that assert or affirm anything—except where there is a danger of confusion.

to distinguish between "Hesperus = Hesperus" and "Hesperus = Phosphorus."

It is of course easy enough to distinguish them as sentences. Distinguishing them in terms of their semantic function, in terms of what they say, is quite another matter. Indeed, both sentences seem to assert the same thing. Both sentences, that is, pick out the same thing twice and affirm the identity relation of it. If they really do "say the same thing," however, how can it be that one is trivial and the other clearly not? Doesn't this obvious difference in "cognitive significance" clearly indicate that they say two different things?

Frege, discussing this question in his early *Begriffsschrift*, distinguishes two ways of thinking about identity: as "a relation between things" and as "a relation between words." If I say "Hesperus is larger than Earth," I assert that a certain relation holds between the heavenly bodies in question. The relation of *being larger than* is thus a relation between the objects denoted by the relevant names. "'Hesperus' has more letters than does 'Earth,'" by contrast, formulates a relation not between the relevant heavenly bodies, but between the linguistic expressions in question. How are we to understand the claim formulated by an identity sentence, for example, "Hesperus = Phosphorus"? Does this sentence formulate a relation between things, the relation *being the same thing as*, as we assumed above, or rather, contrary to syntactical appearances, a relation between words, the relation of co-referring? Does it say that "this is the same thing as that," or rather "this name refers to the same thing as does that name"?

Taking *identity* to be a relation between names really is contrary to the syntactical appearances. In "Hesperus = Phosphorus," for example, the names certainly seem to be used, not mentioned. One who utters this sentence certainly seems to be talking about the relevant things and not about linguistic expressions. Moreover, the relation that is affirmed certainly seems to be *being the same thing as*, not *referring to the same thing*. Nevertheless, Frege, in the *Begriffsschrift*, adopted the metalinguistic solution, the idea that identity statements formulate the claim that two names co-refer. This account recommended itself to Frege, for it solved his informativeness puzzle. Taking identity statements to assert that two names co-refer accounts nicely for the distinction between the content of "Hesperus = Phosphorus" and that of "Hesperus = Hesperus." We now have two different things said by the respective sentences. It also explains why the claim formulated by the former is indeed nontrivial, for it is not trivial that two different names refer to the same thing.[6]

Frege found this *Begriffsschrift* explanation of the informativeness of identity statements ultimately unsatisfying, for he found the idea that names function metalinguistically in identity contexts objectionable.[7] He thus felt the need for a different account of the informativeness of identity statements. Frege might have noticed, however, that his *Begriffsschrift* account does not in any case constitute a general solution. It is easy to generate problems that are of a piece with his problem about informative identities but that have nothing to do with identity. The central problem about the cognitive dimension of language about which Frege was so exercised goes far deeper than the problem of informative identity statements.

Consider two garden variety, non-identity sentences, "Hesperus appears in the evening" and "Phosphorus appears in the evening." These two sentences, no less than the two identity sentences, seem to assert the same thing. Each predicates a property, that of *appearing in the evening,* of the same object. Notice, however, that these two sentences, no less than the two identity sentences, differ from one another along the cognitive dimension. Let us utilize an idea about the cognitive dimension to which Frege himself appeals: Someone might understand both sentences but maintain that one of them expresses a truth and the other a falsehood. How can this be, if they really assert the same thing?

These two non-identity sentences, then, appear to raise the same sort of problem that the puzzling identity sentences did. Frege's

[6] Indeed, and this is related to a point of Kripke's in "A Puzzle About Belief" (in A. Margalit, ed., *Meaning and Use* [Dordrecht: D. Reidel, 1979]): it is not always trivial that "Hesperus = Hesperus." One might have learned the name in two different sorts of contexts so that one might think that there are two Hesperuses in question. Thus the identity sentence might express a new insight. This, of course, does not negate the force of Frege's problem. It only emphasizes it. Contrary to what one might suppose, there is a problem about the informativeness of identity even where the same name is used twice.

[7] His difficulty, as I understand his discussion in the first paragraph of "On Sense and Reference" (in P. Geach and M. Black, eds., *Translations from the Philosophical Writings of Gottlob Frege* [Oxford: Blackwell, 1966]), is related to the fact that on the *Begriffsschrift* view, the heavenly body ordinarily referred to by the names never gets mentioned. The speaker claims that these two names refer to the same thing but never tells us which thing that is. But, on the face of it, "Hesperus = Phosphorus" seems to tell us something about this heavenly body. Objections other than Frege's also seem available. For one thing, as I will soon discuss, Frege's early view posits a dubious systematic ambiguity for all names. They function one way in garden variety assertions and in quite another in identity sentences.

Begriffsschrift theory, while it tells a special story about names in identity contexts, a story that resolves the puzzle, tells no special story about the sentences just considered. The problem of informative identities, far from being the main problem, now appears to be just a special case of a more general phenomenon.[8,9]

Frege, in "On Sense and Reference," provides a solution to the problem of informative identities, a solution that applies quite generally to the wider range of problems about the cognitive dimension. Indeed, Frege's solution, despite his focus upon informative identity statements, does not really single out identity sentences for any special treatment. Another virtue of Frege's new approach is that it avoids positing the dubious systematic ambiguity that the *Begriffsschrift* view maintained for proper names. Names, according to the *Begriffsschrift*, ordinarily refer to the things so named. In identity sentences, however, names were supposed to refer to themselves. Names, on the sense-reference view, function in identity sentences just as they ordinarily do. The identity sign, moreover, is now held to formulate the relation of *being the same thing*, as opposed to the relation of *ordinarily referring to the same thing*, and this seems to be a more natural account, just what one would have naively supposed.

I now briefly rehearse the outlines of Frege's well-known sense-reference view and then turn to the new account of cognitive significance. Any possible object of reference may be thought of in several, indeed indefinitely many, ways. Aristotle, for example, may be thought of as "the teacher of Alexander the Great," or as "the most eminent student of Plato," or in countless other ways. Some of these ways in which objects may be presented, "modes

---

[8] Nathan Salmon, in *Frege's Puzzle* (Cambridge, Mass.: MIT Press, 1986), argues similarly that identity was not the real issue here, but he formulates the real issue in a somewhat different way than I do. Salmon's point is that we can replicate the difference between trivial and nontrivial sentences—where the difference involves the sorts of substitution we are considering—in sentences that are not identity sentences, for example, "Aristotle wrote the *Nicomachean Ethics*" versus "The author of the *Nicomachean Ethics* wrote the *Nicomachean Ethics*." John Perry made a similar point to me in conversation some time ago. I agree with Salmon and Perry, but I think we can go a step further. The fundamental question exercising Frege was not the difference between trivial and nontrivial sentences. Indeed we have seen the same problem with respect to two sentences neither of which is trivial.

[9] We will see later that there is a still more general category of problems of cognitive dimension of language. The relatively general problem just discussed is simply one such problem. For the moment, however, let's rest content with our relatively general problem that cannot be solved by proposing a novel account of identity sentences.

of presentation," as Frege characterizes them, may be of sufficient interest that we conventionally associate linguistic expressions with them. Frege calls modes of presentation, when they are associated with linguistic expressions, "senses" of the latter. Senses, on Frege's view, play a crucial role in all reference, indeed *the* crucial role. The idea is that a name or definite description refers to something by expressing a sense, a mode of presentation that applies to the item in question. Indeed the linguistic item refers derivatively. It is the sense expressed that bears the primary referential relation to the referent.[10]

Frege, as is often noted, never gives us much help with the nature of senses. What are these "ways of thinking," "modes of presentation"? This much is clear: Senses do not reside in the physical world, nor in the minds of those who apprehend them. They are abstract entities that populate a "third realm." Senses are, you might say, Plato-friendly.

A naïve reading of much of what Frege tells us about senses suggests an identification with descriptive concepts of rationalist notoriety. Frege's insistence that it is the sense of an expression that refers in the primary sense now becomes natural. The expression itself, after all, is associated with a sense *by convention*. The sense, on the other hand, is not associated with a referent by convention. It has, or so the story of concepts goes, a sort of intrinsic connection to the object that satisfies it.[11] The concept expressed by, say, "the first president of the United States," for example (the concept—not the piece of language that expresses it), fits George Washington in virtue of Washington's possession of the property in question, not in virtue of linguistic convention.

How does the sense-reference picture of language provide a solution to the problem of informative identities? The usual explanation, the one that a student in a philosophy of language course is likely to hear, runs roughly as follows. What is new, in Frege's new picture, is the notion of sense. It is in terms of this notion of sense that the informativeness of identity statements is to be explained. Consider the informative identity statement that "Hesperus = Phosphorus." 'Hesperus' and 'Phosphorus', although they both refer to the same thing, refer in very different ways, by means of different senses, different "modes of presentation." 'Hesperus', perhaps, ex-

---

[10] "The regular connexion between a sign, its sense, and its reference is of such a kind that to the sign there corresponds a definite sense and *to that in turn* [italics added] a definite reference." From "On Sense and Reference," pp. 56–57.

[11] The connection is intrinsic, *given the way the world is.*

presses the sense of "the heavenly body seen at a certain location in the evening"; 'Phosphorus', "the heavenly body seen in that (or some other) location in the morning." Accordingly, it may not be trivial to a speaker that there is one thing in question, since whatever thing or things are in question are characterized in quite different ways. "Hesperus = Hesperus," by contrast, is trivial—not because the same thing is referred to twice, but rather because it is referred to *in the same way*, and so the speaker will know that it is the same thing.

There is surely something correct about this standard account. Frege surely holds that the informativeness of identity statements is to be explained by appeal to senses. The difficulty with the explanation just roughly formulated is that even at the time of the *Begriffsschrift*, Frege had the idea, or at least the rudiments of the idea, of the sense of a singular term. He speaks in the *Begriffsschrift*, for example, of co-referential singular terms differing in *the ways they determine a referent*.[12] Frege would have maintained early along, then, that "Hesperus = Hesperus" and "Hesperus = Phosphorus" were very different in that in the former, the same referent is determined twice in the same way, while in the latter, the same referent is determined in different ways.

If so, why did identity statements pose such a problem for Frege in the *Begriffsschrift*, a problem that required as implausible a move as the metalinguistic account? Why didn't the difference in sense, as Frege would later call it, between 'Hesperus' and 'Phosphorus' explain why only "Hesperus = Phosphorus" is informative? What, moreover, is so new about the sense-reference picture, if indeed Frege already had the idea of "the way the reference is determined" in the *Begriffsschrift*?[13]

What is really novel about the sense-reference picture, I want to suggest, is Frege's conception of the *propositional content* of a sentence, about what is asserted by an utterance of a sentence, about—as Frege would put it—the *thought* expressed by a sentence—not just with respect to identity sentences, but generally speaking. I turn, then, to the topic with which we began, Frege's explication of the notion of proposition. I will return in section 3 to the question of how this new way of thinking about proposi-

---

[12] "The same content can be fully determined in different ways . . .," "On Sense and Reference," p. 11.

[13] In my answer to this question in the text, which I mention in the next paragraph and develop in section 3, I am indebted to Richard Mendelsohn's seminal essay, "Frege's *Begriffsschrift* Theory of Identity," *Journal of the History of Philosophy* 22, no. 3 (July 1982): 279–99.

tional content opened the way for Frege to a more satisfying account of cognitive significance.

2. Fregean Thoughts

Frege's mature account of propositions might be called the classical view of propositions. Quine, when he argues that we can do very well without propositions, is arguing against something very much like Frege's notion.

What is Frege's view? First, as was noted earlier, whereas I have spoken of propositions, Frege speaks of "thoughts." A thought is not, however, a private mental entity or activity: "By a thought I understand not the subjective performance of thinking but its objective content, which is capable of being the common property of many thinkers."[14] Thoughts are, for Frege, the bearers of truth and falsity: "Without wishing to give a definition, I call a thought something for which the question of truth arises."[15]

What are these items for which the question of truth and falsity arises? Frege here makes a crucial identification of thoughts with *senses*. Just as the subject and predicate terms in a subject – predicate sentence have senses, so does the sentence as a whole. Just as the senses of the component expressions are roughly what the competent speaker understands by those expressions, the sense of the sentence is what the speaker understands by the sentence. What the speaker understands by the sentence is, holds Frege, what the sentence says, the thought it expresses.

> . . . the thought is the sense of the sentence . . . [16]

> . . . when we call a sentence true we really mean its sense is. . . . It is for the sense of a sentence that the question of truth arises in general.[17]

To say that thoughts are to be identified with sentential sentences is not, however, to say that all sentential senses are thoughts.

> One does not wish to deny sense to an imperative sentence, but this sense is not such that the question of truth could arise for it. Therefore I shall not call the sense of an imperative sentence a thought. . . . Only

---

[14] "On Sense and Reference," note on p. 62.
[15] "The Thought," p. 511.
[16] "The Thought," p. 511.
[17] "The Thought," p. 510.

those sentences in which we communicate or state something come into the question.[18]

Central to Frege's account is the idea that every thought is a *complete thought*. The relevant notion of completeness emerges in Frege's argument that thoughts possess truth values eternally.

> Are there not thoughts which are true today but false in six months time? The thought, for example, that the tree there is covered with green leaves, will surely be false in six months time. No, for it is not the same thought at all? The words "this tree is covered with green leaves" are not sufficient by themselves for the utterance, the time of utterance is involved as well. Without the time indication this gives we have no complete thought, i.e. no thought at all. Only a sentence supplemented by a time indication and complete in every respect expresses a thought. But this, if it is true, is true not only today or tomorrow but timelessly.[19]

Notice that Frege does not first raise the question of whether thoughts are complete and then attempt to resolve this question by arguing that since they possess truth values eternally, they must be complete. He instead motivates the view that thoughts have truth values eternally by reference to what he takes to be the more fundamental intuition that thoughts are, so to speak, essentially complete.

Frege's doctrine of the completeness of propositional content has been challenged, at least by implication, by those who maintain that the bearers of truth do not possess truth values eternally. A sentence like "The president of the United States is a Republican" might be true at one time, it has been argued, but false at another.

Frege's intuition here—whether or not it is decisive—is powerful. Consider a different kind of example. Someone says, "This tree is covered with leaves," of two different trees. Has the same thing been asserted, or are there different propositions at issue? Intuitively, very different things have been asserted. Someone might maintain, on the contrary, that the same thing has been asserted on both occasions, a proposition that may have one truth value *at*

---

[18] "The Thought," p. 512. Frege distinguishes between the sense or content of such a sentence and the assertive force that "lies in the form of the indicative sentence." Thus he thinks that certain nondeclarative sentences can have the same sense as a declarative sentence, e.g., the kind of interrogative sentences he calls "sentence-questions," such as "Is it the case that *p*?" Perhaps there is some tension between this view and the idea that only the sense of a declarative sentence can be true or false. We can ignore, for our purposes, such complications.

[19] "The Thought," p. 533.

the first tree and another *at the second.* Propositions vary in truth values, it thus might be said, not only with respect to times, but with respect to the references of demonstrative expressions such as "this tree." A notion of proposition would thus emerge that is even "thinner" than that of the philosopher who takes propositions to be true and false relative to times. Propositions not only would not be specific with respect to time, they would not even be specific with respect to the identity of the things referred to by expressions such as "this tree." Such a view seems possible. It is surely not incoherent. It seems, however, quite artificial. Something different, Frege would presumably insist, was said by the two different individuals, each of whom referred to a distinct tree. Intuitively, the content of the respective assertions was different.

Similarly, two utterances of "This tree is covered with green leaves," with respect to the same tree but at different times, seem intuitively to have very different contents. To say now that the tree has leaves on it and to say this next winter is to say different things, to make two different claims. Indeed that different things have been said explains the fact that the utterances may have different truth values, or so the Fregean intuition goes.

My discussion of propositional completeness is not intended to plumb the depths of that topic. I have not, for one thing, offered any detailed account of the relevant notion of completeness. How, for example, is one to specify the respects in which a proposition must be complete (other than to say "in all respects")? For another thing, I did not consider the arguments of Frege's opponents. As with some of the other questions raised but not fully discussed in this chapter, a full discussion of these matters will not be relevant to what I will try to accomplish in this book, and so, given limited resources of time and space, I let these questions go for the present.

Let us briefly consider a final, crucial feature of Frege's view, one that will figure prominently in the discussion of Russell in the next chapter: Frege's account of the constituents of a thought. The reader, even if he has never read Frege, might well anticipate Frege's view here. Fregean thoughts are, as we know, sentential senses. Moreover, the proper parts of sentences also have (sub-sentential) senses. One would expect then that the constituents of a thought would be the senses of the parts of the sentence. In his argument (which we can gratefully bypass) that the relationship of a thought to a truth value is not one of subject to predicate but rather of sense to reference, Frege notes: "A truth value cannot be part of a thought, any more than, say, the sun can, for it is not a sense but an object."[20] Whatever Frege's thesis concerning truth values as objects, his thesis about the range of possible thought constituents is clear: objects are disqualified. The sun, for example, cannot be a thought constituent, for it is not a sense but an object. The sense of the phrase, "the sun," by contrast, is the sort of thing that can be a constituent of a thought.

I conclude this section by noting an immediate consequence of Frege's view that a thought is a sentential sense, constituted by the senses of the sub-sentential parts. This consequence is a "principle of interchange": If we replace one expression in a sentence with a different one that nevertheless has the same sense, then the sense of the whole, the thought expressed by the sentence, does not change. On the other hand, if we replace one such sub-sentential expression with one that is not equivalent to it in sense, the sense of the whole will change. A new thought will be expressed.

> If we replace one word of the sentence by another having the same reference but a different sense, . . . the thought changes; since, e.g., the thought in the sentence "The morning star is a body illuminated by the Sun" differs from that in the sentence "The evening star is a body illuminated by the Sun." Anybody who did not know that the evening star is the morning star might hold the one thought to be true, the other false.[21]

> We must distinguish between sense and reference. "2 + 4" and "4 + 2" certainly have the same reference, i.e. they are proper names for the same number; but they have not the same sense; consequently, "2 + 4 = 4 + 2" and "4 + 4 = 4 × 2" have the same reference, but not the same sense (which means, in this case: they do not contain the same thought).[22]

3. Concluding Remarks: Frege's Solution to the Problem of Informative Identities

Let us return, armed with Frege's notion of a thought, to informative identities. The questions were these: Frege already had modes of presentation in his intellectual repertoire in the *Begriffsschrift*. Why then was there any special puzzle about the informativeness

---

[20] "On Sense and Reference," p. 64.

[21] "On Sense and Reference," p. 62.

[22] "Function and Concept," in P. Geach and M. Black, eds., *Translations from the Philosophical Writings of Gottlob Frege* (Oxford: Blackwell, 1966), p. 29.

of identity statements? And what was so new in "On Sense and Reference"?

Let's begin with what might seem to be an unrelated question: Frege's interest in *language* vis-à-vis his interest in *thought*. Michael Dummett attributes the following three theses to Frege.

> [F]irst, that the goal of philosophy is the analysis of the structure of *thought* [that is, the objective and eternally existing contents of thought]; second, that the study of *thought* is to be sharply distinguished from the study of the psychological process of *thinking*; and, finally, that the only proper method for analysing thought consists in the analysis of *language*.[23]

Frege's interest in language, then, was indeed secondary to and derivative from his interest in, as Tyler Burge puts it, the "eternal structure of thought."[24]

Frege's thought orientation provides the key to the question of why modes of presentation did not supply an early solution to the informativeness puzzle. Here as elsewhere, Frege's interest was not so much in the properties and problems of *linguistic interaction* as with the properties and problems of *thought contents*. Frege's puzzle, contrary to the way this is often put, was not the question of how someone might become informed by an utterance of "Hesperus = Phosphorus." Were that his problem, then modes of presentation, already available in *Begriffsschrift*, would indeed have supplied a solution. If "Hesperus" takes us to its referent in a very different way than does "Phosphorus," then it is easy to see how someone might not know that there is only one heavenly body in question, and might become informed by the utterance in question. What puzzled Frege was not the explanation of informativeness—in the sense just explicated—but rather the explanation of how the mere substitution of one co-referring name for another could so change the thought content.

Granted that Frege was concerned not so much with communicative interaction as with thought content, how does this fact explain why modes of presentation didn't supply Frege with an early solution? The answer is that it is one thing to believe that names are associated with modes of presentation that determine their references, and quite another to construe the modes of presentation as constituents of propositions. Until Frege took thought contents to

---

[23] *Truth and Other Enigmas* (London: Duckworth, 1978), p. 458.

[24] "Sinning Against Frege," *Philosophical Review* 88 (July 1979): 398–442. The quotation is from p. 398.

be constituted by the modes of presentation—and this is what didn't occur until later—he had no good explanation of the difference in thought content between the two identity sentences.

How, then, was Frege conceiving thought contents in the *Begriffsschrift*? Names, Frege tells us in the *Begriffsschrift*, ordinarily function as "mere proxies for their content[s]," where by "content[s]" he clearly means "references." This remark, with its implication that the linguistic function of a name is simply to make its referent a subject of discourse, is not one that Frege would have made during his sense-reference period. A proper name, for the mature Frege, was surely not a mere stand-in for its referent. If a name was a stand-in for anything, it was (something like) a stand-in for a sense. Indeed, Frege's "proxy" remark seems more in the spirit of Mill's doctrine that proper names are "purely denotative," or Russell's views concerning "logically proper names."[25]

This is not to say that the early Frege held a Millian or Russellian "pure denotationalist" view of proper names. Let's not forget Frege's early adoption of modes of presentation. Nevertheless, Frege, in the *Begriffsschrift*, does seem to hold that the *function* of a name is just to refer, that the contribution of a name to the content of the assertion is limited to making its referent a subject of discourse. This is a far cry from his later view that the function of a name in a sentence is to introduce its associated mode of presentation into the thought content.

If the semantic function of a name is just to refer, then "Hesperus" and "Phosphorus" are identical in semantic function. The presence of one of these names, or the other, in a sentence would not affect the function of the entire sentence, what it expresses, its thought content. "Hesperus is large" and "Phosphorus is large" would thus have the same thought content, as would "Hesperus = Hesperus" and "Hesperus = Phosphorus." Thus the problem that Frege faced both in the *Begriffsschrift* and later on: According to Frege's early account of thought content, these sentences have identical contents, yet since these sentences differ in cognitive significance, they obviously differ in thought content.

To summarize my proposal: There is an important, but usually unrecognized, distinction between two very different problems about "cognitive significance." First, there is a problem about communicative interaction involving factually correct identity sentences. This is the problem of how it is that one can become informed by

---

[25] These latter views will be discussed later.

the utterance of such a sentence. Second, there is Frege's problem of how the thought content of a factually correct identity sentence can be nontrivial.

That these are very different problems becomes striking when we consider a position, one that I have attributed to the early Frege, according to which the reference of a proper name is indeed determined by its associated sense but the semantic function of a proper name is not, as it is in Frege's later theory, to introduce the associated sense into the proposition expressed. The semantic function of the name is solely one of referring. One who maintained such a position could easily explain the communicative interaction problem—if she were interested in so doing—Frege was not, I have argued. He could not explain, however, how it is that the thought content of "Hesperus = Phosphorus" is nontrivial.

This chapter has been an introduction to two of the most fundamental questions in the philosophy of language. We started with the question of the nature of the things that we assert, the problem of propositions. This led us to Frege, the father, in our times at least, of what deserves to be called the classical account of propositions, the idea that a proposition is the sense of a sentence. Since propositions were analyzed by Frege in terms of senses, it was not possible to understand Frege's account of propositions without a grasp of his sense-reference distinction. Here we were led to the second fundamental question, that of the relation between language and the world. Frege, here also, advanced what deserves to be called the classical account (or at least *a* classical account), epitomized by the idea that the reference of a linguistic expression is derivative from, even parasitic upon, the reference of its associated mode of presentation.

I shall argue, in the course of this book, that Frege was fundamentally mistaken and that there is a more natural way to think about these things. Russell, although his remarks on the subject are often opaque, and although his views about these questions are deeply connected with epistemological and metaphysical doctrines that don't recommend themselves, at least to me, advanced views on these two topics that suggest a way forward. Let us turn to Russell.

2

Russell (and
More Frege)

*All thinking has to start from acquaintance; but it succeeds
in thinking about many things with which we have no
acquaintance.*

Bertrand Russell, "On Denoting"

1. Propositions That Contain Objects, the Principle
of Acquaintance, and Direct Reference

Russell was not shy about the difference between his account of
propositions and Frege's.

> I believe that in spite of all its snowfields, Mont Blanc is itself a com-
> ponent part of what is actually asserted in the proposition "Mont
> Blanc is more than 4000 metres high." We do not assert the thought,
> for this is a private psychological matter. We assert the object of the
> thought, and this is, to my mind, a certain complex (an objective prop-
> osition, one might say) in which Mont Blanc is itself a component
> part.[1]

Russell, in this letter to Frege, is not being altogether fair to
Frege, for Frege surely never suggested that thoughts, in the sense of
private psychological entities, are the items that we assert. Frege's
"thoughts" are apprehended by the mind but don't reside there.

---

[1] "Letter to Frege," in Brian McGuinness, ed., *Gottlob Frege: Philosophical and
Mathematical Correspondence*, abridged ed. trans. Hans Kaal (Chicago: University
of Chicago Press, 1980), p. 169.

Nevertheless, the substantial disagreement between the two fathers of our subject is clear enough. Russell thinks that there are nonconceptual constituents of propositions, that, contrary to Frege, the *references* of expressions, things like you and me, can "occur in what is asserted."

Nor is this the only important difference between them. Frege's views on propositional constituency, as we saw in the last chapter, are intimately related to his basic semantic picture. Senses are, at once, the ingredients in propositions and the items in terms of which the word – world relation is to be understood. Russell's idea that the references of expressions can be constituents of propositions, an idea that sounds bizarre to those of us brought up on Frege, is very much connected to his rejection of Frege's sense-reference view and his substitution of a very different basic semantic perspective.[2]

There is another aspect of Russell's view about propositional constituents worth noting here. Focusing upon this aspect will set the stage for a discussion of just how different Russell's basic semantic picture is from Frege's. It will illustrate, moreover, the important lesson that Russell's semantic views are intimately related to his epistemological views. Russell announces a "fundamental epistemological principle": "Every proposition which we can understand must be composed wholly of constituents with which we are acquainted."[3] This is surely not the place to unravel "epistemological acquaintance." What Russell has in mind, however, is a roughly Cartesian notion of direct, privileged, perhaps even infallible, mental access.

Russell's principle seems to limit the possible constituents of propositions to things with which we are "directly acquainted." Well, not quite. There may still be propositions that contain things with which we are not acquainted. These, however, would not be propositions that we can understand or, presumably, assert. The propositions that we can understand or assert, then, may contain

---

[2] Talk of Russell's perspective (in semantics or elsewhere) is risky. There are various strands to Russell's thinking, and these took on different emphases at different times. Nor did he hesitate to change his mind. I will isolate one important strand that contrasts sharply with Frege's approach, and one that is to me suggestive of a way forward. Russell emphasized this approach in "Knowledge by Acquaintance and Knowledge by Description" (hereafter "KBA"), p. 211, in Bertrand Russell, *Mysticism and Logic* (Garden City, N.Y.: Doubleday, n.d.), as well as in the parallel piece by the same name in *The Problems of Philosophy* (Oxford: Oxford University Press, reprinted 1959).

[3] KBA, p. 211.

only things with which we are acquainted. What sorts of things are these? "We have acquaintance with sense-data, with many universals, and possibly with ourselves [Russell here has Humean worries about the self as a possible object of acquaintance], but not with physical objects, or other minds."[4]

The dispute between Frege and Russell concerning the constituents of propositions, I have said, betokens a fundamental difference in semantic perspectives. Russell maintains that when one is acquainted with something, say a present sense datum or oneself, one can refer to it without the mediation of anything like a Fregean sense. One can refer to it, as we might say, *directly*.[5] Indeed, Russell invents a new linguistic category, the "genuine" or "logically proper" name, that subsumes expressions that function in this most un-Fregean way. A logically proper name—Russell's examples of logically proper names of particulars are 'I' (if indeed we are acquainted with the self) and 'this' (when the latter is used to refer to a present sense datum)—is a "mere noise or shape conventionally used to designate a certain [thing]; it gives us no information about that [thing], and has nothing that can be called its meaning as opposed to denotation."[6]

I have so far called attention to two Russellian notions that depart radically from the Fregean outlook: nonconceptual constituents of propositions, and conceptually unmediated reference. Acquaintance, as we have seen, furnishes a link between them. One can refer directly, by means of a genuine name, only to an object of

---

[4] KBA, p. 223. Query: Given Russell's epistemic constraint on propositional constituency, how can Mont Blanc, an external object to be sure, itself be a constituent in a proposition that we can understand, as Russell says that it can? Perhaps Russell, in telling us that "in spite of all its snowfields, Mont Blanc is itself a component part of what is actually asserted," indulges a desire for a dramatic example of a real thing in a proposition. Clearly, in giving such examples, Russell needs to tell us more. I speculate later in the section "Why Russell Was Not a Neo-Fregean," that such examples betray a tendency in Russell's thought that is at odds with his "fundamental epistemological principle" quoted a few lines earlier.

[5] The terminology of "direct reference" derives from the work of David Kaplan. See his seminal work, "Demonstratives," in J. Almog, J. Perry, and H. Wettstein, eds., *Themes from Kaplan* (Oxford: Oxford University Press, 1989), pp. 481–614. Kaplan uses the terminology of direct reference in a wider way than I do here. As I use the terminology, a directly referential expression will be one that, as Russell says, is a "mere noise or shape conventionally used to designate a certain [thing]; it gives us no information about that [thing], and has nothing that can be called its meaning as opposed to denotation." Kaplan, on the contrary, maintains that many of the expressions that are, for him, directly referential, for example, indexical expressions, possess descriptive meaning.

[6] KBA, p. 218.

acquaintance, and when one does so, the referent itself will be a constituent of the proposition expressed.

2. Frege's Rejection of Sinnless Reference

Russell's idea of direct, *Sinn*less reference is one that Frege does not ever explicitly consider, and one that surely he would have rejected, both early and late. Frege, on the interpretation of the *Begriffsschrift* offered in chapter 1, did have the related idea that the semantic function of a name is not to introduce its sense into the proposition expressed, but rather merely to make its referent a subject of discourse. The early Frege thus shares with Russell the idea that nothing sense-like gets into the proposition. Russell's proposal, however, goes far beyond Frege's early view. Russell, unlike Frege, gives no role to modes of presentation. The connection between linguistic expression and referent, for Russell, is not to be explained by the referent's fitting the term's associated mode of presentation, the referent's having the property associated with the term, for there is no such mode of presentation, or property, associated with the expression.

What was so unthinkable to Frege about *Sinn*less reference? It is sometimes suggested that Frege rejects the possibility of direct reference because of his puzzle about informative identity. This seems unlikely. Remember that the Frege of the *Begriffsschrift* had modes of presentation in his intellectual repertoire. The early Frege (rightly, in my view) did not suppose, though, that this solved the problem of informativeness. Still, one might think, senses were at least necessary (if not sufficient) for a solution. I do not believe that even this much is correct. Frege's *Begriffsschrift* metalinguistic account of identity sentences works just as well for sense-less, directly referential, names as it does for names that have associated modes of presentation. Let 'Hesperus' and 'Phosphorus' be directly referential, mere "noises or shapes conventionally used to designate," giving no information about their referents.[7] Given Frege's metalinguistic account of identity, the proposition expressed by "Hesperus = Phosphorus'" will be the nontrivial proposition that

---

[7] What I am envisaging here is the possibility that ordinary names could function semantically as mere tags for their referents, a position that, as we will see, Mill maintained. 'Hesperus' and 'Phosphorus' would accordingly be tags for a single planet. Russell, of course, would have rejected this idea for epistemological reasons, namely that we are not directly acquainted with the heavenly body. The question here under consideration is why Frege rejects the idea.

the referent of the one name is identical to the referent of the other, quite different name. Thus Frege's puzzle is not, at least to the early Frege's mind, solved by the introduction of senses, and his proposed solution would work as well for *Sinn*less names. All of this suggests that the informativeness puzzle was not the key to Frege's adoption of his fundamental thesis that reference requires an associated mode of presentation.

One gets the feeling from reading and rereading Frege, moreover, that his implicit denial of the possibility of conceptually unmediated reference plays a role much more fundamental than is allowed for by the prior suggestion. It is not merely that the reference-without-sense picture is not adequate to certain puzzles. It is that the very idea of *Sinn*less reference is somehow incoherent. In some strong sense, there could not be reference without sense. Whether or not Frege held this strong view, and I bet that he did, it is certainly consonant with the things that he does say. It is, moreover, a view worth exploring, if for no other reason than because it is the sort of thing one often hears in discussions with philosophers of broadly Fregean orientation. Why might Frege, or anyone else for that matter, think that Russell's idea (and, as we shall see, not Russell's alone) of conceptually unmediated reference is thus incoherent, or impossible, or something of the like?

My speculation is that something deep inclined Frege to suppose that reference without sense was impossible: Frege's underlying conception of thought and of the contents of thought. Here's an analogy. A view sometimes called "the representative theory of perception" maintains that the perception of a physical object consists in the apprehension of sense data that represent the object. Direct perceptual apprehension of physical objects, on such a view, is impossible, perhaps even incoherent. My proposal is that Frege, even early along, held an analogous view about *thought*, a "representative theory of conception." The idea is that thought about an object consists in the apprehension of a concept that represents the object, that thinking of an object is a matter of directly apprehending a mode of presentation that refers to the object.

What I'm calling the representative theory of conception is quite a traditional idea, one that has had considerable appeal. Indeed, what is seen as the alternative might seem almost, and is from time to time alleged to be, magical: The direct, unmediated apprehension of things in thought. When you think about me, for example, don't you have to think about me *in a certain way*, for example, as the author of this book? What would it mean to *just think about me,* to think about me without, so to speak, bringing me under a concept? Such considerations, whether or not they are in the end conclusive—I am suspicious, as will emerge—have certainly made the representative theory tempting, prima facie plausible.

If Frege, even at the time of the *Begriffsschrift,* accepted the representative theory of conception, this would explain why reference-without-sense would seem incoherent. Notice that to accept the representative theory, one need not accept Frege's later view that the conceptual representations constitute the content of the proposition thought. The propositional content might even (or even exclusively) include—as Russell maintained, and as Frege's remarks in the *Begriffsschrift* suggest—the object thought about. There is, of course, a certain tension between this Russellian conception of propositional content and the idea that to be thinking of Hesperus is just to be entertaining a concept (that happens to be satisfied by Hesperus). It is this tension, I want to suggest, that gets resolved with Frege's "On Sense and Reference" conception of propositional content.

3. Russell's Anti-representationalism and Russell's Representationalism

When one stands in direct epistemic contact with something, thinks Russell, one needs no representational intermediaries in order to think about it or to refer to it. Russell was, in this respect, an arch-anti-representationalist. Notice, however, the role of the epistemic immediacy. *It* is what precludes the need for any representational intermediary. What about examples in which one speaks or thinks about something with which one is not acquainted? Here Russell's representationalism comes to the fore. One cannot directly apprehend external objects, held Russell. The only way one can make cognitive contact with such things, albeit a kind of inferior contact, is (roughly) by apprehending concepts that represent the things. I say "roughly" because Russell's approach to these matters is so different from Frege's that talk of Russellian "mediating concepts" needs substantial qualification—which I will provide in my discussion of Russell's theory of descriptions. Russell, in any case, although—as I will temporarily put it—he endorsed a kind of conceptually mediated reference, never made it ubiquitous, as did Frege. We revert to mediating concepts—more specifically, to definite descriptions in place of genuine names—only when we wish to speak of something with which we lack epistemic intimacy.

This is not to say, however, that Russell took conceptually mediated reference to be a kind of unusual exception. The overwhelming majority of the things about which people ordinarily speak, Russell is the first to admit, are not objects of acquaintance. Ordinary names of other people, since they refer to things with which I cannot be acquainted, surely don't function for me as genuine names, but rather as disguised definite descriptions. Even demonstratives like 'this' and 'that', expressions that indeed seem like pointing devices,[8] that do not seem to refer by conceptual characterization, are ordinarily used to refer to external objects. Most ordinary singular terms, then, are surrogates for definite descriptions. Logically proper names, despite their theoretical interest, don't seem to have much to do with ordinary linguistic practice.

> Common words, even proper names, are usually really descriptions. That is to say, the thought in the mind of a person using a proper name correctly can generally be expressed explicitly if we replace the proper name by a description. Moreover, the description required to express the thought will vary for different people, or for the same person at different times. The only thing constant (so long as the name is rightly used) is the object to which the name applies. But so long as this remains constant, the particular description involved usually makes no difference to the truth or falsehood of the proposition in which the name appears.[9]

Sounds just like Frege, doesn't it?

> In the case of an actual proper name such as 'Aristotle' opinions as to the sense may differ. It might, for instance, be taken to be the following: the pupil of Plato and teacher of Alexander the Great. Anybody who does this will attach another sense to the sentence 'Aristotle was born in Stagira' than will a man who takes as the sense of the name: the teacher of Alexander the Great who was born in Stagira. So long as the reference remains the same, such variations of sense may be

---

[8] When I introduced the Russellian idea of a logically proper name earlier, I did not emphasize that such devices might usefully be thought of as pointing devices, devices of ostensive reference. Russell sometimes emphasizes this, as when he says, "For the name itself is merely a means of pointing to the thing, and does not occur in what you are asserting . . . " ("Philosophy of Logical Atomism," in Marsh, *Logic and Knowledge*, p. 245, n. 1). Also see Ruth Barcan Marcus's remark that (ordinary) proper names are the "long finger of ostension" ("Dispensing with Possibilia," in *Proceedings and Addresses of the American Philosophical Association, 1975–76*, vol. 49 [Newark, Del: American Philosophical Association, 1976], p. 45).

[9] KBA, p. 208.

tolerated, although they are to be avoided in the theoretical structure of a demonstrative science and ought not to occur in a perfect language.[10]

We seem to have arrived at a Frege-Russell consensus. Ordinary singular terms, at least the great majority of them, are not directly referential. They refer by expressing concepts.

This is, of course, not to say that Frege and Russell agree on all the essentials. Russell, but not Frege, thinks that at least some singular terms are directly referential. Russell's reason, moreover, for thinking that the great majority of singular terms express concepts is that the great majority of the things about which we wish to speak are not objects of acquaintance. Frege certainly never suggests that epistemic immediacy with an object would somehow make possible *Sinn*less reference to it. Finally, a point to which I will return, talk of Russellian mediating concepts needs serious qualification.

Nevertheless, Frege and Russell seem to share something of a common perspective. The connection between ordinary singular terms and the things in the world for which they stand is conceptually mediated. The propositional constituents that correspond to ordinary singular terms, moreover, is, even for Russell and certainly for Frege, the mediating representation and not the reference. Russell, one might suppose, was the first in a long line of neo-Fregeans.

4. Why Russell Was Not a Neo-Fregean

Russell, however, seems to take pains to distance himself from Fregean representationalism. His view, contrary to the suggestion of the last paragraph, was not that Frege's approach successfully accounts, at least in general, for the linguistic phenomena, that it misfires only with regard to the theoretically interesting but rarely occurring phenomenon of logically proper names. Russell believed, on the contrary, that the sense-reference picture was fundamentally mistaken.[11] How then shall we construe Russell's representationalism as opposed to Frege's?

Let us begin by drawing a distinction, crucial from Russell's point of view, between two sorts of definite descriptions, ones like

[10] "On Sense and Reference," in P. Geach and M. Black, eds., *Translations from the Philosophical Writings of Gottlob Frege* (Oxford: Blackwell, 1966), p. 58, footnote.

[11] His reasons are another matter. See Russell's notoriously obscure discussion, in "On Denoting" (Marsh, *Logic and Knowledge*, pp. 41–56).

'the most long-lived of men', as opposed to ones like 'the material object causally responsible for this' (where 'this' refers to a present sense datum).[12] The relevant difference is that only the first is, as we might say, "purely qualitative," or "purely descriptional." The second, insofar as it contains what Russell would consider a genuine name, is a sort of hybrid. Russell held that the definite descriptions our ordinary singular terms conceal are not purely descriptional.

> [A] description known to be applicable to a particular must involve some reference to a particular with which we are acquainted. . . . All names of places—London, England, Europe, the earth, the Solar System— . . . involve, when used, descriptions which start from some one or more particulars with which we are acquainted. I suspect that even the Universe, as considered by metaphysics, involves such a connection with particulars. In logic, on the contrary, where we are concerned not merely with what does exist, but with whatever might or could exist or be, no reference to actual particulars is involved.[13]

When I say, "London is ugly," or, to use an indexical phrase instead of a name, "This pen ran out of ink," the respective singular terms, 'London' and 'this pen', purport to refer to things that are not possible objects of acquaintance, and so, thinks Russell, those terms must be surrogates for definite descriptions. 'London' and 'this pen' are, at the same time, terms that I "know to be applicable to particulars," and so the descriptions that each of these terms conceals must involve reference to things with which I am acquainted. The description concealed by 'this pen' might be, for example, 'the pen causally responsible for this' (where the demonstrative refers to some relevant sense datum).

Russell's notion of genuine name thus plays a role much more central than we had supposed. It is not merely that Russell makes theoretical room for direct reference, even as he admits that, in practice, ordinary singular terms are by and large descriptional. Direct reference is involved even in our conceptually mediated references to ordinary things. Russell's representationalism is thus a far cry from Frege's.

What led Russell to make the hybrid description the effective paradigm, to reject the Fregean purely qualitative paradigm?

> [A] description known to be applicable to a particular must involve some reference to a particular with which we are acquainted, if our

---

[12] Both descriptions derive from Russell.

[13] KBA, p. 210. Russell is not here singling out place names for special treatment. The same holds for proper names like 'Bismarck', as the context makes clear.

knowledge about the thing described is not to be merely what follows logically from the description.

There is, Russell thinks, a certain sort of knowledge about the denotation of a purely qualitative description that is, in principle, unattainable: knowledge that "the description is applicable to a particular," knowledge that goes beyond the information contained in the description. So if ordinary names abbreviated such descriptions, we could not have this sort of knowledge of their denotations. Russell holds, however, that, in the case of ordinary names, we surely do have this kind of knowledge.

One thing that is confusing about Russell's discussion is that he has characterized the impossible-to-attain knowledge in two ways that do not sound like they come to the same thing. We cannot know, he tells us, that a purely qualitative description is "applicable to a particular." And we cannot know "anything that does not follow from the description itself."

Let's begin with the second, and more tractable, formulation. One can know, perhaps one automatically knows, that the denotation of 'the most long-lived of men', if such exists, must be a man and must have lived longer than any other man. This much presumably "follows from the description." One cannot go beyond such knowledge, however, and come to know that the denotation of this description is, say, Chinese or is the man standing before me now. (Why not? I return to this issue shortly.)

What about Russell's other characterization of the unattainable sort of knowledge, "knowledge that the description is applicable to a particular"? Russell apparently does not here intend to rule out the possibility of coming to know that a purely qualitative description has a denotation, that something or other satisfies the description. He tells us, for example, that "'the most long-lived of men' is a description which must apply to some man, but we can make no judgements about this man which involve knowledge about him beyond what the description gives."[14]

The knowledge Russell apparently means to exclude as "knowledge that the description is applicable to a particular" is knowledge that, as Russell sometimes says, the description applies to a "partic-

---

[14] KBA, p. 210. I'm not sure why Russell, of all people, says that this description "must apply to some man." If two men share the honor of being longer lived than anyone else, so that there is no unique most long-lived man, then the description lacks a denotation, as Russell's famous theory of definite descriptions reminds us. But let's not worry about this. Russell seems in any case willing to allow that we can come to know that a description like 'the most long-lived of men' has a denotation.

ular particular." That is, one cannot come to know to *which thing it is* that the description applies. One cannot, for example, come to know who was the most long-lived man.[15]

The case is quite different, according to Russell, for hybrid descriptions, or names that abbreviate the latter. I can know not only that the name 'Jonathan Wettstein', the name of my son, has a denotation; I can also know which thing it is to which the name applies. It applies to my son, the very person sitting across the table from me now, and so on.[16]

I propose that we don't worry too much about the intricacies of Russell's two formulations. This much, at least, is clear. Russell thought that we cannot, in principle, come to know anything substantive about the denotation of descriptions like 'the most long-lived of men'. It's time that we asked, why in the world not? Why, in principle, couldn't we conduct a study, and come to learn that there is a uniquely longest-lived person, that she is Chinese, that her name is such-and-such, and so on. Indeed, allowing ourselves Russell's intuitive talk of *knowing who*, we could presumably meet the relevant person and thus come to know who she is, for example that she is the person standing before me now. Why should, and how could, the fact that our initial specification was in purely qualitative terms preclude such knowledge?[17]

[15] The identification with *knowing who* is suggested by much of Russell's discussion in "Knowledge by Acquaintance and Knowledge by Description" and in his parallel piece in *The Problems of Philosophy*. See, for example, Russell's discussion of his idea that even one who knows Bismarck only through history—and this is not for Russell a case of having a mere purely qualitative description that denotes Bismarck—knows who he was; p. 58.

[16] Russell sometimes appears to deny that in cases like that of my son's name, I can know who is in question. He says, e.g., that only when I am acquainted with something can I know which thing is in question. At the same time, he clearly holds that we can know who is in question in cases in which knowledge by acquaintance is out of the question, for example, the Bismarck case just mentioned in note 15. Perhaps the point is that there is a strong sense of "knowing who" according to which one knows who *x* is only if one is acquainted with *x*. But in another perfectly legitimate sense one can know who someone is if one knows enough about the individual, even if one is not acquainted with him or her. See the discussion on page 45 of Russell's Bismarck example and accompanying footnotes for further discussion of "knowing who." The topic of "knowing who" is extremely complicated, as recent philosophy testifies, and no serious attempt at resolving the perplexities involved can be carried out here. For a recent illuminating discussion, see Steven E. Boer and William G. Lycan, "Knowing Who," *Philosophical Studies* 28 (1975): 299–344.

[17] Perhaps, on a sufficiently "strict," Cartesian-inspired view of knowledge, according to which we can have knowledge only of the things with which we are acquainted, such knowledge would indeed be impossible. Russell, however, is operating with no such strict notion here. His topic is "knowledge by description," the sort of knowledge we can attain in the absence of acquaintance with the thing about

I suspect that Russell has not expressed himself well, that he would have agreed that we can have knowledge of the denotation of a purely qualitative description that goes beyond the information contained in the description. Russell's motivation for the thesis that ordinary names are descriptional but not purely descriptional is not, I want to suggest, quite what it appears to be.

Russell tells us in *The Problems Of Philosophy* that

> [T]here are various stages in the removal from acquaintance with particulars: there is Bismarck to people who knew him; Bismarck to those who only know of him through history; the man with the iron mask; the longest-lived of men. These are progressively removed from acquaintance with particulars; the first comes as near to acquaintance as is possible in regard to another person; in the second, we shall still be said to know "who Bismarck was"; in the third, we do not know who was the man with the iron mask, though we know many propositions about him which are not logically deducible from the fact that he wore an iron mask;[18] in the fourth, finally, we know nothing beyond what is logically deducible from the definition of the man.[19]

Let's distinguish, along Russellian lines, three ways of making epistemic contact with particulars. At one extreme, one makes the most direct sort of epistemic contact. Bismarck, for example, is acquainted with himself. At the other extreme, one makes direct contact not with a particular, but with a constellation of purely qualitative universals, the sort of thing expressed by a purely qualitative definite description. If such a constellation of universals is uniquely instantiated, say by an external material object or another person,

---

which something is known. He allows, for example, that we can come to know that a certain physical object, such as my pen, is the denotation of a hybrid description like 'the object causally responsible for this [sense datum]'. If, however, we can come to know that a description like the latter is "applicable to a particular," then why not one like 'the most long-lived of men'?

[18] Russell's "man with the iron mask" example is confusing since the description would seem to be purely qualitative, and so Russell ought to deny that we can know anything about the denotation beyond what is implied by the description. Perhaps Russell took this description, in some ordinary use, to be a truncated form of a description that contained a directly referential element. If, however, the more complete description is really hybrid, then why should it differ from, say, one utilized by "those who know of Bismarck only through history"? In other words, why does the use of this description, "the man with the iron mask," represent still a further stage in the removal of acquaintance with particulars? Perhaps the answer to this latter question lies in the considerations briefly discussed later in note 23, that hybrid descriptions don't guarantee *knowing who*, or perhaps Russell has something else in mind.

[19] P. 58.

then one might be said to be making a kind of inferior, mediated epistemic contact with that thing.

There is an intermediate case. One might make direct contact with a constellation of universals *and* acquainted-with-particulars, the sort of constellation expressed by a hybrid description, for example, 'the person who is my only daughter' (as used by me). Such a constellation affords me a mediated but still intermediate level epistemic access to my daughter, for she is being presented as related to a particular with which I am directly acquainted—in this case, me.

It's crucial to note here that Russell links this intermediate epistemic access to *knowing who.*[20] Not only Bismarck's friends, but even someone who knows Bismarck only through history, can be said to know "who Bismarck was." Russell's idea here, I think, is that if I am competent with the name 'Bismarck', then either I have met Bismarck and have been introduced to him by name, or I have learned the use of the name from others. Either way, I stand in the intermediate epistemic position just discussed. That is, I am acquainted with a constellation of universals-cum-particulars that together specify Bismarck. If I've met Bismarck, the relevant particulars with which I'm acquainted are "certain sense-data which [I] connect [rightly, we will suppose] with Bismarck's body."[21] For those of us who have not met Bismarck, the relevant objects of acquaintance consist in "testimony heard or read."[22] In either case, thinks Russell, as in the case of "my daughter," I have an epistemic fix strong enough for it to be reasonable to say that I *know who* is in question.[23]

---

[20] In the weaker sense of "knowing who" distinguished in note 16 of this chapter.

[21] P. 209.

[22] Here I adapt a remark of Russell: "If however, we say, 'the first Chancellor of the German Empire was an astute diplomatist,' we can only be assured of the truth of our judgment in virtue of something with which we are acquainted—usually a testimony heard or read." KBA, p. 210.

[23] Actually, there are varying strengths of epistemic access afforded by constellations of universals-cum-(acquainted-with-) particulars. The constellation expressed by 'my daughter', after all, should be quite different in this respect than that expressed by 'the individual, whoever that may be, who is standing closest to a point exactly 4,000 miles due west of me at the moment'. Russell would surely agree—he himself distinguishes in the passage quoted earlier between the "stage in the removal from acquaintance" represented by Bismarck's friends, and that represented by one who knows Bismarck only through history. Russell, then, would presumably not want to say (or at least he might well not want to say) that in cases such as 'the individual, whoever that may be, who is standing closest to a point exactly 4,000 miles due west . . . ', despite the agent's possession of a "hybrid concept," the agent

Russell maintained that ordinary names were surrogates for hybrid descriptions, descriptions that provide intermediate-level epistemic contact with the denotations. One who is competent with an ordinary name, he further held, *knows who* it names. It begins to look as though Russell took there to be a strong epistemic requirement for the use of names, not only of genuine names. One who uses a name, genuine or ordinary, must know about whom he is speaking. One who uses a genuine name must of course satisfy a much more stringent epistemic requirement than need one using an ordinary name. Only the former requires direct acquaintance with the referent. But even the use of an ordinary name requires identifying knowledge.

We now almost understand why Russell insisted that ordinary names could not abbreviate purely qualitative definite descriptions but necessarily abbreviate hybrid descriptions. I say "almost" because the epistemic constraint just mentioned does not yet fully explain why names cannot disguise purely qualitative descriptions. The epistemic constraint does entail that the name user be in possession of identifying knowledge, but this is compatible with the name abbreviating a description that is purely qualitative, a description that doesn't convey such identifying knowledge. Let the name user, for example, know that some appropriate hybrid description, for example 'the person causing this sense datum', applies to the denotation of the original purely qualitative description, for example, 'the longest living person'.

The mere presence of an identifying knowledge requirement for ordinary names, then, while it seems related to Russell's insistence on the hybrid-description picture, does not by itself do the trick. The missing link—what is needed to see why names could not abbreviate purely qualitative descriptions—is provided by what I take to be Russell's intuition that not only do names require identifying knowledge for their use, but the names themselves indeed capture or convey that knowledge. They do this by abbreviating hybrid descriptions that formulate this knowledge. What names do for us— and this is Russell's "datum," the epistemological intuition that

---

automatically knows who is in question. So possession of a hybrid concept may not supply a sufficient condition for *knowing who*, and Russell never even hints at what further conditions might be relevant. In what follows I will ignore this complication and speak as if the possession of any hybrid description ensures the appropriate sort of identifying knowledge of the denotation.

fuels insistence on the hybrid-descriptions model—is to *identify* their bearers or denotations, to indicate *which things* are in question.

Russell, in motivating his idea that ordinary names conceal hybrid descriptions, misspoke. His point, if I understand him, was not that there is any sort of knowledge that one cannot have concerning the denotation of a purely qualitative description. His point was rather that the use, or understanding, of such a description—as opposed to the use, or understanding, of an ordinary name—does not capture or convey or express the sort of knowledge in question.

Russell's views about ordinary proper names seem to me underexplored. I have been focused upon the epistemic motivation for Russell's hybrid-descriptions account, but there is still more. There is in "Knowledge By Acquaintance and Knowledge By Description" a distinct, semantic motivation for his view of ordinary names. Consider these two passages.

> Suppose some statement is made about Bismarck. Assuming that there is such a thing as direct acquaintance with oneself, Bismarck might have used his name directly to designate the particular person with whom he was acquainted. In this case, if he made a judgment about himself, he himself might be a constituent of the judgment. *Here the proper name has the direct use which it always wishes to have, as simply standing for a certain object, and not for a description of the object.* [Italics added.] But if a person who knew Bismarck made a judgment about him, the case is different. [In this case since the speaker is not acquainted with Bismarck, the name must stand for a description.][24]

> It would seem that, when we make a statement about something only known by description, we often *intend* to make our statement, not in the form involving the description, but about the actual thing described. That is to say, when we say anything about Bismarck, we should like, if we could, to make the judgment which Bismarck alone can make, namely, the judgment of which he himself is a constituent. In this we are necessarily defeated, since the actual Bismarck is unknown to us.[25]

Russell's remarks are confusing. In the first he tells us that all names, even ordinary ones, want, so to speak, to reach out and touch someone. What does this mean?

[24] KBA, p. 209.
[25] KBA, p. 210.

Russell suggests, in the second passage quoted, that the use of an ordinary proper name involves a frustrated referential intention. Surely, however, Russell is not speaking seriously here about referential intentions and their failures analogous, say, to the remark that the ancient Greeks intended to refer to Zeus but were frustrated in this intention because of Zeus's lack of existence. Imagine that I really intend to use an ordinary name as a genuine name, that is, I do not mean to put forth a descriptive characterization of the object of reference. If I am not in an epistemic position to refer directly, then my intended reference should turn out to be a real reference failure, not a successful use of a device that abbreviates a definite description. What then is Russell's point?

Perhaps Russell has in mind, in this second passage—the first remains mysterious—not referential intentions but rather referential wishes. Perhaps his point is that we would like to refer to Bismarck directly, which is not to say that we utter the name with the intention of directly referring to him. As much as we would like to so refer to him, we cannot and so we do what is second best: express a descriptive characterization of him. How coherent is this solution? I'm not sure. It unrealistically seems to assume great semantic sophistication on the part of ordinary speakers: They would like to refer directly, but since they know that this is impossible, they go in for the descriptive mode of expression. Referential wishes do not seem to help here, any more than did referential intentions.

I want to suggest a different interpretive direction. Russell gives voice in both of these passages to a lingering sense that somehow names, ordinary ones, do not quite *feel* descriptional. Isn't it just this sense that Russell attempts to evoke with the remark that 'Bismarck', as Bismarck himself uses it, has the direct use *that it always wishes to have,* or with the comment that even when I use 'Bismarck', *the name tries to directly get through to the man himself?* If not for what we know about the epistemic conditions for real naming, we can imagine Russell musing, it would be tempting to treat all names, ordinary ones included, as directly referential. Russell, if I am not mistaken, felt a conflict between the dictates of his semantic ear,[26] according to which names are directly referential, and his epistemological conscience.

---

[26] The expression is Joseph Almog's. Almog has argued in conversation that there are direct semantic intuitions to the effect that ordinary proper names are directly referential. I find this appeal to intuition difficult to evaluate. It is not one that plays any role in my argument in this book.

I see in Russell's discussions of ordinary names, then, a tension between two conflicting pictures of the semantics of ordinary names. Russell's dominant tendency, the one that gets all the press, is to treat ordinary names as disguised definite descriptions. One may begin to get the scent of a conflicting tendency when Russell so often uses ordinary proper names as examples of genuine names, and characteristically remarks in such contexts that he is speaking *as if* mere ordinary names were real names. Perhaps, but Russell's direct-reference impulse shines through most clearly, I think, in the quoted passages.

What we might call "Russell's compromise," his idea that ordinary names are descriptional-but-not-purely-so, might well represent, at least in part, his attempt to do justice to the conflict between his semantic ear and his epistemological scruples. Ordinary names fail to make direct semantic contact with their referents—as dictated by epistemology—yet they do not merely talk about things by indirection, as do purely qualitative definite descriptions. Ordinary names, since they abbreviate definite descriptions that contain genuine names of particulars, make a kind of semi-direct contact with their bearers by specifying the latter in terms of directly referred-to particulars.

I have explored two philosophical motives for Russell's hybrid-descriptions theory of ordinary names, epistemic and semantic. Russell's ideas here are, as usual, ingenious, intriguing, and frustrating. I find his epistemological ideas especially troublesome, at least in part because of their Cartesian inspiration. At the same time, one cannot deny their suggestiveness, as in the idea that the use of even ordinary proper names requires some kind of identifying knowledge. This idea is independent of, although of course not unrelated to, the thesis that names are description surrogates. The epistemic requirement thesis, like so many of Russell's ideas, shows up, albeit in different dress, in contemporary discussions,[27] and it is one to which I will return in later chapters.

It is striking how differently Frege and Russell respond to the challenges that names present. Russell, unlike Frege, was impressed, almost obsessed, with proper names, even ordinary ones. Ordi-

---

[27] Keith Donnellan, e.g., a defender of a direct reference view for ordinary names, nevertheless argues that one must stand in a privileged epistemic relation to an individual in order to refer to it by name. See, e.g. his "Rigid Designators and the Contingent A Priori," in P. French, T. Uehling, and H. Wettstein, eds., *Contemporary Perspectives in the Philosophy of Language* (Minneapolis: University of Minnesota Press, 1979).

nary names, as we have seen, constituted a very special category to
him. Indeed, if my reading of Russell is on track, ordinary names—
both semantically and epistemologically—are much more like genuine names than the usual talk of the "Frege-Russell description theory" would suggest. Frege, by stark contrast, introduces a category of
"proper name" with the remark: "The designation of a single object
can also consist of several words or other signs. For brevity, let every
such designation be called a proper name."[28] Frege is thus not all
that worried about what is distinctive about actual proper names.
Semantically, they are of a piece with definite descriptions.

It is unfortunate that Russell never really develops, or even
makes fully explicit, his semantic motivation, what I have referred
to as the dictates of his semantic ear. Here, in a way that is entirely
independent of his Cartesian epistemology, Russell's deepest differences with Frege are highlighted. And here, Russell anticipates a
most influential idea in contemporary philosophy of language, one
that I will discuss later, the idea that an ordinary name is a "mere
noise or shape conventionally used to designate a certain [thing]; it
gives us no information about that [thing], and has nothing that can
be called its meaning as opposed to denotation."[29]

5. More on Russell's Representationalism: The Theory of Descriptions

Despite the deep differences uncovered between Russell and Frege,
there remains, at least so far, this substantial agreement: Ordinary
singular terms like names and indexical expressions refer by expressing concepts. Well . . . perhaps "concepts" are not quite right
for Russell. Ordinary singular terms, after all, express constellations of universals-cum-(acquainted-with-)particulars, and referring
to these as concepts is perhaps distorting Russell's view, exces-
sively assimilating it to Frege's.[30] Still, Russell apparently shares
with Frege the idea that ordinary singular terms make mediated
contact with their referents. The mediating agents may be Fregean
senses, or Russellian universal-cum-particular constellations, but

---

[28] "On Sense and Reference," p. 57.

[29] KBA, p. 218.

[30] At issue here is not Russell's, nor Frege's, use of the term 'concept' (or 'Be-
griff'). I am using the term 'concept' as I have all along, to refer to something like
Fregean senses (as opposed to the things Frege calls 'concepts', i.e., the references of
predicates, or that Russell does, i.e., universals). My point in the text is that it is
stretching things to attribute to Russell the view that hybrid descriptions express
such concepts.

they mediate nevertheless. Or so it seems. The problem is that Russell's famous theory of descriptions suggests otherwise, for according to it, definite descriptions do not really express constellations of concepts and particulars, nor do they even really refer to anything.[31] Let's see why.

One thing that is novel about Russell's approach to the semantics of definite descriptions, and that is particularly relevant here, is Russell's idea that a sentence of the form "The *F* is *G*" is, to dramatize a bit, almost ill formed. Less dramatically, the grammatical structure of such a sentence, its subject-predicate form, gives a misleading picture of the content of the sentence, of what the sentence is actually putting forth as true. Contrary to the grammatical appearances, such a sentence does not attribute a property, *G*, to a thing, the *F*, as do sentences of the form "*a* is *G*," where '*a*' is a logically proper name. How, then, are we to understand such sentences? What exactly do they assert?

Russell's well-known answer[32] is that the content of such sentences is perspicuously formulated thus: One and only one thing has *F*, and that very thing also has *G*; or, more long-windedly, something has *F*, anything that has *F* is identical to this first thing (so that no more than one thing has *F*), and that very thing also has *G*. One who says, "The president of the United States who emancipated the slaves was a Republican," should not be thought of as, strictly speaking, attributing the property of being a Republican to Lincoln. Don't think of this utterance as mentioning Lincoln at all. Think of it as saying something very general about the universe: There is one and only one thing that has a certain property, *being a United States president who emancipated the slaves*, and, further, this very thing has an additional property, *being a Republican*.

While the general direction of Russell's approach is clear, the details are quite another matter. For one thing, the example just given, like many of the examples that spring to mind, including many of Russell's examples, would be extremely complicated to work out in detail. We might symbolically represent the reformulation just discussed as

$$(Ex)\ \{(Px)\ \&\ (y)\ [Py \rightarrow (y = x)]\ \&\ Rx\}$$

---

[31] I haven't forgotten Russell's view that definite descriptions have "denotations." I will return to this shortly.

[32] See "On Denoting" for Russell's reasons for denying that the apparent grammatical structure reflects what is really going on, as well as his reasons for the positive view sketched here.

What property does '*P*' designate? Remember, the predicate 'is a United States president who emancipated the slaves' embeds another description, 'the slaves', as well as the name 'United States'. The latter name in turn abbreviates a hybrid description, according to Russell. So we should think of the above reformulation as a mere first step toward a final version in which all descriptions are eliminated.

Even more troublesome is obtaining a precise account of the semantics of Russell's perspicuous formulations. This would involve, among other things, an account of the semantics of quantifiers, and Russell himself talks about this question in confusing, and on different occasions quite different, ways. Who knows how all of this is ultimately to get spelled out?

Let's be content, then, with Russell's basic idea, that the old, description-containing sentence ought to be scrapped in favor of one that employs quantifiers, variables, and so on, so as to formulate the proposition perspicuously.

I want to focus upon the great gap between the look of the original sentence and that of the reformulation. A radical metamorphosis seems to have transpired. The definite description does not simply get replaced by some other expression that better exhibits the description's function. We might think of Frege's view in this latter, less radical, way: A name, according to Frege, fails to make explicit its informational content, and so were we to replace it with a definite description, this would have the virtue of making the content explicit. This latter kind of reformulation leaves the basic structure intact.

Russell's reformulation, by contrast, yields a radically new structure. What looked like (but never really was) a reference to Lincoln is gone, and instead we have references to various properties, acquainted-with-particulars, and so on (including whatever references are involved in the use of quantifiers, possibly propositional functions, second-order properties, and who-knows-what). The result is a new sentence that, as a whole, is supposed to be functionally equivalent[33] to the original, but not at all, so to speak, piece by piece. The

---

[33] There is more than one way to understand the relation between the original sentence and the Russellian reformulation. I have been proceeding with Russell's dominant trend: to view the reformulation as making explicit the thought in the mind of the speaker, a thought that is misleadingly put by the original sentence. One might do it differently (in the spirit of Quine, for example) and see the original as muddled (who knows what ordinary folk think when they use descriptions, and who cares?) and see the reformulation as coming as close to the original as possible

basic structure of the propositions we express by ordinary sentences is, according to Russell, radically different from the structure suggested by the grammar of those sentences, and radically different from what, Russell admits, one would have naturally assumed.[34]

Consider now a Russellian reformulator, one who takes his Russell very seriously. (There is one in every crowd.) The Russellian reformulator looks at definite descriptions as mere artifacts of the misleading grammar of ordinary language. Definite descriptions don't really exist for him, at least not at the level of, as he likes to say, logical form. When a Russellian reformulator hears someone utter a sentence that contains one or more definite descriptions (or description abbreviations), he barely hears the vulgar form(s) of expression. What registers is "what the speaker is 'really' saying," the perspicuous Russellian reformulation. (Think of yourself "translating" a child's poorly constructed remarks.)

Does it make any sense, given this Russellian perspective, to speak of "the constellation of universals-cum-particulars expressed by a definite description"? If we took the unanalyzed sentence at face value, if we left the grammatically unified definite description intact, it would have been natural to speak of "what *it* expresses," a concept, constellation, or whatever. We are, however, not leaving this expression intact. When we straighten out what is being said, there is no unified expression that plays the role of the description.

---

while meeting serious standards of acceptability, intelligibility, etc. For more of the latter see W. V. O. Quine's *Word and Object* (Cambridge, Mass.: Harvard University Press, 1960), esp. "The Ordered Pair as a Philosophical Paradigm." Also see Russell's remarks in this Quinean direction in Russell's "Mr. Strawson on Referring," in *My Philosophical Development* (New York: Simon and Schuster, 1959), chapter 18, part 3.

[34] At one point in "On Denoting," after formulating how things should go according to his own theory, Russell says, "This may seem a somewhat incredible interpretation; but I am not at present giving reasons, I am merely stating the theory"; p. 44.

There is an interesting methodological contrast here with Frege, as Kaplan notes in "What Is Russell's Theory of Descriptions?" in D. F. Pears, ed., *Bertrand Russell: A Collection of Critical Essays* (Garden City, N.Y.: Doubleday, 1972), pp. 227–44:

> Russell and Frege were both interested in removing the logical imperfections of ordinary language but their methods were quite different . . . Where grammar called for entities whose nature was obscure, Frege attempted constructions, as with numbers, or a theory about the purported entities, as with propositions. Thus he sought to preserve the integrity of ordinary language with ontological ingenuity. Russell's response, at least in the case of definite descriptions, was by grammatical reconstrual and replacement.

The Russellian reformulation *eliminates* the description, and disburses those expressions that derive from it. There is thus no expression left that can be thought of as expressing such a constellation. Nor, to speak more ontologically, is there any such constellation of universals-cum-particulars that enters as a unit into the proposition.

Talk of names and descriptions expressing semantically mediating entities fits hand-in-glove with Frege's approach, but does not seem felicitous with respect to Russell's perspicuous reformulations. Strictly and philosophically speaking, then, Russell does not think of descriptions, nor of the ordinary names and indexicals that abbreviate descriptions, as expressing constellations of concepts and particulars. What has become of what we took to be Russell's Fregean tendency, his representationalism?

It will be instructive here, before we get carried away with strict and philosophical talk, to take brief note of Russell's introduction of the notion of "denotation." Russell maintains that although it's no part of the linguistic function of a definite description to pick something out (how could it be since these expressions don't exist at the level of logical form?), we can still speak of the "denotation" of a description. The perspicuous reformulation of "The president who emancipated the slaves was a Republican" may not contain any expression that refers to Lincoln, but there is still a sense in which it is "about" Lincoln. That sense emerges when we note that we can inquire as to who is (roughly speaking) the unique individual particularly relevant to the truth or falsity of the perspicuous formulation. Russell suggests that we call this individual, if indeed there exists such, "the denotation."

> Thus if '*C*' is a denoting phrase [e.g. a definite description], it may happen that there is one entity *x* (there cannot be more than one) for which the proposition '*x* is identical with *C*' is true, this proposition being interpreted as above. We may then say that the entity *x* is the denotation of the phrase '*C*'.[35]

Definite descriptions may not really function to pick something out, but it is harmless enough to speak as if they did, since, in the felicitous case at least, there will be a unique individual particularly relevant to the truth or falsity of the perspicuous formulation.

---

[35] "On Denoting," p. 51.

Russell's "philosophy of 'as if'" approach to denotation seems applicable as well to talk of the concept or constellation expressed by a definite description. The Russellian reformulator, although he may balk at talk of definite descriptions expressing concepts, is not altogether ignorant of what *we* might reasonably call "the meaning" of individual descriptions (even considered "in isolation," perish the thought). Give him a definite description and he will be able to associate with it a group of universals, acquainted-with-particulars, and so on. These are the items that will get mentioned, albeit in a disbursed fashion, in the perspicuous reformulation. He knows (thankfully) much better than we do precisely which universals and acquainted-with-particulars constitute the remains of, for example, 'the president of the United States who emancipated the slaves'.

Given that definite descriptions can thus be "associated with" universals and acquainted-with-particulars, in the sense just indicated, we can, so to speak, mentally collect these disbursed remains of a description and speak as if there were a unified entity expressed. Properly understood, such talk is harmless, and it facilitates recognition of what still can be called the "representationalist character" of Russell's approach. Just as the description can be said to be about someone, in the sense of having a denotation, it can be said to be about that individual in virtue of the individual's fitting the reconstituted constellation.

Russell's representationalism, it turns out, is a trickier business than Frege's, trickier than we had supposed. Indeed, in one important respect it is a more severe representationalism than is Frege's. Not only can one not speak in a conceptually unmediated way of, for example, external things (or more generally, of anything that is not an object of acquaintance); one can never refer to such things at all. Such an epistemically removed item can never be the subject of a subject-predicate proposition, at least not one that we can understand. One can, however, still "talk about" such things in the oblique fashion of Russell's perspicuous reformulations. We can, in this oblique sense, "talk about" Lincoln by asserting that one and only one thing was a presidential slave emancipator, and that thing was a Republican. Such talk crucially involves reference to universals and particulars with which we are acquainted. It is these latter sorts of things, specifically the ones that I induced my Russellian reformulator to count as constitutive of the "meaning" of the description, in the "as if" sense discussed above, that together can be said to represent the things obliquely talked about.

6. Concluding Remarks: Propositions
and the Intentionality Intuition

Russell and Frege seem worlds apart on the major questions under scrutiny here: the nature of propositions, the viability of the sense-reference distinction, the intelligibility of conceptually unmediated reference, and, as we saw in the preceding section, the integrity of the syntax of natural language. Even where they seem to agree, moreover, one needs to take a closer look. They seem to agree, for example, that proper names have descriptive content. What this comes to, though, is very different for Frege than it is for Russell.

This chapter concludes with brief discussions of two issues that play a major role in what is to follow.

6.1. Russellian Propositions

Russell wants no part of Fregean senses. Propositions, on his view, contain not senses but rather references, things like you and me, as well as universals, the references of general terms. Russell's idea that ordinary things can be constituents of propositions has proved startling to many. Is such a notion even coherent? Philosophers with broadly Fregean sympathies, and others no doubt as well, find the idea unintelligible. Propositions, they argue, are concept-like entities, and surely cannot contain things like you and me as constituents. Russell's sympathizers argue that abstract entities, sets for example, can contain things like you and me, so that it is not clear that there is a real problem here. The opponents then point out that propositional constituency is not at all the same thing as set membership, and the debate continues.

I have always found Russell's idea of objects in propositions both appealing and troubling, and in the end I do not want to defend it. Indeed, for reasons that will emerge, propositions play no important role in my approach. (Had I read those words at the time of my dissertation, I would have been incredulous. Surely, I would have thought, notwithstanding the urgings of the ontologically stingy, we need some distinction between what is uttered and what is asserted. We also need something to serve as bearers of truth and objects of belief. And so propositions are central to my project.) Nevertheless, I think that Russell's conception is powerfully motivated, and I will devote further attention to it later.

For now, at least this much can be said. If one wants a distinction between a sentence and its content, if one wants something like the notion of proposition, and one is committed to direct reference, to the idea that some expressions refer without any sort of conceptual mediation, then it is difficult to see how one can avoid putting the referent itself into the proposition.

So it is important, and it will be important to the discussion of Russellian propositions, that Russell restricts cases in which a particular is a propositional constituent to cases of direct reference. The latter idea, conceptually unmediated reference, is for me the most exciting to have emerged in this discussion of Russell. Direct reference, after we have distilled it a bit and extracted it from Russell's Cartesian epistemology, will constitute one of the central ideas of this book.

6.2. The Intentionality Intuition

While the stark contrasts mentioned earlier between Russell and Frege deserve emphasis, perhaps especially in light of contemporary talk of a Frege-Russell approach, it is nevertheless useful to revert to a level of abstraction at which we find agreement between the two fathers of the subject. The deepest, most fundamental point of contact concerns what I will call the "intentionality intuition." This is the traditional idea—and it will play a major role in what follows—that if one is to speak or think about a thing, one must possess a discriminating cognitive fix on the thing, that something about one's cognitive state must distinguish the relevant item from everything else in the universe. Otherwise, so the intuition goes, what would make *this* thing the referent.[36]

Even here, Frege and Russell approach the matter in very different ways. They disagree on what counts as the appropriate sort of cognitive fix, on just what sort of cognitive relation is required between thinker (speaker) and object of thought (referent). Frege's idea was that reference to an object required that the object be brought under an individuating concept, that only the possession of an individuating concept puts one in a position to refer to that which satisfies the concept. Russell—an intentionality zealot—was dissatisfied with the idea that the possession of a concept might supply

---

[36] As I am using this fancy word, it has nothing special to do with the problem, associated with Brentano, of how it is possible to think about something that does not exist. 'Intentionality' here concerns the more general phenomenon of the "aboutness" of thought. The traditional picture to which Frege, Russell, and many others subscribe has it that thought can be about something only if that something is intellectually discriminable by the thinker.

the required cognitive grip. One might possess a purely qualitative concept that in fact applies to a certain entity and yet, Russell reasoned, have absolutely no idea who or what satisfies that concept. On the other hand, were one to be directly acquainted with an object, were one to have the object, as it were, smack up against one's mind, one would really be making contact, one would know which thing was in question.

Having identified fundamental Frege-Russell agreement—the intentionality intuition—we can now see that their respective ideas about cognitive fix are pivotal in their controversy about direct reference. Frege's approach to the cognitive-fix requirement makes direct, conceptually unmediated reference an impossibility. Russell, thinking about intentionality in terms of direct acquaintance, sees no problem with direct reference but only with respect to the epistemically intimate.

There is another candidate in the literature for a point of important agreement between Frege and Russell: their accord on the descriptive character of ordinary proper names. This does not seem to me to go nearly as deep.[37] For one thing, Russell does not espouse a description theory for what he took to be the real names, a fact that is too often noted but quickly set aside in an enthusiasm for (or against) their shared descriptivism. While Russell's descriptivism is thus mitigated, his view about the necessity of a strong cognitive fix, especially for genuine names, is not. Russell's tendency, moreover, was not to assimilate names to descriptions—as was Frege's—but to emphasize the differences. Even ordinary names, as we have seen, involve for Russell a kind of epistemic intimacy with their referents not characteristic of purely qualitative descriptions. If I'm correct about Russell's semantic ear, moreover, he would have loved to find a way to view ordinary names as directly referential, if only their epistemology would take care of itself.

Nor is it even clear that descriptivism is at the heart of Frege's approach. Indeed, there is a controversy in the literature about whether Frege was a descriptivist at all, whether Frege took the senses of names to be given by purely qualitative definite descriptions. What is uncontroversial is that Frege took modes of presentation to be essential to reference. While it is difficult to imagine

---

[37] It has become widely (but not universally) accepted nowadays that it is a mistake to see names as surrogates for definite descriptions. If so, descriptivism, in both its Fregean and Russellian (very different) embodiments, is incorrect. I agree. However, it's important to me that this topic not divert our focus from the more fundamental area of agreement, the intentionality intuition.

Frege as movable on the latter question, it is much easier to see the description theory as negotiable. For both Frege and Russell, then, it is not the description theory, but the cognitive fix requirement, that goes deepest.

The idea that reference indeed requires some sort of substantive cognitive fix may look unassailable, but it is not trivially true. Perhaps one can refer to an object simply by using an expression conventionally associated with the object, even if the speaker himself, in terms of his own knowledge or belief, has no way of distinguishing that object from a lot of other things. But the Frege-Russell intuition here is very strong, and if the reader is coming to these questions fresh, then it would certainly not be unreasonable to find the Frege-Russell orientation congenial.

3

Revolution in the Philosophy of Language

During the late twentieth century there was talk of a new, even revolutionary, approach to the philosophy of language. Something radically different from the perspectives of Frege and Russell was in the wind.[1] It is my aim in this book to develop this alternative, but in quite a different way from that envisaged by the key figures in the movement—Donnellan, Kaplan, Kripke, Marcus, and Putnam. For even as they effected substantial change, they remained locked within traditional patterns of thought. I will recommend a way of thinking about language, and about the character of its philosophic study, that likely will seem foreign to *both* traditionalists and revolutionaries. My hope, though, is to bring into sharper focus what was at the heart of the dissatisfaction with the traditional approach.

Philosophy, as it has been practiced in the Anglo-American philosophic community during the last few decades, consists too much in the sophistication, in a pejorative sense, of what often began as interesting and intuitive ways of construing various philosophic subject matters. I'll have more to say about this tendency,

---

[1] What is really a tendency is sometimes badly described—I have done so myself—as the "New Theory of Reference."

but for the moment I want to emphasize that my aim here is not to produce another intellectual twist on the insights of those just mentioned, a new wrinkle that makes the approach immune to some crucial range of counterexamples. If I am correct that the revolutionaries remain tied to traditional patterns, what is needed is no mere twist, but rather a deepening of our understanding of what was essential to the traditional patterns, and in what the real revolution consists. The epicycles already offered, ingenious as they sometimes have been, have make it even more difficult to discern the heart of the revolution.

1. Language vis-à-vis Thought: Two Perspectives

I want to begin by contrasting in a rough and ready way two philosophic perspectives, the clash of which lies beneath the surface in current debates. The first is a broadly Cartesian outlook that gives priority to thought over language. One crucial respect—call it "functional priority"—concerns the paramount function of language, its raison d'être: the expression of thought. If not for our need to communicate our thoughts to one another—as it is sometimes, perhaps naïvely, put—there would be no need for language.

This functional priority is closely related to an ontological priority. While thought is in no way dependent upon language, language without thought is scarcely coherent, a body without soul, noises or marks on paper without significance.

Other respects in which the Cartesian outlook gives primacy to thought are (more or less) epistemological. It is customary to distinguish thought, more precisely, thinking (an act or process), from the *contents* of the thinking. A broadly Cartesian approach may take the contents of thought to reside in the mind, in the head, or in an objective third realm, accessible to the mind or maybe even to the head. Thought contents, wherever they live, tend to be seen as well behaved, even clear and distinct. Moreover, thought contents are transparent to the thinker. One has a privileged—on some variants, infallible—access to the contents of one's thoughts.

Actual language, on the other hand, is from this broadly Cartesian standpoint a relative swamp, not particularly well behaved, about which theorizing does not come easy. In the way that ordinary things are for Plato highly imperfect reflections of the Forms, so actual talk awkwardly and imprecisely mirrors the pristine thought that constitutes its content. To jump centuries, and from Platonic metaphysics to Cartesian epistemology, Descartes' dictum that the mind is better known than the body finds a modern linguistic analog in the remark that thought is better known than speech.

Such an approach contrasts starkly with that of Walker Percy in "The Delta Factor": "Instead of starting out with such large, vexing subjects as soul, mind, ideas, consciousness, why not set forth with language, which no one denies, and see how far it takes us toward the rest."[2] The nature of thought, on this dramatically contrasting perspective, is a difficult and elusive matter, one with respect to which it is relatively easy to lose one's bearings. Questions about the nature of thought are surely not the place to begin.

What is relatively out in the open is not thought but linguistic practice, a set of social, institutional arrangements. Here we are not nearly as apt to get lost. It may even turn out that clarifying the character of linguistic practice will illuminate some of those "large, vexing subjects." Indeed, it becomes tempting on this second approach, although it is no doubt much too simple, to see thought—silent thought, that is—on the model of silent utterance. Less ambitious is the idea that in verbally communicating, we are sometimes not conveying preexistent thoughts that lie behind our utterances, but rather thinking out loud quite literally. Consider, in this connection, a lively discussion in which you and your interlocutor are animatedly "figuring it out as you go." Such external speech episodes count as thinking no less than does silent thought. These tempting speculations aside, the central idea is that, as it were, the body—unkempt as it is—is nevertheless better known than the mind.[3]

---

[2] Walker Percy, "The Delta Factor," collected in Walker Percy, *The Message in the Bottle: How Queer Man Is, How Queer Language Is, and What One Has to Do with the Other* (New York: Farrar, Straus, and Giroux, 1984), p. 17.

[3] Cf. Anthony Kenny's remark in "Cartesian Privacy" in George Pitcher, ed., *Wittgenstein: The Philosophical Investigations, A Collection of Critical Essays* (Garden City, N.Y.: Doubleday, 1966), p. 352:

> Medieval Aristotelians had taught that the human mind, as we know it, was most at home in the study of the nature of physical bodies. Intellect is a capacity, so their theory ran, and capacities are known through their exercise. But the proper exercise of the human intellect as we know it is the investigation of the physical universe. Knowledge of the human mind, therefore, must be secondary to, almost parasitic on, knowledge of the external world.

2. The Cartesian Character of Frege's Philosophy of Language

So much for a rough sketch of the clashing perspectives. Where does Frege fit in?[4] Frege, as Michael Dummett emphasizes,[5] has played a crucial role in the twentieth-century anti-Cartesianism. Frege's revolutionary contribution consisted in making the philosophical study of meaning, rather than skepticism and the theory of knowledge, the starting point in philosophy.[6]

Clearly Frege wants no part of Descartes's making the theory of knowledge the place to begin. At the same time, there is more deeply buried a bond between Frege and the Cartesian tradition. I have in mind not Cartesian epistemology but rather Cartesian tendencies concerning the relations between thought and language.

Frege, as writers like Burge and Dummett have pointed out, and as I noted in chapter 1, was less interested in language per se than in "the objective structure of thought."[7] It was the realm of eternally existing thought contents, what Frege calls "the common treasure of mankind," that was his primary quarry, and not a mere set of social practices.

Frege, moreover, gives thought contents the characteristic sorts of priority over their linguistic embodiments that I delineated earlier. Clearly the key function of language on Frege's view is the expression of thought. Thought contents, moreover, are ontologically prior to their linguistic embodiments. The Fregean thought (or proposition) that the sun is larger than the earth would exist and be true even if no one ever expressed it, or even apprehended it, even if it had no linguistic embodiment.

---

[4] Russell's story, as we saw in the last chapter, is quite complicated. For many purposes, however, we can follow the customary practice of the revolutionaries, and where it is of no consequence assimilate Russell's views to Frege's, discussing their differences when it becomes important to do so.

[5] *Frege: Philosophy of Language* (London: Duckworth, 1973). See esp. chapter 19, "Frege's Place in the History of Philosophy," a chapter well worth reading even for nonspecialists.

[6] This phrase, "the starting point in philosophy," covers a multitude of sins. Did Frege take the philosophical study of language to be *foundational*, in some sense at least roughly analogous to the sense in which Descartes took epistemology to be foundational, as Dummett seems to suggest? Or, as I am inclined to suppose, did Frege merely take this study to be deep and intellectually fundamental? Thankfully, we need not pursue the matter further here.

[7] Tyler Burge, "Sinning Against Frege," *Philosophical Review* 88 (July 1979): 398.

Thought also enjoys the (roughly) epistemological priority discussed earlier. Frege emphasizes the gap between the pristine contents of thought—a concept without sharp boundaries, we are told, is no concept at all—and our rather imperfect representations of such contents in natural language. The transparency of thought, moreover, is a fundamental Fregean idea. A thinker has a privileged (maybe even infallible) grasp on the content of his thought. One who apprehends the same proposition twice knows that it is the same. The contents of thought are surely better known than the messy linguistic practices, to allude to the Cartesian analogy once again.

None of this inclines Frege to downplay the enormous importance of the philosophical study of language. If language is thought externalized, then the study of language ought to be of great utility for the understanding of thought. Philosophical interest in language may be derivative, but concern with language is at the heart of philosophy.

Frege's view has a distinctly individualistic flavor, an additional point of contact with the notoriously individualistic Cartesian tradition. Frege's individualism is obscured by his making the representations abstract and therefore public entities. Think, though, about how proper names, for example, or indexical expressions, get attached to the in-principle public senses. The reference of a proper name depends, for Frege, not upon anything like the role of the name in the public language, an idea to which we will return, but rather upon the individual speaker's associating a particular sense with the name. Nor will it be clear, in many cases, which of the public senses a particular name user is attaching to his use of a name. (This is why I referred to the senses as public "in principle." Audiences will often have no way of telling how the speaker is thinking of his referent, and thus no way of knowing which public-in-principle thought is being expressed.)

3. The Vitality of Language and the Intentionality Intuition: More on Frege's Cartesianism

Descartes, in the *Meditations*, tells us that it seemed very strange to him that parts of nature appear to move themselves. How, he must have been thinking, could mere constellations of atoms do such a singular thing? That mere pieces of nature *signify* might seem even more singular. How are we to explain what, following Wittgenstein, we might call the vitality of language, the fact that linguistic expressions—also mere constellations of atoms—are for us alive? Whence the magic? This, by my lights, is among the most fundamental questions for philosophical reflection on language.

The Cartesian picture of the mind provides a powerful account of significance. The Cartesian sees the mind as, to use Rorty's wonderful expression, a "mirror of nature," as a repository of representations that naturally, intrinsically—at least not by human convention—represent (or fail to represent) things. Words come to life when we associate them with the intrinsically significant representations. The meanings, the associated representations, are, as Wittgenstein says, the souls of words, and they provide the magic. There is a striking parallel between agent-induced locomotion and significance. In both cases, magic is provided by the soul, enlivening the body.

This approach, of course, is almost exactly Frege's. Of course Fregean senses are most emphatically not residents of the mind, but rather of a third realm of abstract entities. His way of thinking about significance is nevertheless Cartesian spirited. There is for Frege a realm of intrinsically significant representations, distinct from the things represented and accessible to (even if not residing in) the mind; linguistic expressions come to life when they come to be associated with these representations. Fregean senses—and not their linguistic embodiments—refer in the primary instance.[8] The connection between words and things is thus derivative from the connection between the conceptual representations and the things they represent. The vitality of language is derivative; the vitality of sense is primary.

At the end of chapter 2 I identified an idea that runs deep in traditional thinking about language, the intentionality intuition— the idea that a substantial cognitive fix is essential to reference. This, I argued, was the most fundamental point of agreement between Frege and Russell. Frege's Cartesian-spirited approach to significance—his making the vitality of sense primary—underlies his commitment to the cognitive fix requirement. Words refer derivatively, in virtue of their being associated with concepts, and so one can speak of something only if one has an adequate concept.[9]

---

[8] "The regular connexion between a sign, its sense, and its reference is of such a kind that to the sign there corresponds a definite sense and *to that in turn* [italics added] a definite reference, . . . " From "On Sense and Reference," in P. Geach and M. Black, eds., *Translations from the Philosophical Writings of Gottlob Frege* (Oxford: Blackwell, 1966), p. 58.

[9] See my discussion in chapter 2 regarding Frege's "representative theory of conception."

I have been emphasizing Frege's Cartesian roots for several reasons. First, Frege never does formulate or even gesture toward, a broad philosophic outlook. In this, of course, he is in company with analytic philosophers generally—ours is a movement to which he provided great inspiration—and with his recent critics specifically. Nevertheless, seeing Frege's semantic outlook as grounded in a broader Cartesian perspective may yield a deeper appreciation of the organic quality of his view. Indeed, I will return in the next chapter to several crucial Fregean themes that seem closely connected with Frege's Cartesian orientation. Seeing Frege in such terms may also yield a better sense of the grip of a broadly Fregean outlook on the philosophic community, a point to which I will also return.

There is a more immediate reason for emphasizing Frege's Cartesianism. Central to my project is the elucidation of what is, or ought to be, at the heart of the revolution against Frege. Anti-Fregeans, not any more fluent than was Frege in the idiom of large philosophic perspectives, haven't really said. Indeed, one might well get the sense from much of the seminal literature that what is at stake is something fairly refined and technical, like the idea that many sorts of singular terms, contrary to the views of Frege and Russell, have an important modal-cum-semantic property, namely that they are, in Kripke's vocabulary, rigid designators, that they "refer to the same thing in all possible worlds."

I believe, on the contrary, that what is at stake is the rejection of what we might call linguistic Cartesianism. The deep lesson, I will urge, is the need for a virtual gestalt switch, a transformation from this broadly Cartesian perspective to the contrasting social practice orientation. The pivotal notion in the latter approach is one brought to life not nearly as much by recent anti-Fregeans as by the later Wittgenstein, the notion of a public language, a set of shared social practices. The public language picture, as I will call it, is what this book is about. Suitably developed, it will suggest a new and very different approach to a host of philosophic questions concerning language, and indeed concerning thought, questions that to many have seemed beyond the grasp of the anti-Fregean revolutionaries.

While the public language picture does not get the focus and development that it deserves in the direct-reference literature, one can certainly detect its traces here and there, from time to time. Kripke, Putnam, and Kaplan come especially to mind here. In the second lecture of *Naming and Necessity*,[10] for example, Kripke suggests that the Fregean conception is fueled by a picture that sees the giving of meanings to expressions as something that one could accomplish in the privacy of one's (I would add, Cartesian) study, whereas, Kripke suggests, his own picture emphasizes the social character of language. In Kaplan's 1982 comments upon John Searle's Pacific APA presentation, Kaplan spoke of the semanticist as "an anthropologist of certain social, linguistic practices," an idea that seems to me extremely suggestive and essentially tied to the public language picture that I will be developing here. I return to Kaplan's suggestive remark in chapter 6.[11]

4. A Kuhnian Revolution?

Thomas Kuhn, in *The Structure of Scientific Revolutions*, provides a sketch of the process of radical theory change, a sketch that illuminates the process of intellectual revolution generally, not just scientific revolution.[12] Let's see how Kuhn's sketch applies to the revolution against the Fregean perspective.

Intellectual revolution, Kuhn taught, begins with difficulties in the received view that come to be seen not as reflecting mere technical problems requiring theoretical refinement, but as revealing fundamental inadequacies.[13] The revolutionary may, for example, take note of examples available for some time, perhaps even pre-

---

[10] See Saul Kripke, *Naming and Necessity* (Cambridge, Mass.: Harvard University Press, 1972), p. 91.

[11] See also Kaplan's "Afterthoughts" to his monograph "Demonstratives," *Themes from Kaplan* (New York: Oxford University Press, 1989), p. 565, esp. his discussion on pp. 600ff of "subjectivist" and "consumerist" semantics.

[12] Indeed, Kuhn's account seems often to illuminate even the process of revolutionary change in the beliefs of individuals, for example, religious beliefs. To find Kuhn's sketch illuminating is not necessarily to find all of its features acceptable. Specifically, I want to keep my distance from some of the relativistic suggestions of Kuhn's original remarks.

[13] The explanation of why previously noticed difficulties come to be seen in this way is no doubt quite complicated. One factor may be simply the striking character of the examples themselves, something that attachment to the received view may tend to obscure for a time. Still another may be the fact that these examples, perhaps all of a sudden, suggest to someone another account of the fundamentals, an account that may have been in disrepute recently but that may have promise after all. A third: a revolutionary may be dissatisfied with the received view on independent grounds and may antecedently prefer a radically different picture and thus be attracted to these examples. One cannot here overlook additional factors such as the force of personality and the impact of the opinions of powerful intellects.

viously seen as problematic for the received view. The revolutionary, however, urges that we see such examples as *counterexamples*
to the received view, and as suggesting a radically different conception of the fundamentals, both of which suggestions seem extravagant to defenders of the received view. Such indeed seems to be the
gross structure of the anti-Fregean revolution, with anti-Fregeans
seizing upon a number of striking examples, at least some of which
had been under discussion for some time,[14] and Fregean sympathizers refusing to see these examples as requiring anything more than
refinements.

One of the snares of such intellectual confrontations, a snare
that is encouraged by much of our training in analytic philosophy
and one that is exemplified in too much recent work, is an excessive reliance on counterexamples and a lack of attention to the fundamental questions at stake. Instead of seeing the counterexamples
as revealing points of pressure for the opposition, and as suggesting
a different fundamental conception, the revolutionary may wield
the counterexamples like blunt instruments, as if such examples
could themselves put the opposing view to rest. The revolutionary
may well not be clear about what exactly he wishes to put in place
of the traditional conception. It may thus be tempting to attempt
to win, as it were, on a technicality.

On the other side, that of the traditionalists, there is the style
of response to such criticism that we might call "philosophy as
epicycles on what was once an interesting idea." All too often one
gets the sense—and many have so commented upon the epistemological discussions subsequent to the famous Gettier counterexamples to the traditional conception of knowledge—that the central
ideas are getting lost in the steady stream of counterexamples, new
theoretical refinements, further counterexamples, new and still
more sophisticated refinements, and so on. [15]

The following discussion of the initial counterexamples is not
meant to obliterate the Fregean picture as technically inadequate.

---

[14] At least some of the examples that I will be discussing, like cases in which a
speaker refers to Aristotle despite having many false beliefs about him, were discussed by Fregeans such as Searle, but they were seen as requiring not fundamental
change but rather relatively modest readjustments. See his "Proper Names," *Mind*
67 (1958): 166–73.

[15] For a helpful survey of the literature spawned by Gettier's "Is Justified True
Belief Knowledge?" (*Analysis*, 25 [1963]: 121–23), see Robert K. Shope, *The Analysis
of Knowing: A Decade of Research* (Princeton, N.J.: Princeton University Press,
1983).

Doing this, it seems to me, would be a waste of time, given the potential for sophistication of philosophical positions.[16] Nor will I review the recent literature that is replete with elaborate discussions of the counterexamples along with proposals for how to elaborate the Fregean picture so as to sidestep the now notorious problems, as well as with putative refutations of these later proposals. My idea—and this is my task for the remainder of this chapter—is simply to present the examples so as to make plain why it has been felt that they reveal something seriously amiss with the traditional approach.

The counterexamples suggest that something or other is amiss with Frege's approach, and Russell's. My idea, though, is that it is something fundamental that is amiss. In chapter 4 I will turn to the question of why these anti-Fregean data should be seen as suggesting *radical* change, an alteration in fundamental outlook. The anti-Fregean counterexamples, I will urge, point to a dramatically different and more natural (in part because more naturalistic) way of thinking about language (and related phenomena). In chapter 4, then, I will attempt both to motivate the need for a fundamentally different account and to adumbrate the new picture.

To overthrow a paradigm, however, requires more than the presentation of problematic data, even if that data can be seen as pointing to a different fundamental conception. The received view, after all, presumably has its own intuitive motivation, a range of examples or considerations that have made it seem attractive and natural. Before the revolutionary can rest, then, he needs to take seriously the considerations that motivate his opponents' view, data that may well be difficult to accommodate on the new picture. In chapters 6–9 I will turn to just such data, to puzzles that are alleged to find natural solutions on Fregean approaches. Chapter 6 begins with Frege's famous puzzle concerning "the cognitive significance of language." If my preferred account cannot accommodate all such Frege-friendly phenomena in a natural, organic fashion, if epicyclical sophistication is required (or, what seems just as bad, biting the bullet and settling for relatively unintuitive judgments dictated by theory), this consequence will count heavily against my approach.

---

[16] Philosophical theories don't often get obliterated, as Arthur Collins once said to me, they just go away. They are, as it were, pressured into hiding, often lying in wait until conditions are ripe for a return.

5. What's Wrong with the Sense-Reference Picture?

Let's begin with an observation about the methodology of the revolutionaries, an observation that will become important later: The
attack on Frege has been not as philosophical, as it were, as it has
been empirical. One might have found fault with Frege's approach
in a more philosophical vein. First, as is often noted, Frege does not
tell us much about the pivotal notion of sense. As I suggest in chapter 1, to understand senses as the rationalists' *concepts* only helps
a bit, since we have no clear understanding of these either. Second,
one might have expressed worries about the explanatory adequacy
of senses.[17] Has one truly explained the vitality of language when
one appeals to the intrinsic vitality of concepts or senses? Do we
understand how anything—physical, mental, third realm, or whatever—could represent or stand for things not by convention but
intrinsically? Additionally, one might have objected to the very
idea of a purely qualitative way of individuating things. Perhaps the
ways of individuating things available to us always, maybe even
necessarily, involve some sort of reference to particulars—a Russellian sounding point. Perhaps there are deep metaphysical and/or
epistemological reasons for this.[18]

The anti-Fregean attack, however, has been less philosophical,
more earthbound. Frege's foes—in effect taking Walker Percy's advice that we attend to linguistic practice—have pointed to the empirical inadequacy of the sense-reference approach. When one sur-
veys examples drawn from ordinary linguistic practice, it has been
urged, Frege's theses that propositional contents include senses and
that reference depends upon sense seem clearly mistaken.

For one thing, speakers have no trouble speaking about things
even when they lack anything like purely qualitative specifications
of the things of which they speak. Think about all the historical
individuals you can refer to by name, people such as Cicero, Ploti-
nus, Gorgias, Marie Curie, Roger Bacon. Can you provide purely
qualitative descriptions that individuate each of these people, that
distinguish them from everyone else who ever lived? Forget providing "purely qualitative" descriptions, perhaps a difficult or even impossible task even for things with which you are very familiar. Russell's view, at least, doesn't require such descriptions in any case.

---

[17] As I will do in chapter 5.
[18] See Tyler Burge, *"De Re* Belief," *Journal of Philosophy* (1977): 338–62.

Can you provide any substantive sort of description that even begins to individuate in many of these cases? Kripke points out, rightly I believe, that many people who are perfectly competent with 'Cicero' don't have the slightest idea "who he was," over and above that he was, say, "a Roman orator." There were, of course, lots of Roman orators, and so the descriptions available to people fall far short of what Frege, or even Russell,[19] required.

Reference in the absence of individuating information suggests that something is very wrong with the Fregean perspective. If typically or even frequently speakers use names competently but don't associate anything like senses with them, this fact strongly suggests that we look elsewhere than to senses for whatever factor(s) determine the references of names. It also suggests that we look elsewhere than to senses for an account of the constituents of the propositions expressed.

Here's another garden variety linguistic phenomenon that is prima facie problematic for the Fregean outlook. People may have mistaken ideas about the items to which they refer by name. Some of our students' concepts of, say, Aristotle, unfortunately fit Socrates better than they fit Aristotle. Imagine that an introductory philosophy student identifies Aristotle as the Greek philosopher who taught Plato and was executed for corrupting the youth of Athens. The student might mistakenly remark, "Aristotle taught Plato." His remark expresses a straightforward falsehood. He would be so graded on an exam, and so told in conversation.

Notice, though, that if Frege or Russell were correct and the name were a mere surrogate for the student's preferred descriptions, then the student's remark, "Aristotle taught Plato," would express a truth. 'Aristotle', after all, was supposed to abbreviate the speaker's identifying descriptions. So 'Aristotle taught Plato' in the student's mouth would express roughly the proposition that the Greek philosopher who taught Plato and was executed . . . taught Plato. If Frege or Russell were correct, the student's utterance would express not only a truth but a trivial truth! But no one, not even the student himself after he is apprised of the facts, would be at all tempted by the suggestion that the student's remark was true, no less that it

---

[19] Russell indicates that in the case of historical figures, the identifying description will specify the individual in terms of some aspect of my immediate experience pertaining to "testimony heard or read." Can you really identify say, Cicero, in such terms? Do you remember where and when you heard of Cicero? See note 18 of chapter 2 in this book.

was a trivial truth—no one, that is, other than one defending a philosophical theory.

I shall make no attempt here to formulate all or even most of the Fregean difficulties highlighted by reflection upon linguistic practice. I cannot forbear, however, to mention one final problem. The Fregean tradition maintains that a name is a linguistic manifestation of a mode of presentation, that someone who says "Aristotle was a philosopher" expresses a thought content that has, in place of the name, a way of thinking about Aristotle. If this idea were correct, we would presumably be able to find out which mode of presentation lies behind the use of the name by asking the speaker.

Let's assume that the speaker knows a great deal about Aristotle (to bypass the problems highlighted earlier). Still, he will often be in no position to provide much help here.

> I was thinking about Aristotle, but I'm not quite sure how to answer your question as to *how* I was thinking of him. I know, of course, that he wrote various works, that he studied in the Academy with Plato, that he taught Alexander the Great, and lots of other things as well. But I don't know that I was thinking of him in any particular one of these ways, or in a way that combines several (or all) of them.

I take this "phenomenological" point to be highly significant. Which proposition is asserted, on Frege-style views, depends crucially upon which sense is being entertained, upon how the speaker is cognizing the referent. Surely this Fregean idea stands in tension with speakers' inability to provide much help with the question of which is the operative sense.

Such reflections upon ordinary linguistic practice put great pressure upon the views of Frege and Russell. It may be, of course, that Frege or Russell meant something far richer and more complicated than what their words have suggested to many of us. One might, moreover, develop a sophisticated Fregean- or Russellian-spirited view that promises to avoid these and similar objections. The point remains, however, that these sorts of considerations put pressure on what the fathers of our subject certainly seem to maintain. And that's all I want, for the moment.

Although my focus in recent paragraphs has been upon proper names, the problems for the Fregean tradition upon which I have been focusing are not at all specific to proper names. Indeed, in my own case at least, these problems seemed most forceful with respect to other sorts of referring expressions, specifically indexical expressions such as 'I', 'he', 'that', and so on, expressions—to give a rough characterization—that are unambiguous but whose reference shifts with context.[20]

Frege seems committed to the view that indexicals, no less than proper names, express purely qualitative, individuating senses.[21] Frege's view, particularized to indexicals, seems incorrect, however, and for the same sorts of reasons as were discussed for the case of proper names.

First, there are many quite ordinary contexts in which someone refers to something by means of, say, a demonstrative but fails to have a correct, individuating description of the referent. Someone might say, "That is one smart cookie," pointing to someone he sees across the quad, or, alternatively, referring to Aristotle. The speaker's "concept" of the person to whom he was pointing, or of Aristotle, may be quite incomplete, however—that is, it may fall far short of being individuating—and may well contain considerable misinformation. So just as in the case of proper names, if we were to go with the speaker's concepts as determining the reference, we might get no referent at all, or a different referent from the obvious one.

Similar problems arise for other indexicals, say, 'I'. Someone feeling under the weather might say "I feel sick" and might be speaking the truth, despite the fact that his self-concept might be (1) inadequate to individuate anything, and (2) almost radically disordered. To begin with (1), I don't really know if any of us can provide purely qualitative characterizations of ourselves, but even if we can do so, it is less than obvious that, say, an amnesiac, unaware of who or where he is or when he is speaking, can provide such a characterization of himself. Such a person, however, no less than you and I, can truthfully say, "I feel lousy," thus referring to himself. Nor does one's belief that he is the Creator of the universe prevent one from referring to himself and speaking falsely when he says, " . . . and then I rested."

Back to the real world: There was a third problem for the Fregean account of proper names. In many cases speakers will know

---

[20] Kaplan, in "Demonstratives," also takes indexical expressions as the best case from which to launch the anti-Frege revolution. Kaplan's idea, however, is that in the case of indexicals—as opposed to proper names—we can devise a fairly simple positive theory of their semantical workings. I disagree both with Kaplan's proposed theory and with the idea that such a theory is readily available. See my "Turning the Tables on Frege," in *Has Semantics Rested on a Mistake? and Other Essays* (Palo Alto, Cal.: Stanford University Press, 1991), and chapter 6 in this book.

[21] See especially his discussion in "The Thought: A Logical Inquiry," in P. Strawson, ed., *Philosophical Logic* (Oxford: Oxford University Press, 1967).

many things about the referent and there will be no natural way, even for the speaker, to select some particular description or descriptions as *the* way that he was thinking of the referent. If Frege were correct, however, there must have been some particular sense that was actually functioning as the reference determiner and that was a propositional constituent.

Now this problem seems very striking for the case of indexicals. Someone says, pointing to a cup on his desk, "That's good coffee." If asked to what he was referring, he can give lots of answers, corresponding to the many things he may know about that coffee, for example, its present location, where it was grown or purchased, whether or not it is the speaker's favorite kind, and so on. How can anyone—including the speaker himself—tell how much of this information was, from a Fregean point of view, part of the operative sense? "I know that I was talking about that coffee," we can imagine him replying to the Fregean request, "but I'm not sure that I was thinking of it in one of these ways in particular, or in a way that involves all or some particular subset of them."

One way to conceptualize the Fregean view is this: Frege makes definite descriptions the paradigm referring expressions. It is striking that the problems for the Fregean view that I have been discussing arise not only for the cases of names and indexicals, but even for definite descriptions. Many of the garden variety definite descriptions actually used by people are rather incomplete and indefinite. "The man over there looks drunk." "The movie is far from faithful to the book." And while it might be tempting to suppose, as it has been sometimes suggested, that such incomplete descriptions are elliptical for descriptions that are more adequate from Frege's point of view, this idea is not really very promising. For when we try to fill out the meager, explicit information contained in the actually used description, we run into precisely the problems we have been seeing again and again. Often the information available to the speaker will be incomplete, often it will be incorrect, and so on.

So much for the anti-Fregean counterexamples.[22] Why do these suggest the need for a *radical* alternative? What shape would such an alternative take? Turn the page.

---

[22] I have explored these difficulties with Frege's view in considerably more detail in my dissertation and several essays, reprinted in *Has Semantics Rested on a Mistake? and Other Essays*. See esp. "Indexical Reference and Propositional Content" and "Demonstrative Reference and Definite Descriptions."

4

Supplanting Linguistic Cartesianism

1. Every Revolution Needs a Motto

Linguistic Contact
Without
Cognitive Contact

To many philosophers, my candidate motto will seem bizarre if not outright crazy—and this is no mere prediction.[1] It goes to the very heart of the Cartesian perspective that a speaker needs to stand in a substantive cognitive relation with anything to which he refers, that he needs to possess, in the vocabulary of chapter 2, a *discriminating cognitive fix* on a referent.

Frege and Russell, as we saw in chapter 2, construe the requisite

[1] It is of the essence that a motto be splashy, simple, and unqualified. The question at issue is whether reference by a proper name, for example, requires a substantial cognitive grip on the referent. I mean to stay far from such questions as whether a community that was somehow systematically misled about things could use language to talk about the world.

cognitive fix in very different terms and motivate it quite differently. They concur, however, that in the absence of an appropriate cognitive fix, reference is unthinkable. Russell—Cartesian in epistemology—maintains that genuine reference, that is, reference by means of a genuine name, requires that the speaker or thinker be *directly acquainted* with the referent. Even the use of an ordinary name requires a kind of epistemic acquaintance for Russell, albeit an attenuated kind.

Frege, while he seems relatively free of Cartesian *epistemic* scruples, maintains a broadly Cartesian standpoint in the philosophy of mind, or so I have been arguing. Frege requires not that the referent be smack up against the mind of the speaker or thinker, but rather that the latter can intellectually individuate the former, that he possess a discriminating conception of it.[2] Again, a substantial cognitive fix is indispensable.

It is, inter alia, this central feature of linguistic Cartesianism, the cognitive fix requirement, that the anti-Fregean counterexamples call into question. We regularly refer by name to historical and contemporary personalities, to places, theories, works of literature, and so on, knowing (or even believing) very little about the references of the names we utter, even having many false beliefs about the things in question. My motto—and its radical rejection of the traditional approach—is thus strongly suggested by an elementary survey of ordinary linguistic practice.

It is here that we can expect the thought-oriented theorist to dig in his heels. The cognitive fix requirement is, from his point of view, not negotiable. Anti-Fregeans, accordingly, must have overlooked something. Perhaps we need to take a closer look at the putative counterexamples, possibly to recover overlooked pieces of accurate information available even to such apparently ignorant speakers.[3] Or perhaps, given the power of the examples, we need to negotiate the nonnegotiable—to loosen up our conception of just how strong a cognitive fix is required.[4] These alternatives, and numerous variants on them, have been suggested.

---

[2] Frege's reason is *not* that without the requirement of a discriminating conception, a speaker might not know of what he speaks. Frege's requiring such a cognitive fix, as I argued in chapter 2, is grounded in his "representative theory of conception."

[3] In this spirit it has been suggested, originally by Russell, that the speaker will inevitably know that the referent, whom he can't otherwise identify, was "called Cicero." Perhaps we can make this knowledge do the job of providing an identifying concept, or so it might be thought.

[4] I have in mind here approaches like Searle's cluster theory, according to which a speaker may have some false beliefs about his referent, the latter being determined

Let us take stock. Attention to actual linguistic practice suggests something radical, that reference in the absence of a substantial cognitive fix is indeed possible. This idea, as we have seen, stands in tension with the Cartesian perspective. One person's *modus ponens*, as we in the business sometimes quip, is another's *modus tollens*. If we follow the lead of actual linguistic practice, then, we may well wonder about the Cartesian picture, not just the details of Frege's account, or Russell's, but the thought-oriented conception itself.

2. What Then? Toward a Social-Practice Conception

Recall Walker Percy's remark quoted in the last chapter: "Instead of starting out with such large, vexing subjects as soul, mind, ideas, consciousness, why not set forth with language, which no one denies, and see how far it takes us toward the rest."[5]

It is Percy's advice I am suggesting we follow: Let's put the big questions on the back burner for a while, questions about thought, the mind, cognition, and so on. Let's approach our linguistic practices directly, unfettered by preconceptions of what those practices must be like. Unfettered in this way, it will no longer seem trivial, virtually a priori, that reference requires a substantial cognitive fix. Nor will the cognitive fix requirement reemerge as a empirical generalization from actual practice. It never was, after all, put forward on such a basis. It was rather the product of philosophical thinking about what must be the case. Scrutiny of our practices certainly seems to suggest that there is no such requirement.

A great deal changes if we begin as I am suggesting. To occupants of a Cartesian perspective, understanding the commonplace linguistic phenomena highlighted by anti-Fregeans is a matter of bringing those phenomena into line with the cognitive requirements for reference. This task has all the charm of boxing one's way out of a paper bag. On our new perspective, this formidable task yields to a considerably more tractable challenge. When we think about the counterexamples, no longer problematic, we may be led to wonder whether it is perhaps an important feature of ac-

---

by something like the majority of those beliefs he associates with the name. See Searle's well-known article "Proper Names," *Mind* 67 (1958): 166–73.

[5] Walker Percy, "The Delta Factor," collected in Walker Percy, *The Message in the Bottle: How Queer Man Is, How Queer Language Is, and What One Has to Do with the Other* (New York: Farrar, Straus, and Giroux, 1984), p. 17.

tual practice that there is no cognitive fix requirement. Might there be, for example, important ends served by *not requiring* a substantial cognitive fix?

In fact, the lack of a cognitive fix requirement has enormous utility for communication and thought. If one can refer by name to things concerning which one knows very little, one can then ask, "Who was Cicero?" not having the foggiest idea who he was. One can hypothesize various things about him, come to believe some of them, find out that one was right about some and wrong about others. *Proper names thus allow individual speakers to bridge great cognitive gulfs, to speak about things despite a lack of anything close to individuating beliefs about the things in question.* Far from making our practices with names unintelligible, the lack of a cognitive fix requirement seems most understandable, an extremely important feature of our practices with proper names.[6]

The benefit that thus accrues to us simply because we have no cognitive fix requirement is impressive. Reflections like these, however, will not silence the misgivings of traditionalists, and for good reason. I have, in effect, shifted focus from one dimension of the intelligibility of linguistic practice to another, deemphasizing the individual's epistemic situation in favor of considerations of social utility. Such a shift of focus leaves a crucial question untouched. What, on our social-practice picture, connects an utterance of a name with a referent? What indeed, our opponent will urge, could possibly accomplish this other than some sort of cognitive contact with the referent, something like acquaintance, or an individuating conception, or something of the like? If the mind's grip on a referent does not drive reference, what does?

One wishing to develop an alternative to the traditional approach needs to keep one's balance here. One needs to be diligent, on one hand, not to succumb to the temptations of the thought-oriented picture. This is no mean feat given the power and degree of entrenchment of Cartesian ways of thinking. On the other hand, one needs to face squarely the Fregean's good question: What, other than some sort of cognitive contact, could possibly connect a piece of language with what it's about? How is it possible for there to be linguistic contact in the absence of cognitive contact?

---

[6] Bernard Reginster, as a member of my seminar on these questions at the University of Notre Dame, remarked that perhaps in place of the traditional cognitive fix requirement we should impose a new condition of adequacy, that of explaining, and not explaining away, our ability to ask, "Who was x?"

3. Keeping the Faith

Reference in the absence of a substantial cognitive relation is by no means a new idea. Kripke advances the idea in *Naming and Necessity*.[7] Even Russell found the prospect tempting: Remember the distinction I drew in chapter 2 between Russell's semantic ear and his epistemological conscience? Although Cartesian scruples precluded Russell from adopting this supposition, he writes as if he were tempted to suppose that ordinary names, no less than logically proper names, are directly referential, that they refer to their assigned bearers without conceptual mediation.[8] Nor is the idea of recent vintage. John Stuart Mill's remarks on proper names encourage a similar conception.

> Proper names are not connotative: they denote the individuals who are called by them; but they do not indicate or imply any attributes as belonging to those individuals. When we name a child by the name Paul, or a dog by the name Caesar, these names are simply marks used to enable those individuals to be made subjects of discourse. It may be said, indeed, that we must have had some reason for giving them those names rather than any others; and this is true; but the name, once given, is independent of the reason. A man may have been named John, because that was the name of his father; a town may have been named Dartmouth, because it is situated at the mouth of the Dart. But it is no part of the signification of the word John, that the father of the person so called bore the same name; nor even of the word Dartmouth, to be situated at the mouth of the Dart. If sand should choke up the

[7] I have often thought that there is a conflicting, albeit subordinate, tendency in Kripke's thought, as when he suggests in Lecture II of *Naming and Necessity* (Cambridge, Mass.: Harvard University Press, 1972) that the paradigm case of the introduction of a name is not introduction by ostension of the object-to-be-baptized, but rather is introduction by description of the item in question, as if descriptive characterizations were needed to get names afloat. In an informal discussion session at the University of Notre Dame during a series of talks given by Kripke in the spring of 1986, he defended this view further. Not that Kripke can be held accountable for such informal remarks, but they may be illustrative of the tendency. When confronted with difficulties facing such a descriptional view of *name introduction* (indeed the difficulties were analogous to some that Kripke himself originally raised for the description theory of names), Kripke replied that perhaps what is needed here is a "cluster theory" (see note 4 in this chapter), a view of the sort that Kripke rejects for the theory of names generally.

[8] I discuss the matter in chapter 2, section 4 of this book. Russell makes a number of suggestive remarks along these lines. He tells us that ordinary proper names "try [unsuccessfully] to directly get through to the man himself," and that the name 'Bismarck', as Bismarck himself uses it, has the "direct use that it always wishes to have."

mouth of the river, or an earthquake change its course, and remove it to a distance from the town, the name of the town would not necessarily be changed. That fact, therefore, can form no part of the signification of the word; for otherwise, when the fact confessedly ceased to be true, no one would any longer think of applying the name. Proper names are attached to the objects themselves, and are not dependent on the continuance of any attribute of the object.[9]

The view is not, then, a new one, but the question of its intelligibility remains. Russell, in the end, rejected the dictates of his semantic ear, for nonepistemically grounded reference seemed to him unintelligible. Contemporary anti-Fregeans, insofar as they roundly affirm the possibility of cognitively innocent reference, and they rarely do so,[10] seem never to discuss adequately the question that the Fregean rightly poses: What, if not something cognitive, might possibly connect a piece of language with a referent?

I said earlier that on the perspective I am encouraging, we should "put thought on the back burner and approach our linguistic practices directly." If we are to see cognitively innocent reference as unproblematic, and indeed as the natural view, we will need to emphasize not only the thought-language contrast, but also the contrast between a Cartesian-inspired individualism and a more social orientation. It is *our linguistic practices* that we will need to approach directly. If one restricts one's focus to the individual, his cognitive states,[11] and his use of symbols—if one is thinking of the individual language user in isolation from the linguistic community—it is difficult to see how language might make contact with the world other than in traditional terms, Fregean or Russellian. If one attends to the social dimension, however, the Fregean's question may no longer seem so formidable, almost unanswerable. It may no longer seem obvious, or even plausible, that semantic contact is driven by cognitive contact. So I will argue.

Mill's idea that ordinary names are, as it is sometimes said, mere tags for their bearers constitutes another central component in my approach.[12] Anti-Fregeans have often acknowledged their

---

[9] From John Stuart Mill, *A System of Logic*, 10th ed. (first published 1843), Book I, chapter 2 (London, 1879).

[10] See section 3.1, "Anti-Fregeans and Cognitively Innocent Reference."

[11] The terminology of "cognitive states," insofar as it is suggestive of the idea that a person's cognitive situation resolves into his "states," is quite natural on an individualistic picture, but much less so on the orientation I want to encourage.

[12] Wittgenstein, in the *Philosophical Investigations* (§15 and §26), and Ruth Barcan Marcus ("Modalities and Intensional Languages," *Synthese* 13 [1961]: 303–22) both use the picturesque "tag" and "label" characterizations of ordinary proper names.

debt to Mill and have advanced a number of treatments of names that are, or have been taken to be, "Millian," but it is Mill's original "pure tag" idea in which I am interested. To situate my view, I begin in section 4 with a brief discussion of such allegedly Millian ideas.

3.1. Additional Note: Anti-Fregeans and Cognitively Innocent Reference

Kaplan is one who does not roundly affirm the idea of nonepistemically grounded reference. His groundbreaking work, "Demonstratives,"[13] defends a view of indexical reference that concedes quite a bit to Fregean intuitions: indexical reference, contrary to orthodox Fregeanism, does not require that the speaker possess an individuating description of the referent. But it does require that the speaker possess a characterization that is individuating *in the context of utterance.* This is not the way Kaplan presents his own view, but it is implicit in his "character-content" approach to indexicals.

Turning to proper names, Kripke and Donnellan famously suggest that a "historical chain of communication" bridges the gap between name and referent. The rough idea is that a name is introduced, paradigmatically in some sort of name-bestowing ceremony, and it is passed along in conversation from one speaker to another. In some such fashion I now possess the name 'George Washington' in my vocabulary, and the name, in my mouth, refers to Washington in virtue of its social history—in virtue, that is, of the chain of communication that extends from the first use of the name until the present.

This notion might seem like an explicit rejection of the idea of a cognitive bond between name and referent, but the matter is not this clear. Actually the views of Kripke and Donnellan are not quite the same here. To consider Kripke's view first, there is the nondominant tendency in his thought of which I spoke in note 7. Its application here is as follows. The role of the historical chain of communication is, for Kripke as opposed to Donnellan, to connect a present utterance of the name not so much with the referent as with the name as given in something like a baptismal event. Kripke's preferred paradigm for the baptismal event, what sets up

---

[13] The view is elaborated in a famous underground monograph, "Demonstratives," which appeared after many years in J. Almog, J. Perry, and H. Wettstein, eds., *Themes From Kaplan* (New York: Oxford University Press, 1988). I discuss Kaplan's view at more length in chapter 6.

the name as a name for the item in question, however, is a description, as is discussed in note 7 of this chapter. At least for this aspect
of Kripke's discussion, then, the tie between name and named is
more intellectual than it might appear. In Donnellan's case, this is
even more clear. As is suggested by his "The Contingent A Priori
and Rigid Designators,"[14] the role of the historical chain of communication is somehow epistemic; when one stands in some appropriate causal or historical relation to an entity, this position somehow puts one in a favorable enough *epistemic* relation to the entity
to refer to it.

4. Millian Names, Rigidity, and Historical Chains of Communication

Kripke, in *Naming and Necessity*, advanced the view that proper
names are "rigid designators," that they—ignoring niceties—"refer
to the same things in all possible worlds." Clearly Kripke, both in
this work and later, thinks of his idea as Millian,[15] but how Millian
is it? Is rigid designation just a modern-day, perhaps clarified, rendering of Mill's pure denotation idea?

Mill's issue, we should remember, was whether or not proper
names connote properties and thereby denote, or whether they
purely and simply denote. Mill, unlike Kripke, does not seem concerned with the modal properties of names. Notice that one who
has never given a moment's thought to questions of modality might
well have given a great deal of thought to the viability of pure,
connotationless reference. Likewise a philosophical skeptic about
modality might like (or dislike) Mill's conception of proper names.[16]
The notions—Millian proper name and rigid designator—seem
quite different.

This is not to suggest that Kripke himself thought otherwise.
But many have confused the matter, taking the anti-Fregean approach to amount to a thesis about the rigidity of names (and perhaps other expressions). As Kripke remarks about other conceptual
distinctions,[17] even if it were to turn out that the two notions of

---

[14] Keith Donnellan, "The Contingent A Priori and Rigid Designators," *Midwest
Studies in Philosophy* 2 (1977): 12–27.

[15] As he says in the First Lecture. See esp. p. 29 and surrounding text. Also see
his discussion of Millianism in his later article, "A Puzzle About Belief," in A. Margalit, ed., *Meaning and Use* (Dordrecht: D. Reidel, 1979).

[16] As Joseph Almog emphasized.

[17] In Lecture I of *Naming and Necessity*. See p. 38 and the preceding discussion
of the notions of necessity and *a priority*.

Millian tag and rigid designator were coextensive, they would still be quite distinct notions. Clearly, however, they aren't coextensive, for the category of rigid designators includes even certain "connotative singular terms," definite descriptions for example. 'The successor of 2', no less than 'Aristotle', refers to the same thing in all possible worlds.

Kripke's contention, as I understand it, was not that Mill's notion was or should have been that of rigid designation. Indeed, without invoking Millian assumptions, Kripke argues that names are rigid designators. But the rigidity of names, says Kripke, is incompatible with the traditional Frege-Russell approach to their semantics[18] and is fully compatible with a Millian approach. "Rigid designation," in any case, is not Mill's idea, and it is Mill's idea in which I am interested and of which I will make use in what follows.

There is a second idea that needs to be distinguished from Mill's. Donnellan and Kripke advanced the view that what ties a name to a bearer is a "historical chain of communication." This, like rigidity, is a topic that could bear lengthy discussion; the issues raised by the historical chain idea have loomed large in the literature. Is the chain of communication best thought of as a causal chain, as several of Kripke's remarks in *Naming and Necessity* suggest? If the chain is causal, does this fact suggest a causal theory of names or, even more ambitiously, a causal theory of reference, as some—but neither Kripke nor Donnellan—have suggested? Would such a theory make plausible or at least possible a reduction of the notion of reference to something physicalistically more acceptable, a project explicitly disavowed by Kripke?[19]

---

[18] Some definite descriptions are nonrigid; some, like 'the successor of 3', are rigid. The rigidity of names was initially seen as incompatible with the traditional approach because the sorts of descriptions traditionally proposed as defining proper names, e.g., "the teacher of Alexander the Great," are nonrigid. In other words, Kripke argues that 'Aristotle' cannot mean "the teacher of Alexander," for the former expression but not the latter is rigid. Neo-Fregeans and neo-Russellians have countered that perhaps there are rigid descriptions that provide the content of proper names. Plantinga (In "The Boethian Compromise," *American Philosophical Quarterly* 15 (1978): 129–38) and others have suggested that while "the teacher of Alexander" will not do, for Kripke's reasons, other rigid descriptions will work, such as "the actual teacher of Alexander" or "the teacher of Alexander in α," where α is a proper name for the actual world.

[19] See *Naming and Necessity*, p. 97. Donnellan, it should be noted, avoids causal terminology altogether. Donnellan explains in "Speaking of Nothing," *Philosophical Review* 88 (1974): 3–32, note 3, that he "wants to avoid a seeming commitment to all the links in the referential chain being causal." See Wettstein, "The Causal Theory of Names," in the *Cambridge Dictionary of Philosophy* (New York: Cambridge University Press, 1999).

What is important for our purposes, however, is that, as with rigidity, Mill tells us nothing about such chains of communication. *His* semantical story, or so it would seem, is merely that a name is a tag for its bearer. Perhaps Mill's story is inadequate as it stands and it needs to be supplemented by talk of historical chains of communication. Perhaps not.[20] The conception I want to emphasize, in any case, is not that of "historical chain of communication" any more than it was "rigid designator," but it is rather Mill's "tag" idea itself.

The approach to be developed here, then, places considerably more emphasis on the social character of language than has been customary in the anti-Frege literature. Moreover, rigidity and the historical chain idea (with or without a causal interpretation), ordinarily taken to be at the heart of the revolution against traditional semantics, play no role in my account.

My intention in what follows is not to lay claim to a historically accurate interpretation of Mill. Rather, I wish to take Mill's brief remarks and place them in the context of a broader social practice conception. Mill's view[21] might be adaptable to a different, more traditional, overall outlook. Russell's account of genuine names, for example, is a highly epistemologized Millianism. Russell, after all, is with Mill in denying that names "connote" properties. Russell's approach, though, is very far from my Millianism, for it merely replaces one sort of cognitive contact with another.

5. Millian Names and Cognitively Unmediated Reference

How does Mill's "tag" conception help us understand how there might be reference in the absence of substantive cognitive contact? Consider a hypothetical linguistic community in which parents, or the community, assign "official" numbers to children at birth— think here of social security numbers. The numbers provide tags, as it were, for the relevant individuals. When a member of the community uses a number to refer to a particular person, the number's reference does not depend upon the number user's knowledge or beliefs, upon which properties he associates with the number. The reference of a number depends upon whose number it is. Indeed,

---

[20] Cf. Joseph Almog, "Semantical Anthropology," *Midwest Studies in Philosophy* 9 (1984): 479–90. I am indebted to Almog for discussions of both issues discussed in this section, rigid designation and historical chains of communication.

[21] As Eli Hirsch pointed out to me.

this is an important feature of the practice, since it allows speakers to make reference to individuals about whom they are rather in the dark.[22]

Typically, of course, speakers know many things about the people to whom they refer by number. Indeed, some of the number bearers are famous, and some of their properties are very well known. The bearer of "2342," for example, might be the first president of the United States, and this fact may be a commonplace to most members of the community. Noting this, it may be tempting, especially if one approaches linguistic phenomena from a broadly Cartesian standpoint, to suppose that such properties constitute something like the sense of the number, and further that all official numbers must possess such senses if they are to refer.

One need only remind oneself, however, of the sorts of considerations adduced at the end of the last chapter—which we will assume hold in the hypothetical community as well—and one will not succumb to this temptation. Speakers can refer by using official numbers even when they lack appropriately rich beliefs; they sometimes have mistaken beliefs, and even when their beliefs are "adequate," there is often no way to privilege some property or properties as the one(s) to be included in the sense of the number.

Having provided a rough sketch of the practice, let's return to the traditionalist's challenge. Is the practice I've been sketching, one that involves cognitively unmediated reference, intelligible? Let's begin with the question of whether making the practice more Fregean would help make it more intelligible. Let's stipulate that although the official numbers are assigned at birth, the referent of an uttered number depends upon the properties the current speaker associates with the number. It seems to me that we will have rendered the practice less intelligible! Isn't there something almost baroque about assigning to an individual an official device for identification and yet allowing that the reference of the device depends upon the vagaries of the beliefs of the user?

Indeed, we are noticing a tension in Frege's original conception: Names have *bearers*, and yet they only sometimes apply to them. That is, the reference of a name depends not upon to whom it was

---

[22] The hypothetical practice might be made to mimic our actual practices with names in other respects. We might specify, for example, that the parents are not restricted in which numbers they pick. There would then be no guarantee that any particular number, say 17468, picks anyone out. Nor would there be any guarantee of uniqueness of reference for a particular number. The number 37456 might, for example, have been given to several different people, and the reference of this num-

given, but rather upon who satisfies the condition that the current name user associates with the name. Intuitively, the notion of a "bearer" and that of a "satisfier" (of a definite description) seem very different. A bearer is an assignee, and the job of the name is, as Mill says, simply to make its assignee a subject of discourse. A description, by contrast, is like a recipe or an instruction for finding its satisfier. To adapt some imagery from David Kaplan, while a name bears its assignee, a description is always searching, searching, searching for its satisfier. Frege's approach sees proper names under both aspects, and this duality makes for an uneasy tension.[23]

So much for making the practice more Fregean. Where do we stand on the intelligibility of the practice as originally described? Imagine a linguistic engineer designing a set of linguistic practices for a community. Given the utility of official numbers, can't we imagine the engineer implementing some such practice, without even noticing its violation of traditional cognitive fix ideas? If the traditional conception was true to the ways we think about these things, something should seem amiss here. But nothing does seem amiss. What other than the grip of Cartesian ways of thinking would rule out such a practice as unintelligible?

Tradition has taught—and this makes a kind of a priori sense to us—that reference depends upon the speaker's grasp of the referent. When we picture, in an abstract sort of way, someone using words without the appropriate sort of cognitive relation to the referent, we suppose that something has misfired badly. However, when we shift attention from the individual's cognitive situation to her participation in a full-blown communicative practice, then despite the lack of cognitive fix, it no longer appears that anything has gone awry.

We should not suppose that the burden of proof, or even of argument, is on the advocate of cognitively innocent reference. This supposition seems natural when and only when we view matters individualistically. Attention to an individual qua participant in a name-using community diffuses the sense that the referential tie supervenes on the agent's cognitive fix.

---

ber, on some occasion of utterance, would depend upon whatever factors determine the reference of real proper names on particular utterance occasions. (See section 6 in this chapter for more on this question of names with multiple references.)

[23] In an unpublished essay, "Frege's Millianism," Genoveva Marti emphasizes that even Frege gives weight to the notion of name as having a bearer in the sense in question.

6. Objection: Real Names Have Many Bearers

In this last section I will develop further my Millian approach to names by considering an objection that immediately threatens to reinstate something more traditional, Fregean or Russellian.

It is sometimes thought that Mill's conception of names is widely off the mark for natural language, since real names have many bearers, and the Millian conception—and of course my Millian number fantasy—seems to presuppose that a single name picks out a unique individual. Indeed, my case for the intelligibility of cognitively unmediated reference seemed to rest upon there being a single referent for each official number. What makes a particular person the referent of an uttered number, I argued, is that it is *his* number.

Not only does Mill's view apparently not accommodate this datum, Frege's and Russell's seem to do so. On a descriptional account of names, a single name might accommodate many referents. The referent on a given occasion depends upon the specific description the name abbreviates on that occasion.

I agree that it's easier to explain Mill's conception on the simplifying assumption of "one name-one referent," but I don't think doing so is at all essential. Nor do I think that the fact that our practice with names fails to obey the "one name-one referent" stricture lends any credence to the traditional conceptions.

Let's begin with this latter, purely negative point, that the so-called ambiguity of names doesn't help the Fregean or Russellian. If the traditional approach proved adequate up to, so to speak, the ambiguity of names, then pretty clearly it would be adequate to that problem as well. If speakers in general associated individuating conceptions with proper names, then we would indeed have a natural way of dealing with multireferenced proper names.

However, a survey of ordinary linguistic practice strongly suggested that the traditional account was inadequate. For all the reasons surveyed, individuating conceptions seem like the wrong idea for actual practice. Accordingly, it's difficult to get excited about an approach that makes individuating conceptions the key to understanding multireferenced names.

Nor is it at all clear that individuating conceptions make for a natural account even for names with multiple bearers. Quite the contrary. As we have seen, one can use the name 'Cicero' for the Roman orator without possessing accurate individuating information about the man. But one can use that name both as a name for the man and as a name for the city without an accurate individuating conception of either. Likewise, a student can speak of Aristotle the philosopher and of Aristotle the shipping magnate without accurate individuating conceptions of either. The many arguments, reviewed at the end of the last chapter, which indicate that names don't require the backing of individuating conceptions, apply to names with several bearers as much as they apply to uniquely borne names.

The remarks just made about 'Cicero' and 'Aristotle' make vivid the question of how we manage to use multireferenced names to refer to single individuals. It might be useful here to remind ourselves that names with more than a single bearer are to some extent like ambiguous expressions. Not that we should be confident that "ambiguity" is precisely the right idea here. It seems worthwhile, though, to pursue similarities (and differences) between such names and ambiguous expressions more generally. Perhaps a better understanding of what is often, with insufficient attention to poetry, called "disambiguation" would provide us with an understanding of how we use names with many bearers to refer to particular individuals.

What is needed here, or so it seems to me, is not philosophical ingenuity, but a good nose for what we actually do. Let's begin then with a garden-variety ambiguous expression. When someone uses an ambiguous word such as 'bank' in an everyday context, it is typically clear which sort of bank (financial bank, river bank) is in question, but very far from clear what sort of factors determine this. To what extent does it depend upon the speaker's intentions? Need he have a *definition* of the two sorts of bank in order to mean one of them? (Implausible.) And if he really does intend one of them, whatever this takes, say he intends to speak of a river bank, does that guarantee that his utterance of 'bank' counts as a reference to a river bank? Can't we imagine a context in which his intention is overridden by certain contextual factors, a context, for example, in which it is completely obvious to the most casual observer that a financial institution is in question?[24]

---

[24] My interest here is reference, what Kripke calls "semantic reference," as opposed to intended reference, what Kripke calls "speaker reference." For the latter concept, it will be true by definition that the speaker's intention is determinative. With respect to the former, my own view and Kripke's is that the speaker's intention is not determinative. See Kripke, "Speaker's Reference and Semantic Reference," in *Contemporary Perspectives in the Philosophy of Language* (Minneapolis: University of Minnesota Press, 1979), and Wettstein, "How to Bridge the Gap Between Meaning And Reference," in *Has Semantics Rested on a Mistake? and Other Essays* (Palo

A better understanding of disambiguation, of how we actually proceed, will result from serious attention to our practices. Perhaps some relatively simple, straightforward account will be forthcoming, according to which speaker's intentions, context, and so on will be given their rightful places. Or perhaps there is no simple theoretical account available here. Perhaps disambiguation is itself highly context dependent, and different sorts of factors get weighted differently according to the specifics of the communicative situation.

Let's return to proper names, armed, we will imagine, with a better understanding of disambiguation. We can picture a number of scenarios. First, a subsequent empirical study of multiply assigned names might reveal that such names behave just like ambiguous expressions generally. What makes one Cicero, rather than another, the referent of some utterance of the name may have something to do with the speaker's intentions (he meant to be speaking of Cicero the orator rather than the city), the context of utterance (the conversation had been focused upon a particular Cicero), or whatever.

Notice that if this were correct, if the determination of the reference of a multireferenced name were just like disambiguation, then Mill would have told us more or less the whole story about the semantics of proper names! Mill, that is, would have told us what is distinctive about proper names. He would not have explained our general practice of using expressions that have more than one official function to perform a specific one of those functions. It's difficult, however, to fault his remarks on proper names on this point.

Consider an analogy. We are all familiar with age-old debates about universals and general terms. Does 'blue' apply to blue things in virtue of their instantiating a universal? Or does it somehow apply directly to blue things without the mediation of a universal? Imagine that after several millennia someone finally provides a truly promising account but does not address the topic of ambiguity. Someone objects that 'blue' also means "sad" and that the new account, promising as it is, provides no way of discerning the correct interpretation of 'blue' in a given context. This objection would be misplaced. True, we won't fully understand the functioning of

---

Alto, Cal.: Stanford University Press, 1995) for arguments that intentions are not determinative of semantic reference. Keith Donnellan, in a number of articles, has defended the idea that speakers' intentions in general are determinative of reference.

'blue' in any context until we understand why it functions in one of these ways instead of in the other in a given context. Nevertheless, the ambiguity of 'blue' certainly seems like a distinct problem and not something that vitiates the accomplishment.

I have been proceeding on the supposition that multiply referenced names are, in the relevant respect, like ambiguous general terms. There is, of course, no guarantee that our study will have this result. Perhaps the determination of reference for multiply assigned names has peculiarities, special features not shared by disambiguation generally. Perhaps the context of utterance, as opposed to the speaker's intentions, counts more (or less) than in cases of ambiguity. Perhaps the context is relevant in some different respect than usual. Still, whatever our study reveals ought to be fine with the Millian. His topic was names, not the distinct problem we have been discussing. The "one name – one referent" idea was a simplifying myth, a way of making the pure denotation idea dramatic and easy to see.

Let's return to the question that motivated this discussion. How is it possible for there to be reference, linguistic contact with things, in the absence of substantive cognitive contact? The key to my answer has been the notion of what we might call a public name. Our language provides us with a way of getting at things which does not depend much upon the vicissitudes of our epistemological situation. A minimally competent speaker who acquires the name in some usual way[25] is in a position to use it to make its bearer a subject of discourse. Doing so does not depend upon knowledge of the bearer, or even upon more or less accurate beliefs about the bearer. There is, then, no special problem about reference in the absence of a substantial cognitive fix. Indeed, that there might be such reference is one of the points of the practice, one of its virtues. Reflecting upon Mill's remarks on proper names, or, more accurately, placing Mill's remarks in the context of our developing social-practice picture, thus yields the result that epistemically ungrounded reference is by no means unintelligible.

---

[25] I speak of the need to pick up the name "in some usual way," for one may, I suppose, pick up a name in various unusual ways and then not be in a position to use it to speak of its conventional assignee. Making up a name with no special bearer in mind, for example, doesn't put one in a position to speak of someone who actually happen to bear the name. To say that the name has a public, social role is not to say that there are no requirements at all for who is in a position to make use of the social instrument.

5

A Father of
the Revolution

Never complain; never explain.
Attributed to Henry Ford II.

1. Wittgenstein and the Anti-Fregeans

When I was a graduate student in the late 1960s, Wittgenstein was very fashionable. Remarks like "meaning is use" rolled off one's tongue as easily as "Hell no, we won't go," or "It's not the case that necessarily the number of planets is greater than seven." I vowed to avoid the *Philosophical Investigations,* and I was true to my vow until some years later when a friend commented that my approach to indexicals[1] exhibited what he called a social perspective. Difficult and quirky as Wittgenstein's text might be, I reluctantly concluded, it might well be a source of insight concerning the social character of language.

There was a second reason for taking the plunge into the *Investigations.* Wittgenstein, it was well known, defended a variant of the description theory of names, specifically the cluster theory. It was additionally well known that Wittgenstein opposed in a radical sort of way making naming any sort of key to language. A study of the *Investigations,* then, would provide an excellent test of my developing anti-Fregean approach.

[1] In "How to Bridge the Gap between Meaning and Reference," in Wettstein, *Has Semantics Rested on a Mistake? and Other Essays* (Palo Alto, Cal.: Stanford University Press, 1995).

Imagine my surprise when I found that what I've been calling the Cartesian orientation was for Wittgenstein almost an obsession. It is just such ways of thinking that, according to Wittgenstein, paralyze us, that create puzzles and quandaries. Wittgenstein's remedy is to attend closely to actual practice. "Look at our practices," he urges, "don't think about what they must be like." But this, I reflected, is just what contemporary anti-Fregeans have done, the outcome being a host of examples that strike at the heart of traditional philosophy of language. I was finding, contrary to what I expected, something of a convergence of views.

Even more startling, Frege himself was one of Wittgenstein's central targets. This fact didn't emerge right away, but by the time I hit Wittgenstein's discussion of "concepts with blurred edges" in §71,[2] it was clear. Indeed Wittgenstein often sees Frege as the foremost advocate of the targeted traditional views.

And while Wittgenstein roundly opposed the assimilation of other forms of speech to names he certainly took naming to be of central interest. Names and namelike pieces of language are focal, for example, in the elementary language games. The idea that Wittgenstein advocated a descriptional account of names, moreover, didn't fit very smoothly with remarks like, "It will often prove useful in philosophy to say to ourselves: naming something is like attaching a label to a thing."[3] Not to speak of, "And the *meaning* of a name is sometimes explained by pointing to its bearer."[4]

It's not as if Wittgenstein advances all sorts of views characteristic of the later anti-Fregeans. Surely not: no rigid designation, possible worlds, or propositions with objects as constituents. Nor should we infer from the two passages just quoted that Wittgenstein advocates the sort of Millian position about names I've been defending here. Perhaps most important, Wittgenstein's work suggests a very different treatment of the notion of reference itself.[5] Still, Witt-

---

[2] "Frege compares a concept to an area and says that an area without clear boundaries cannot be called an area at all. This presumably means that we cannot do anything with it." For Wittgenstein, the utility of ordinary concepts is closely connected with their lack of "clear boundaries." The metaphor of boundaries has a number of implications. An important one concerns definition: our concepts typically lack clear definitions.

[3] *Philosophical Investigations*, §15

[4] *Philosophical Investigations*, §43

[5] This is an IOU not cashed out in the present work. I hope to do so elsewhere. The short version: Wittgenstein opposes the idea that the concept of reference constitutes a kind of master key to the relation between language and the world. There is no single such relation.

genstein not only anticipates important features of the later anti-Fregean approach, he often provides a deeper and more satisfying rationale than in recent work. And where Wittgenstein sharply diverges from the anti-Fregeans, it often seemed to me that Wittgenstein was pointing the way forward.

That Wittgenstein might be something of an ally was surprising enough. Even more so was anti-Fregean assistance in understanding Wittgenstein. His work not only represents a radical departure from traditional philosophy, it is also quite obscure, difficult to penetrate. Wittgenstein maintains—to mention some ideas that will be pivotal here—that meaning is use, that he has no interest in explaining anything, that philosophical puzzles do not require solutions. How to understand any of this, not to speak of all of it! The antecedent likelihood of finding the anti-Frege literature helpful in understanding Wittgenstein was very slight. Nevertheless, that literature provided considerable assistance, as I'll explain.

The convergence of views to which I'm drawing attention seems to me almost universally unappreciated. It is unappreciated by Wittgenstein sympathizers, whose vision is obscured by the rigid designation/possible worlds/singular propositions aspects of the anti-Fregean literature. It is unappreciated by the anti-Fregeans, who tend to see Wittgenstein sometimes as an arch-anti-theorist who is happy to leave matters muddy, sometimes as a sort of description theorist of proper names, an obscure one at that. The lack of recognition of the Wittgenstein link by anti-Fregeans has been particularly costly, for such recognition might help reveal the very large stakes at issue in their own debate. Insufficiently focused on these larger questions, anti-Fregeans have often proceeded as if their project amounted to what John Perry once called a conservative revision of Frege.

My aim in this chapter is to develop further the social-practice conception of the last chapter. I'll do so by bringing Wittgenstein into the picture more explicitly and by locating and developing some key points of congruence between Wittgenstein and the anti-Fregeans. One such point will be central: an approach to the vitality of language, the fact that words, mere pieces of nature, have a kind of life for us. The shift from the Cartesian orientation is considerably more radical than we have yet supposed.

2. Convergence: Meaning Ain't in the Head

A further bit of stage setting will be afforded by a brief return to the anti-Fregean counterexamples of chapter 3. In a discussion with graduate students, I was reviewing my favorite objection to Frege's approach,[6] discussed briefly here in chapter 3, when a student remarked that it was the sort of objection Wittgenstein might make. Let's think about names of people we know very well, or indexicals used to refer to things that we can identify in any number of ways. That is, let's bypass the problems anti-Fregeans have highlighted concerning the facts that ordinary speakers often lack uniquely identifying beliefs, that their beliefs may be mistaken, and so on. Still, in many cases there will be no way to select some discrete bit of identifying information from the mass of such information available to the speaker, and to conclude that *this* bit of information functions as the sense of the name on the occasion in question. There will often be no reason to select some particular description, nor conjunction (or disjunction) of available descriptions, to play this role. And Frege's view, that on such occasions a distinct proposition was asserted, requires that it not be arbitrary which bit of identifying information is to play this role. So even where there is no problem with the speaker's identifying information—even where she possesses a cognitive fix—it is implausible to suppose that this knowledge plays the role assigned to it by the Fregean orientation.[7]

The connection between my line of argument and the general tenor of Wittgenstein's work is positively striking—at least once it has been pointed out. The connection is perhaps especially striking in the context of the other anti-Fregean counterexamples mentioned in chapter 3. Think of my "too many descriptions" point in connection with the Donnellan-Kripke idea that the use of a name requires very little identifying information. The result of putting these together is this: *Reference does not require a cognitive fix, and even where there is one the cognitive fix does not do the work it was supposed to do, the work assigned to it by the Fregean orientation.* Turning to the *Philosophical Investigations*, with its more general concerns, I read one central theme thus:

There is likely to be considerably less in the head[8] than traditional philosophy has supposed. And what is in the head (for example, mental

---

[6] Its being my favorite is related to its being my own. The argument played a pivotal role in my dissertation.

[7] This problem, it should be noted, applies to Russell as much as to Frege. Let the name or indexical abbreviate a nonpurely qualitative definite description, say one that contains an expression that directly refers to something in my immediate experience, as Russell would have supposed. Still, there will likely be a multiplicity of such descriptions, and no way to choose between them in many cases.

[8] I am not being careful here with a distinction that is for some questions quite important, the distinction between what is in the mind and what, although not in

images, occurrent intentions—in the sense of conscious acts of decision) is likely to be playing less of a role in the workings of language than philosophers have assumed.[9]

It seems to me remarkable that such fundamental points of contact have received so little attention.

Hilary Putnam, in his early discussion of "natural kind" terms, remarked that "meaning ain't in the head."[10] Putnam's remark, although he may or may not have been thinking of Wittgenstein, nicely focuses this important point of contact with Wittgenstein. But it isn't only this negative proclivity that anti-Fregeans share with Wittgenstein. There is a corresponding positive conception. (I had been led to believe not only that Wittgenstein was something of a description theorist but also that he had no positive views.) Wittgenstein, more than anyone else in recent times, brings to life the central idea of the revolution, that of a public language, understood as a set of shared social practices.

As with many philosophers, Wittgenstein found it easier, I think, to formulate what he was against than what he was for. Nor was his emphasis on the negative simply a matter of ease of formulation. Wittgenstein is preoccupied with the task of freeing us from the grip of a disputed picture, and in his (to my mind) darker moments may even suggest that there is no positive philosophical work to be done. In what follows, I'll try to attend to the positive as well as the negative.

3. The Life of the Sign Revisited

That linguistic significance is not explained by associated representations is pivotal for both Wittgenstein and the direct-reference advocate. Yet the contrary idea has both the weight of tradition and powerful intuitive support. In *The Blue Book*, Wittgenstein criticizes the traditional view:

---

the mind but in a third realm of abstracta, is merely accessible to the mind. Wittgenstein himself is often not careful about this; that's fine in contexts when it does not matter for what exercises Wittgenstein. For example, in his discussion of Frege's views about meaning (I discuss this in section 3 of this chapter), Wittgenstein moves freely between criticizing Frege (who sees meanings as denizens of a third realm) and the mentalist, as if Frege himself saw meanings as mental entities.

[9] Such things also play less of a role in the workings of *thought* than philosophers have supposed. So maintains Wittgenstein, as I read him. I return later to the question of thought. For the moment, however, language is more than enough.

[10] "The Meaning of 'Meaning,'" in Hilary Putnam, *Philosophical Papers: Volume 2, Mind, Language and Reality* (Cambridge: Cambridge University Press, 1979).

Frege ridiculed the formalist conception of mathematics by saying that the formalists confused the unimportant thing, the sign, with the important, the meaning. Surely, one wishes to say, mathematics does not treat of dashes on a bit of paper. Frege's idea could be expressed thus: the propositions of mathematics, if they were just complexes of dashes, would be dead and utterly uninteresting, whereas they obviously have a kind of life. And the same, of course, could be said of any proposition: Without a sense, or without the thought, a proposition would be an utterly dead and trivial thing. And further it seems clear that no adding of inorganic signs can make the proposition live. And the conclusion which one draws from this is that what must be added to the dead signs in order to make a live proposition is something immaterial, with properties different from all mere signs.

But if we had to name anything which is the life of the sign, we should have to say that it was its use.

The passage continues:

If the meaning of the sign (roughly, that which is of importance about the sign) is an image built up in our minds when we see or hear the sign, then first let us adopt the method we just described of replacing this mental image by some outward object seen, e.g. a painted or modeled image. Then why should the written sign plus this painted image be alive if the written sign alone was dead?—In fact, as soon as the image thereby loses its occult character, it ceases to seem to impart any life to the sentence at all. (It was in fact just the occult character of the mental process which you needed for your purposes.)

The mistake we are liable to make could be expressed thus: We are looking for the use of a sign, but we look for it as though it were an object *co-existing* with the sign. (One of the reasons for this mistake is again that we are looking for a "thing corresponding to a substantive.")[11]

These remarks perhaps typify what many find wondrous, in all its senses, about Wittgenstein's writings. A striking difficulty with the last two passages is that the view criticized—meaning as mental image—is not Frege's. Perhaps, though, Wittgenstein mentions Frege's remarks on formalism only because those remarks afford easy entry into a quite general tendency of thought, the latter being Wittgenstein's target. Still, one wants to know how Frege's view itself, if it is supposed to exemplify the broad representationalist tendency, is subject to the stated attack. Why, moreover, doesn't

[11] P. 4.

Wittgenstein go after a relatively strong version of representational-ism? The meaning as mental image view is arguably no more than a straw man.[12]

Let's agree that Wittgenstein's comments certainly need to be enlarged upon if they are to apply to the general case (or to Frege, for that matter). Wittgenstein, I'm sure, would agree. What he wants from the mental image view, I believe, is a kind of intuitive model, one variant, of the broad tendency he is attacking. His immediate target is this variant, the mental image conception of meaning. However, the considerations brought to bear are no doubt intended to be at least suggestive of what's wrong with the general tendency, Frege's variant included.

Such "straw-man" arguments have, as I see it, a genuine and important role in philosophy. In *Naming and Necessity*,[13] Kripke criticizes the "Frege-Russell description theory," which perhaps neither Frege nor Russell held precisely in the form described, and which might be strengthened in any number of ways by a contemporary Fregean or Russellian. Still, Kripke's argument is very powerful.

Important here is the distinction between the strongest form of a view and the purest. To put the point in a rather extreme way, while advocates of a view may well prefer discussing some latest epicycle, produced with one eye on the latest counterexample, it may be easier to get hold of a view by viewing some more original, naïve, or sometimes even oversimplified form of it. The naïve form is more easily refutable, it is true. Its refutation surely doesn't entail the refutation of other forms. Still, seeing what's wrong with the naïve form may be just what's needed to see what's wrong with the tendency itself. By contrast, exclusive attention to the most sophisticated form may often obscure the intuitive idea at its core.[14]

---

[12] And some will think of it as obviously correct. Speaking to psychologist colleagues some years ago, I was stunned to realize that for them the mental image model was the (almost obvious) literal truth about meaning. I say this not because it is obviously not, although I find it difficult to take to seriously, in part because of the sorts of reasons Wittgenstein offers. I say this rather because it illustrates the dominant role of intellectual fashion. I wrote this section of the book while on leave at the Center for Ideas and Society at the University of California, Riverside, where many of the Fellows took it to be completely obvious that all facts are social constructions, an idea that I was unable to get under control. I was on leave at the time from the Department of Philosophy, where, as I saw the matter, the social dimension often got less than its due.

[13] As David Kaplan pointed out to me.

[14] I'm thinking here of the more and more sophisticated forms of theoretical response to the Gettier counterexamples to the traditional definition of knowledge, as well as the increasingly sophisticated analyses of belief sentences.

The distinction between pure and sophisticated versions, and the utility of such straw-man arguments, are important topics, but not ones to be explored further in the present context. Nor will I explore Wittgenstein's argument against the meaning as mental image view. My interest here is in Wittgenstein's positive alternative to representationalism, his idea that "the life of the sign" is its use. He provides a bit more assistance (but only a bit more) in the passage that immediately follows that just quoted.

> The sign (the sentence) gets its significance from the system of signs, from the language to which it belongs. Roughly: understanding a sentence means understanding a language.

> As a part of the system of language, one may say, the sentence has a life. But one is tempted to imagine that which gives the sentence life as something in an occult sphere, accompanying the sentence. But whatever accompanied it would for us just be another sign.

To understand the distinctive way in which linguistic symbols are alive for us, maintains the Fregean, look past the symbols to their meanings, to the intrinsically alive representations. Wittgenstein redirects our focus to the symbols themselves, not in isolation but "as part of the system of language."

But this can't quite explain the matter. First, to see a particular sentence as situated in language is to see it in relation to other sentences of the language. But, as Wittgenstein says, "no adding of inorganic signs can make the proposition live." Second, having told us that the life of the sign is its use, an idea that cries out for explanation, it doesn't help much to add that what vitalizes the sign is its inclusion in a language. This doesn't help because it doesn't sound much like an explanation of use. It sounds rather like quite a different idea. The use of a sentence and its inclusion in a system of sentences are not, after all, in some obvious way the same idea. So what's going on?

That symbols are alive for us, that they are significant, is to be understood in terms neither of the association of symbols with representations, the traditionalist's meanings, nor of the mere inclusion of the symbols in a system of symbols. Linguistic vitality is rather a matter of the embeddedness of symbols in social, communicative practice. When Wittgenstein speaks of the inclusion of a sentence in a system of language, he means the inclusion of a sign, among other systematically related signs, in a living language, in a system of communicative practice.

This is, of course, only a beginning, for now we will want to ask how embeddedness in social practice breathes life into a symbol. But let's press on. Talk of the life of the sign is of course metaphorical. What is at stake is significance, the fact that words mean. Wittgenstein's quoted remarks about the life of the sign somewhat parallel his remarks about meaning and use. In discussing meaning and use, Wittgenstein sometimes (only sometimes) seems to identify the two notions, albeit qualifiedly: "For a *large* class of cases—though not for all—in which we employ the word 'meaning' it can be defined thus: the meaning of a word is its use in the language."[15]

Larry Wright points out that the positivists, in discussions of meaning and verification, sometimes used to say that meaning *just is* the mode of verification. Sometimes they would put the point more helpfully by urging that instead of asking for the meaning of a statement we rather inquire about how it is to be verified. So, Wright continues, perhaps the formula "meaning *is* . . . ," as used by midcentury philosophers, should not be heard as suggesting theoretical identification. Perhaps it was a way of directing attention away from the concept of meaning and toward more illuminating ways of thinking about significance. This brings to mind Wittgenstein's other formulations:

> "Don't ask for the meaning, ask for the use."

> —But what is the meaning of the word "five"?—No such thing was in question here, only how the word "five" is used.[16]

Still other times, Wittgenstein connects meaning with role in the language:

> We seemed to ask a question about the state of mind of the man who says the sentence, whereas the idea of meaning which we arrived at in the end was not that of a state of mind. We think of the meaning of signs sometimes as states of mind of the man using them, sometimes as the role which these signs are playing in a system of language.[17]

One thing—maybe not much else—that seems clear from both discussions, that of vitality and that of meaning, is a general explanatory direction: Significance is not a matter of associated ideas in the mind or concepts in a third realm, but rather of what we do with symbols. While it is difficult to know how to work out such

[15] *Philosophical Investigations*, §43
[16] *Philosophical Investigations*, §1
[17] *Philosophical Investigations*, §1

a view, its naturalism has always seemed to me very attractive. Just as in a naturalistic spirit it would be preferable to characterize human beings without notions like that of a purely spiritual substance, so it would be preferable to account for language without employing any notion like that of Frege's sense. A sense, you might say, is the soul of a word.

The appeal to Fregean third-realm senses seems to violate naturalism. Yet one may develop a Fregean approach along naturalistic lines, for example, by locating significance-giving representations into the brain instead of construing them as abstract or mental. There is an important parallel in the philosophy of mind, where one may develop, and many have developed, a Cartesian approach to mentality in a physicalistic direction.[18] Such naturalisms seem to me unnatural, the products of arranged marriages, as it were. What I see as Wittgenstein's naturalism,[19] by contrast, proceeds from a wholly different direction: Don't look to representations (whether mental, abstract, or physical) to understand significance; attend instead to our practices.

When one comes to Wittgenstein from Frege, more generally from our almost genetically inherited Cartesian ways of thinking, the idea of significance-without-representations—even if this begins to seem attractive—is very difficult to get under control. How, one wants to ask, could linguistic significance not be a matter of something like association with intrinsically representative entities? Doesn't our ability to use symbols, our doing things with them, presuppose that they are significant? Doesn't the significance have to come first? How then can significance be a matter of use, or what we do with the symbols? Nor does bringing more people into the picture resolve anything—as if a bunch of people could accomplish the magic simply by making noises in coordinated ways.[20]

Alvin Plantinga once commented to me that he found Wittgenstein's approach to these matters tantalizing, even if ultimately unacceptable (unacceptable for just the sorts of reasons just men-

---

[18] That the adoption of a physicalistic outlook is no guarantee that a Cartesian orientation has been rejected has been pointed out by a number of philosophers, perhaps under the inspiration of Wittgenstein. For a recent discussion see Hilary Putnam's 1994 Dewey Lectures in *The Journal of Philosophy* 91 (September 1994).

[19] Cf. my article, "Terra Firma: Wittgenstein's Naturalism," *The Monist* 78, no. 4 (1995): 425–46.

[20] Wittgenstein's approach is no more palatable from Russell's standpoint. Again, the life of the sign is derivative from the mind's grasp, this time the direct grasp of a referent.

tioned, as I remember his remarks). Unlike Plantinga, I had the sense that Wittgenstein was on to something, that something more sound, less magical was in the offing. But how, given all these questions, can we get further inside Wittgenstein's picture, to bring it to life as a real alternative?

4. Gaining a Foothold

When we think about significance abstractly, about what makes it possible, it's very difficult to conceive an alternative to a broadly Fregean outlook. Nor does Wittgenstein clearly articulate such an alternative, at least not in a way that makes it readily available.

What is perhaps most helpful in Wittgenstein is his working through many kinds of examples, accumulating insights, and highlighting dead ends engendered by traditional modes of philosophical thinking. But Wittgenstein's approach to the course of the intellectual therapy is notoriously difficult and, not unlike the other sort of therapy, is almost always painfully slow and, until one gets the hang of it, quite frustrating.[21] I want to recommend another mode of access to Wittgenstein's themes, an alternative or supplementary route not only to the rejection of the Fregean orientation but also to the understanding of meaning as use. Enter direct reference.

An important preliminary is to avoid the lofty plane at which discussions of meaning often proceed. My approach to direct reference avoids discussion of significance in general or in the abstract. This might seem strange in light of the tendency among some direct-reference advocates to make names the paradigm, and further—this is a distinct move—to think of meaning as reference, or alternatively to make indexicals the paradigm and to think of meaning as *character* (in Kaplan's sense). These quite general theses are far from what I am after. Instead, let's narrow our focus to particular categories of linguistic expressions—for example, to proper names, or indexical expressions, definite descriptions, predicate expressions—and scrutinize actual practice. The question is this: What does significance come to with respect to this particular practice? This sort of significance-particularism has a Wittgensteinian flavor.

---

[21] The analogies are quite striking. Note how in psychotherapy the articulation of an alternative picture to the patient's is also often not helpful very early. One is unlikely to recognize one's own deep conception and therefore unlikely to be able to make use of an alternative. Early work often involves facilitating the recognition of one's own deep conception and, sometimes simultaneously, the loosening of its grip.

It should go without saying that it does not preclude finding commonalities.[22]

When one asks this question—what does significance come to?—for the case of, say, proper names, one comes to reject traditional representationalism, Fregean or Russellian. So the direct reference literature has argued. It's often assumed that Wittgenstein himself is sympathetic to some form of description/cluster theory of proper names. Whether or not this is right—I'm skeptical— what's striking is the extent to which direct reference criticisms of traditional ideas about names are mirror images of Wittgenstein's ideas about significance.

Consider the traditional idea that an expression's being significant is a matter of its possessing a meaning, where close to the heart of "meaning" is "grasped by the competent speaker." As direct reference advocates have pointed out, proper names just don't fit this model. One does not have to grasp any such meaning-entity to be competent with a name. Simply acquiring a name in some appropriate way (such as conversing with someone who is using the name) puts one in a position to use the name. This is not just an anti-Fregean contention; it is a datum. People are regularly judged competent with names even when they lack familiarity with the bearers of the names.

Notice also that we do not ask what names mean. When we lack familiarity with an expression like 'lugubrious' we inquire about what it means; this is not the case for 'Aristotle' or 'Gell-Mann'. Nor do we, except perhaps in the grip of a theory, think of the name 'Harry' as ambiguous just because there are many Harrys. "Meaning" as a substantive, or "the meaning," seems like the wrong notion for proper names.[23]

---

[22] The tendency among the first wave (Kripke, Kaplan, Marcus, Putnam), as opposed to their followers, was to steer clear of general characterizations of significance. This is certainly true of Kripke, for example, but even Kaplan, who is more theoretically inclined, hesitates in "Demonstratives" to extend his story about indexicals to proper names. I'm (perversely) tempted to say that their ideological purity here often exceeds Wittgenstein's, whose characterization of meaning in terms of use, despite his disclaimers and admonitions, has encouraged a kind of un-Wittgensteinian theorizing, "use theories of meaning," and the like. At the same time, of course, Kripke's short-lived emphasis on the "causal chain of communication" has encouraged others, not him, to advance "causal theories of reference" and the like. Similar remarks apply to Kaplan and Putnam.

[23] This is not to say that if one comes to Millianism with a traditional conception in hand, thinking that meaningfulness requires meanings, one cannot lay one's hand on a candidate. Names, after all, stand for things. Their significance consists,

These negative reflections are at once Millian and Wittgensteinian. As are these positive ideas: When we say that names are significant, meaningful, we gesture to their role in the public practice, their use or function: making things subjects of discourse, as Mill says. What brings names to life, to use Wittgenstein's metaphor, is their function, their role in our practice. In terms of Wittgenstein's (mostly unhelpful) slogan one might say that for proper names their meaning (that is, their significance) just is their use (that is, their function of standing for things).

In §1 of the *Investigations*, Wittgenstein is attacking one variant of the traditional way of thinking about meaning:

—But what is the meaning of the word "five"?—No such thing was in question here, only how the word "five" is used."

Substitute the name "Aristotle" for "five," and you will see the confluence of views of which I've been speaking.

We have been struggling with Wittgenstein's approach to significance, trying to find a way into the picture. The anti-Fregean treatment of names in modeling key Wittgensteinian themes provides a good beginning. In addition, anti-Fregean successes, substantial in my view, constitute a powerful argument for Wittgenstein's approach. Indeed, we have isolated one clear domain in which Wittgenstein's intuitions about significance seem right on the mark.

A traditionalist might here point out the limited character of this argument, its restriction to proper names: Conceding proper names, there is still the rest of language, its Fregean core.[24] After all, as was noted, we don't ordinarily speak of the meaning of a proper name. We don't find their meanings, or definitions, in dictionaries. And while the anti-Fregean can appeal to such facts to

---

we might say, in the fact that they stand for things. It may seem like a short distance between this last formulation and the idea that the significance of the name just is the thing stood for. Accordingly—so said Russell, and later some of the anti-Fregeans—the significance of the name, its meaning, just is the bearer. But there is no need to say this, and one will not naturally do so unless one feels the need to find something to be the meaning of the name. Moreover, it is one thing for Russell to make the referents of names into meanings. Russell, after all, really does think that speakers must grasp the references of names they are in a position to use. But contemporary anti-Fregeans have usually rejected epistemological constraints on name-reference. Accordingly, their talk of name-bearers as meanings seems especially unmotivated.

[24] As Julius Moravcsik argued in conversation.

highlight the insensitivity of Frege's view of names to actual practice, the Fregean can appeal to the same facts to illustrate the viability of Frege's ideas for the rest of language.

Proper names, however, cannot be so easily conceded by the traditionalist without saying significantly more. The Cartesian-inspired picture appealed to representations as essential to linguistic significance. For the Cartesian to suppose that proper names might somehow function without associated meaning-entities would be like a spiritualist supposing that some humans might function without souls.

And of course proper names are hardly the only problem for the traditionalist. Renewed attention to actual practice has paid additional dividends with respect to a variety of types of linguistic expression. As I see it, proper names are hardly the model for direct reference. Or, if we are to generalize from the study of names, if that study is suggestive of a program, that program would emphasize the search for natural ways to characterize actual practice with a variety of expressions. Look, as Wittgenstein said, don't think.

5. Explaining Significance?

One of the aims of Wittgensteinian therapy is to loosen the hold of our almost genetically inherited Fregean impulses about significance. I have tried to accomplish some of the same by modeling Wittgensteinian themes in direct-reference terms. Even so, it is very difficult to lose a sense of uneasiness about significance-without-representation.

One way to highlight the discomfort is to focus on explanatory adequacy. Descartes says that he found it amazing that bodies, mere pieces of nature, could move themselves. If locomotion can seem miraculous, what about reference? That mere pieces of nature can mean, or symbolize, or stand for something really seems extraordinary. It cries out for a philosophical account. Frege's approach seems empirically inadequate, insensitive to actual linguistic practice. But at least Frege tries to explain, to get behind or underneath reference: The reference of a name resolves into two more primary facts, first, that that a name by convention expresses a sense and second, that senses intrinsically, non-conventionally, represent things. My favored alternatives—Millian or Wittgensteinian—seem worse.

Mill's remarks about proper names hardly constitute an explanation of how it is that names signify. Mill's remarks are largely negative: Names do not refer by means of associated connotations, senses, or anything of the like. His positive contention is that names are assigned ad hoc, as it were, and then are used to make their bearers subjects of discourse. If there is anything like an explanation here, it is a matter of explaining the reference of a particular name in terms of the general name-using practice. Try to construe this as an attempt to get underneath the phenomenon of reference and what you get is a pretty obviously circular explanation. We wanted to know how it is possible for one piece of nature, the word 'Aristotle', to stand for another, the man Aristotle. and we are told that in general we use such symbols to stand for things.

Wittgenstein sometimes talks as if *use* is somehow to play the explanatory role of Frege's sense: "But if we had to name anything which is the life of the sign, we should have to say that it was its use."[25]

But again, what we want to understand is how it is possible that a name stands for a thing. It does not help to be told that what makes this possible is that the name is used to refer to the thing. Indeed, additionally, as I've said, the use of a linguistic expression seems to presuppose that the expression is significant. How then can use explain significance?

Moving to the social level, as do Mill and Wittgenstein, doesn't seem to resolve anything. What the intelligibility of linguistic practice seems to require is something like the association of concepts with the words. So it looks like with respect to the project of explaining reference, arguably the most important question of all, Frege's view—problematic as it may be—has a leg up. Frege has a story to tell about how the Red Sea parted, as it were; we remain mute.

But has the Fregean really provided an explanation of significance? Never mind empirical inadequacy; does it explain? The Fregean proposal has only the form of an explanation, as Tom Blackburn once commented. It would represent a genuine explanatory advance if we understood its key ingredient, the intrinsic intentionality of the representations. But how exactly are representations significant; how do they stand for things? Why isn't this as problematic as the aboutness of words—even more so, given how unclear we are about senses? The Fregean explanation, unless further developed, seems like positing a god to explain how it all got here but having little helpful to say about what sort of being is this god,

---

[25] *The Blue Book* (New York: Harper & Row, 1976), p. 4.

about how the god pulled off this "creation," and about how god himself got here (or about why that's no problem).[26]

In the absence of an account of the matter, the Fregean is in an embarrassing position. If the aboutness of the representations is left unexplained, their theoretical utility is cast into doubt. But the representations are a theoretical posit; it's not, after all, that attention to ordinary practice makes plain the presence of suitable representations accompanying our words. So why bother with them?[27] Why not leave things where we found them? This suggests—and this might seem at least mildly depressing (but not to worry, it grows on one)—that perhaps the best we can do is to describe our ways with language, making no attempt to get beyond or behind.

Why does the Fregean—indeed the Cartesian tradition—take it to be plain that the significance of the mental or abstract representations is somehow more primitive, more intrinsically intelligible, than the significance of linguistic signs? Frege's bias, if that's what it is, is hardly parochial. Teaching this material at virtually any level reveals that the Cartesian-spirited idea has substantial appeal.

The importance of this traditional intuition can hardly be exaggerated. It is a favorite topic of Wittgenstein; his discussion in *Philosophical Investigations* does much, I think, to dispel our sense of comfort with the intrinsic aboutness of representations.[28] I'll remark briefly on the matter here.

That the representations seem intrinsically significant perhaps reflects a tendency to model conceptualization on vision.[29] If one

---

[26] There is a delicate question lurking here. I am envisaging the hypothesizing of a god on grounds that we don't understand how the universe came to be. The evidence for the existence of such a being would then be the alleged fact that positing it explains something. The explanatory situation would be considerably different if one had independent knowledge of a god and its traits, as it would be in Frege's case if one had independent knowledge of senses.

[27] Perhaps it's hasty to suggest that we might as well do without the representations. There are, after all, other theoretical purposes served by the representations, other, that is, than to explain intentionality. They purport to provide the makings of an account not only of aboutness, but also of the more specific puzzles upon which Frege and Russell were so focused. My argument against the Fregean approach to the puzzles (in chapters 6–9) supplements the present discussion.

[28] See especially §§ 139–41. My remarks here reflect to some extent the content of those sections.

[29] The idea that conceptualization is often modeled after vision has been emphasized by Richard Rorty. He writes in *Philosophy and the Mirror of Nature* (Princeton, N.J.: Princeton University Press, 1979), p. 12: "It is pictures rather than propositions, metaphors rather than statements, which determine most of our philosophical convictions. The picture which holds traditional philosophy captive is that of the mind as a great mirror, containing various representations—some accurate, some not—

thinks of ideas or concepts along the lines of mental images, where these in turn are thought of as something like mental photographs, it might seem like there is no real puzzle about their significance, no puzzle concerning their aboutness. So an idea or a concept might be intrinsically about what it's about, but surely a mere word is not.

How obvious is it that photographs are intrinsically about whatever they are about? The intrinsic aboutness intuition seems fueled by the thought that a representation does not signify by human convention, by our projecting the representation onto the world in a certain way. It, so to speak, projects itself. Internal to the representation, you might say, is somehow its mode of projection. Is this true of a photograph? It is tempting to think so, to take the photo's visual properties to fix what it's about. But this won't do, as David Kaplan makes dramatic with his remark that there is a picture of him that looks more like Steve Allen than like him. Wittgenstein argues forcefully that photographs, no less than other representations, stand in need of interpretation; they require a method of projection. Perhaps we have some such methods that are natural to us—although training may be relevant—methods that we employ effortlessly, naturally. But this is not intrinsic intentionality. This is projection by us.

When one moves from mental images to concepts, to a more sophisticated representationalism, it becomes more difficult to understand why the aboutness of the representations is supposed to be intrinsic. What exactly is a concept, or a sense, and how exactly is it about what it's about? Concepts are—I thought as an undergraduate—something like intellectual (that is, nonvisual) pictures. And I can't say I understand the traditional rationalist notion any better now. Perhaps again it is the visual model that drives the idea.

It is far from clear that positing intrinsically alive representations to ground the life of the sign constitutes an advance in our understanding. And this criticism of the Fregean approach is quite apart from the empirical failures I emphasized earlier. Where does this leave the Millian? My idea is to turn what looks like a vice into a virtue, not by substantive transformation, but by declaration. The vice is the Millian's begging the questions about intentional-

---

and capable of being studied by pure, nonempirical methods. Without the notion of the mind as mirror, the notion of knowledge itself as accurate representation would not have suggested itself. Without this latter notion, the strategy common to Descartes and Kant—getting more accurate representations by inspecting, repairing, and polishing the mirror, so to speak—would not have made sense."

ity, his helping himself to aboutness. Maybe that's a good idea.
Maybe the attempt to provide an explanation is the mistake.

Let's begin with Wittgenstein's remark: "We must do away
with all *explanation,* and description alone must take its place."[30]

Even allowing for its sound bite quality and attendant over-
statement, this is another one of those remarks that inspires frus-
tration. I admit to experiencing such . . . until I made the connection
with Mill. I now think I see something of the first importance in this
passage, as well as in Wittgenstein's frequent admonishments that
philosophy needs to stay at the surface and avoid hypothesizing intermediate entities and processes. Think of §109, the passage just
quoted, in connection with §18 of *Philosophical Grammar:* "In philosophy one is constantly tempted to invent a mythology of symbolism or of psychology, instead of simply saying what we all know."

Perhaps what is at work in §109 is not hatred of theory, but
something analogous to Aristotle's idea that different degrees of
precision are appropriate to different subject matters. Philosophy is
all about providing intelligibility, Wittgenstein might well agree.
However, the urge to do so drives philosophers to desperate measures, measures that from Wittgenstein's point of view often involve no explanatory progress.

Frege's sense-reference explanation provides a paradigmatic example of this sort of pseudo-explanation. Of course, we don't need
Wittgenstein's radical-sounding rejection of explanation to see the
deficiencies in Frege's approach. But what I see as the suggestion of
§109 may help us take a giant step forward. Perhaps it is not, or not
only, the specifics of Frege's account that are the problem. Perhaps
the question he seeks to answer is itself suspect; perhaps the very
attempt to explain is out of place.

Consider the following picture. Creatures of a certain neurological complexity, appropriately socialized, use pieces of nature as
symbols for other pieces of nature. People, that is, use symbols to
stand for things. Think of this—here is what is new—as primitive
for philosophy, not as something for which philosophy owes or
might provide an explanation in simpler or more primitive terms.
This is not to deny that philosophy and related disciplines can aug-
ment our understanding of this ability in all sorts of ways. We can,
for example, provide detailed characterizations of the ways this
ability is implemented, our practice with proper names being a case
in point. It may also be helpful to study the evolution of such prac-

[30] *Philosophical Investigations,* §109

tices, the question of how they derive from more primitive forms.[31] There may be other such questions to study, but no explanation of the fundamental ability in simpler or more primitive terms is available or appropriate.

Nor is increasing the intelligibility of this fundamental ability strictly a task for philosophy, linguistics, and the like. The natural sciences may provide a characterization of organisms that possess such abilities, and specify the facilitating neurological structures and functions. That is to say, we may come to know that such structures/functions support this ability and that others do not, that still other related structures/functions support related abilities and the like.

It might appear that what I'm saying comes to the idea that philosophy is stymied or limited here and that the real explanatory work is to be done by science. But the question that my imagined scientist is answering is not the same one the Fregean sets out to answer. The scientist wants to know what structures support this ability and what needs to go on neurologically. How could anyone, why would anyone, even Wittgenstein, argue with this? The Fregean seeks quite a different sort of understanding.

Once we have answers to the sorts of questions mentioned—we hear, for example, from the scientist, and we have an adequate account of the ways the ability is implemented in linguistic practice, and so on—there is no further question of explaining how these signs come to life for us. There is nothing further to explain, no explanatory space. When the Millian is asked why 'Aristotle' refers to this particular person, he cites our name-using practice and remarks further about how 'Aristotle' came to be attached to the person in question. If you suppose that the Millian is trying to explain the intentionality of the name, the miracle of its aboutness, then it will indeed appear that he begs the question. In fact, the Millian seeks to explain no such thing. And this is to his credit, on the approach I'm suggesting. The Millian merely seeks to situate this particular name in the general practice. The Millian thus stays at the surface. He says what he knows and resists the temptation to invent a mythology of symbolism or psychology.

Let's come at this from another direction, one suggested by Joseph Almog in conversation. In "Why does 'Aristotle' refer to that individual?" traditional philosophy of language hears a question of great philosophical interest, the "analytic question," as Almog

---

[31] See "Terra Firma," in which I explore Wittgenstein's ideas on the subject.

called it: What connects the name with the referent? What is the mechanism of reference?[32] What, in another idiom of Almog's, is the chemistry of the bond between the name and the referent? As we have repeatedly seen, Frege's sense-reference picture tries to supply an answer to this question, the needed mechanism, the needed bond with its analysis.

There are other questions one might hear in "Why does 'Aristotle' refer to that individual?" questions about the general linguistic practice invoked by a use of the name, questions about how the particular name came to be associated with this particular individual. To these other questions the Millian is happy to respond. But the Millian hears no analytic question, no request for a mechanism that connects name to referent. "All I can tell you is that we have this general practice, and I can of course tell you something about how 'Aristotle' entered this practice as a name for this particular person. In telling you these things, I realize that I'm not supplying what the Fregean is seeking. But there is nothing more to tell."

To say that there is nothing more to tell is to join forces with Wittgenstein. For it is to say that there is no further explanatory space, no genuine additional question to be answered. Intelligibility in this context, the kind that philosophy can provide, is a matter of describing our name using practice and of explaining, really describing again, how this particular name comes to fit in.

Philosophers nowadays distinguish externalist approaches from internalist ones, in any number of domains. In the theory of knowledge, for example, an internalist wants to provide an account of the vexed third condition on knowledge (knowledge is true belief + what?) in terms of features that are internal to the knower, for example, in terms of the justificatory structure of his beliefs. By contrast, an externalist may turn to causal relations between the agent and the environment.

It might be assumed, and I have heard it said (I used to think something like this), that the anti-Fregean proffers an externalist explanation of intentionality in place of Fregean internalism. Kripke's chains of communication might then be seen as anti-Fregean candidates for the mechanism of reference. Indeed, whether or not the chain is causal or wholly causal would then be beside the point. The chains of communication could be externalist either way.

---

[32] This useful turn of phrase was perhaps first suggested by Colin McGinn in "The Mechanism of Reference," *Synthese* 49 (1981): 157–86.

Although I think that this is not Kripke's considered view,[33] some passages in *Naming and Necessity* may suggest it. It is in any case not the view defended here. The envisaged externalism accepts the explanatory project and provides an externalist answer. Wittgenstein and my Millian reject the explanatory project.

6. Concluding Remarks: The Miracle of Reference

Carnap emphasized that semantics, the study of the relations between symbols and the items in the world that the symbols are about, proceeds by abstraction from the use of language, from linguistic practice. Strawson, going a step further, maintained that the use of language needs to be the focus in the philosophy of language and that a more abstract or abstracted view of the relations between symbols and the world may mislead at crucial points; surely something like this is Wittgenstein's view. Of course, there may be both semantic, and perhaps especially syntactic, questions for which such abstraction may be just the ticket—I speak here for myself, not Wittgenstein. The point is not to discourage such approaches, nor to discourage formal treatments. The point is to keep our collective eyes on the ball. There is some danger that a lack of attention to the full-blown practices may skew our questions that we ask and ultimately the way we see language vis-à-vis the world.

Case in point: name reference. Abstract the name from its environment in our practice. Then stare at a name, and then at its referent, and keeping looking back and forth. The connection between these two pieces of nature, that one is *about* the other, can seem dazzling. What is this magical *aboutness?* Perhaps its explanation needs to look beyond the natural world, to Fregean senses in a third realm. Perhaps we need to posit nonnatural relations, unanalyzable relations of intrinsic intentionality between senses and their referents. It might seem that the only alternatives to such spookiness are either *eliminativism*—seeing reference as an illusion—or *reduction;* the suspect nonnatural entities or relations reduced to some-

---

[33] In a discussion after a talk at Stanford University in 1982 Kripke suggested that one should not read him as advocating a causal theory, and in a subsequent conversation at the University of Notre Dame he advocated something much closer to the approach to names I've been defending here. See also Joseph Almog's article, "Semantical Anthropology," *Midwest Studies in Philosophy* 9 (1984): 479–90.

thing physicalistically acceptable, the relation between name and referent, for example, reduced to a causal chain.[34]

Stepping back from the abstraction, attending to the full-blown practice and seeing our use of names as an implementation of an ability that is primitive for philosophy, changes a great deal. Armed with this perspective, my Millian is happy to explain, or maybe merely describe, the function of names in our practice. He is less happy to explain the miracle, how it is possible that mere pieces of nature signify.

And when Wittgenstein identifies the life of the sign as its use, it is not that uses, or linguistic practices, now play the explanatory role that senses play for Frege. Words are paradigm intentional entities, not shadows of the genuine ones. At the same time, our ability to use symbols is something that evolves, that awaits social practice for its implementation. So Wittgenstein can say that the life of the sign is its use, drawing attention to the idea that only in the context of social practice do pieces of nature come to semantic life; only in such ways do such abilities get implemented.[35]

We should reject the Fregean explanatory project. The felt need for a substantive explanation, I've suggested, is in part a product of the failure to maintain focus on the full blown practices. But we need not reject the sense that there is something magical at work here.

> What is the first thing [the Martian anthropologist] notices about earthlings? That they are forever making mouthy little sounds, clicks, hisses, howls, hoots, explosions, squeaks, come of which *name* things in the world and are uttered in short sequences that *say* something about these things and events in the world.[36]

---

[34] Cf. Harty Field, "Tarski's Theory of Truth," *The Journal of Philosophy* 69 (1972): 347–75.

[35] To emphasize the essential place of the social is not yet to suggest that there is some in-principle reason that an individual in isolation could not use a symbol. Perhaps there are considerations that motivate such a very strong conclusion; certainly commentators frequently mention Wittgenstein's private language argument in this connection. But if there are such considerations, they go beyond what we have seen. It is enough for our purposes to appeal to the social as essential in a less extravagant sense. Our ability to perform in such sophisticated ways, to use language, is quite clearly a product of the evolution of practice and of cumulative training that spans countless generations. It is very difficult to imagine a creature who starts off as we did and just somehow begins to use symbols.

[36] Walker Percy, "The Delta Factor," in Percy, *The Message in the Bottle: How Queer Man Is, How Queer Language Is, and What One Has to Do with the Other* (New York: Farrar, Straus, and Giroux, 1984), p. 12.

This is a mood worth encouraging in our students, in ourselves. What to make of something so strange and wonderful, even mysterious, is what our subject is about. There is only a short step from feeling wonderment to asking, as we often do, how the phenomenon in question is possible. This question may be just another expression of wonderment, or it may be an expression of the sense that there is information missing, that a substantive explanation is needed. It is here that we need to be careful. To adapt an optimistic remark of Hume in *Dialogues Concerning Natural Religion*, "The slow and deliberate steps of philosophers here . . . are distinguished from the precipitate march of the vulgar."

6

The Puzzles: Informative Identity

A logical theory may be tested by its capacity for dealing with puzzles, and it is a wholesome plan, in thinking about logic, to stock the mind with as many puzzles as possible, since these serve much the same purpose as is served by experiments in physical science.

Bertrand Russell, "On Denoting"

1. The Puzzles: The Early History

In its early stages during the 1960s the debate in the philosophy of language resembled a personal disagreement in which each party had his favored complaint and only hesitantly and begrudgingly acknowledged those of the others. Traditionalists emphasized anti-Fregean avoidance of the "cognitive significance" puzzles that for traditionalists lie at the very heart of the subject. Anti-Fregeans, for their part, focused on the empirical failures of the traditional account and paid scant attention to the puzzles.[1]

Anti-Fregean avoidance of the puzzles was perhaps especially surprising. Frege and Russell, the fathers of the subject, taught that

---

[1] The work of David Kaplan, certainly a seminal figure in the movement, was always more sensitive to Frege's concerns. Indeed the doctrine of Kaplan's monograph "Demonstratives: An Essay on Semantics, Logic, Metaphysics, and Epistemology of Demonstratives and Other Indexicals," in J. Almog, J. Perry, and H. Wettstein, eds., *Themes from Kaplan* (Oxford: Oxford University Press, 1989) is infused with Frege's spirit and concerns.

the puzzles were at the heart of the subject. It was well known, moreover, that the puzzles were especially problematic for approaches like that of the anti-Fregeans. For example, Frege's early (pre-Fregean, so to speak) view in the *Begriffsschrift* was a cousin to *direct reference:* the "content" of a name was, for the early Frege, the referent itself. And Frege was well aware that this feature of his view makes it difficult to explain the informativeness of identity sentences. Ironically, the anti-Fregean revolutionaries, having made a powerful case against the traditional approach, were themselves seen as naively defending a view with obvious and severe difficulties.[2]

Riding a wave of triumph, theorists might well overlook or postpone even fundamental questions. But anti-Fregean avoidance seems to go deeper, as if they found it difficult to take the cognitive significance puzzles too seriously. There is a curious passage early in *Naming and Necessity*,[3] in which Kripke mentions several puzzles of the traditional sort. Although it would be nice to answer all of them, Kripke says, he is not sure what to say about some of them. Indeed, about the informative identity puzzle, the granddaddy of them all, Kripke says almost nothing in *Naming and Necessity.* "Nevertheless," writes Kripke, "I think it's pretty certain that the view of Frege and Russell is false."[4] Kripke clearly is not thinking of these puzzles as being at the heart of the subject.

My own case is perhaps representative. As one trying to develop an alternative to Frege since the time of my dissertation in the mid-1970s, I never quite felt what one was supposed to feel about the force of the puzzles. They were there. They were not going to go away. And we anti-Fregeans could not go on ignoring them. Yet somehow they did not seem to be at the core of the subject. I was content to think about them later.

How might we make sense of this implicit rejection of the teachings of the fathers of the subject? First, there is a methodological matter, the role of puzzle cases in philosophy. Leonard Linsky once commented to me that he didn't really understand what Kripke was about. Philosophy, Linsky said, is an attempt to resolve crucial puzzle cases. Frege and Russell at least tell us what their

---

[2] Indeed, the view was often seen not only as severely difficult but even as incoherent. The latter charge reflected the traditionalist sense not only that problems were being avoided but that the view offended fundamental principles such as the cognitive fix requirement.

[3] P. 29.

[4] P. 29.

motivating puzzles are; Kripke is mute on the subject. What are his puzzles?

I was mute. What were Kripke's puzzles?[5] What were mine for that matter? I muttered something to the effect that Kripke was interested in how names work. Not much of a puzzle.

Looking back, I was on the other side of a substantial methodological divide from Linsky. My interest was in how language works, in the character of our practices. Puzzles of the sort Frege and Russell articulated seemed quite another matter. Who would deny that puzzling phenomena deserved attention? But I had no inclination to make them the places to begin, or to see their solution as *the* important test for a philosophical proposal in this domain.

Indeed, as I see the procedural question, perhaps the worst place to start is with the puzzling or problematic examples. John Perry once commented to me, in one of those remarks one does not forget, that if one is thinking about perception and begins with the puzzle cases—straight sticks that look bent in water, and the like— one loses the world rather quickly. It likely skews matters to begin with the unusual, the especially puzzling.[6]

So early anti-Fregean avoidance of the puzzles never seemed to me quite a scandal. But there is an even more important reason why an anti-Fregean might not see the puzzles as being of central and pressing concern. We are back to chapter 4's contrasting big pictures.

Frege's dominating interest in thought and its contents makes the informativeness puzzle an urgent matter. Frege looks at language—thought's embodiment—and his gaze is diverted upward toward the originals, toward the realm of senses. He sees "Hesperus is Phosphorus" and immediately thinks: nontrivial thought content. The problem then—it becomes *the* classical puzzle—is to provide an account of the functioning of the words that yields a nontrivial proposition.

The anti-Fregean begins in a very different place. It is language—not thought—that is at the heart of her concern; a system

---

[5] This was before Kripke's article, "A Puzzle About Belief, in A. Margalit, ed., *Meaning and Use* (Dordrecht: D. Reidel, 1979). After the appearance of that article, comments like Linsky's are less likely. But in fact, Linsky was onto something: Kripke's project fails to give the puzzles a very central place. Indeed "A Puzzle About Belief" suggests that the puzzle in question is really no special problem for his view.

[6] Kripke, reminding us that hard cases yield bad law, makes a similar point at the end of "A Puzzle About Belief." I will return to Kripke's comment and the puzzles about belief in chapter 8.

of signs embedded in social practice, not a realm of contents. While Frege's focus was upward, the anti-Fregean's is strictly downward, or perhaps sideways, from the word to the world. Words do their thing—referring is the thing of interest in the present context— only when embedded in social practices. The semantic project is to discern the character of those practices. For example, what, as our practice goes, links a particular name with a referent?[7]

My emphasis in this book has been names. But the anti-Fregean project is broader; there are, for example, indexicals and definite descriptions to consider. And anti-Fregeans had barely begun (and still have barely begun) to rethink the traditional approach to general terms and predication.

Think of yourself as new to all of this, tracking the anti-Fregean enterprise as presented in the last two paragraphs. Someone now asks, "Explain the difference between 'Hesperus is Phosphorus' and 'Hesperus is Hesperus', specifically how only the former can be both true and informative?" The Fregean's question, interesting as it may be, seems to come from left field. Given that it is not immediately implicated in the basic project of discerning the connection between expressions and referents, why not postpone it? Indeed how could one think to locate it at the heart of semantics?

This difference in conception of the enterprise—discerning the contribution of words to thought contents versus discerning the character of the word-world connection—in large part explains anti-Fregeans' lack of urgency about Frege's puzzle.

I have focused on the very beginning of the extended debate because of what I see as the relative theoretical purity of the early discussions. As one tracks the debate through the 1980s and 1990s, it becomes more difficult to isolate distinct tendencies, to discern the larger, underlying issues. After a while it does appear that interapproach communication has much improved, that the parties are talking past each other considerably less. But I see the early limited communicative success as presenting an opportunity (to discern the character of the disagreement), and the later enhanced communication as a dubious improvement.

There is a familiar pattern exemplified here, one I commented on in chapter 3.[8] At first there is a vigorous debate fueled by funda-

---

[7] I emphasized this "anthropological" character of the anti-Fregean semantic project in *Has Semantics Rested on a Mistake? and Other Essays* (Palo Alto, Cal.: Stanford University Press, 1995). I return to it in section 5 of this chapter.

[8] Section 4.

mentally different conceptions, sometimes rather naively formulated. To cite a paradigm example, in the wake of the brilliant Gettier counterexamples to the traditional justificationist conception of knowledge there arose a radically different approach, at first called the causal theory of knowledge. The initial debate was vigorous and exciting; very different ways of thinking about knowledge were at stake. Counterexamples were produced on both sides, and these were met by refined formulations. So far so good. But what sometimes ensues—and many have so commented on post-Gettier epistemology—are theoretical developments that obscure the original conceptions, theoretical developments with increasingly more kinks that seem designed to meet the latest counterexamples. Each side finds itself borrowing pieces of theoretical apparatus from the other, and soon the neo-traditionalists are virtually indistinguishable from the descendants of the revolutionaries.

Theoretical refinement is important in philosophy, and what is often needed is a way to incorporate the insights of apparently competing approaches. Nevertheless, the pattern described sometimes signals not a salutary refinement but a dead end, particularly when it issues in the sense that one is facing epicycles on what were once exciting ideas. It is for these reasons that I worry about the improved communication between the parties, a case in point being the 1990s debate over the semantics of belief sentences, to be explored in chapters 8 and 9.

2. Direct Reference and Cognitive Significance: The Classical Approach

Let's turn from history to the analytical situation. Whether or not Frege's puzzle is a primary agenda item, it cannot be ignored.[9] But the puzzle is formidable, and the known options for solution are limited. Solution requires finding the right sort of difference between co-referring names like 'Hesperus' and 'Phosphorus', a difference that explains the nontriviality of "Hesperus is Phosphorus."

Frege's final way out, the "On Sense and Reference" solution, locates the difference in the different senses associated with the names; Russell's resolution appeals to different associated definite descriptions. And then there is the earlier *Begriffsschrift* idea that

---

[9] See later for considerations suggesting that the solution does not lie within the province of semantics, as I argued in "Has Semantics Rested on a Mistake?" in *The Journal of Philosophy* 83, no. 4 (April 1986): 185–209. I no longer find these considerations compelling, as I'll explain.

names in identity sentences refer to themselves and so the relevant difference is simply the difference between the names 'Hesperus' and 'Phosphorus'. That these are the options does not bode well for the anti-Fregean. Unless he opts for the unintuitive *Begriffsschrift* solution, his Millianism with its rejection of senses and descriptional accounts of names leaves him with no obvious or natural place to go. He has, it would seem, no resources out of which to fashion a solution.

But anti-Fregeans have been enterprising. After the period of avoidance, there has been a characteristic, almost universal, anti-Fregean tack. The core idea of what I'll call the classical direct reference approach is a simple one, and it has proved both attractive and resilient. Whether in the end it makes for a suitable response—I'll argue that it does not—it is clearly the key to the subsequent literature, that pertaining not only to Frege's puzzle but to the literature on the puzzles generally.

The rough idea—details will follow—was to take advantage of Frege's insights, to follow his lead in making modes of presentation the master key to the puzzles. But modes of presentation, the stuff of Frege's solution, were highly problematic for anti-Fregeans; for some, they were *the* problem.[10] Perhaps, however, one might devise a new and improved way of thinking about modes of presentation, one that does not run afoul of anti-Fregean strictures. So armed, anti-Fregeans might provide a Frege-type solution: The difference in associated modes of presentation of 'Hesperus' and 'Phosphorus' explains the informativeness of "Hesperus is Phosphorus." This, in any case, was the hope.

If it seems perplexing that modes of presentation, even new and improved, should be attractive to anti-Fregeans, you are tracking well. In hindsight, what I'm calling the classical direct reference approach to the puzzles seems like a bad idea. Imagine that one could find a way to capture or mimic Frege's modes of presentation within a direct reference framework. Isn't this the old trick of borrowing pieces of apparatus from the opponent's arsenal? This is the road to epicycle, something that often does violence to the coherence of one's own conception.

It is much easier to see the foibles of the move in retrospect, however, than it was as these views were developing. This is not

---

[10] While some anti-Fregeans, most notably Kaplan in his work on indexicals, never gave up on Frege's master key, the anti-Fregean proper names literature suggested something much more radical.

to say that even now the philosophical community generally views the approach with suspicion.

In what follows I'll temporarily eschew hindsight and will retrogress, putting my own antirepresentationalism to the side and talking the language of modes of presentation. Let's see how far modes of presentation will take us.

First, let's formulate the classical direct reference solution in more detail. I'll begin by explaining how a direct reference approach to propositional content—Kaplan's singular propositions can be combined with modes of presentation so as to yield this classical solution I've been discussing. Don't worry for the moment about how to clean up the modes of presentation. I'll return to that in the next section.

Here's the classical direct reference solution:

1. 'Hesperus' and 'Phosphorus' co-refer, and so both names contribute the same entity—their single referent—to the propositional content. So both "Hesperus is Hesperus" and "Hesperus is Phosphorus" express the same singular proposition, one of the form $a = a$.

2. Problem: That's exactly the consequence of direct reference that has looked crazy; "Hesperus is Hesperus" and "Hesperus is Phosphorus" express the same proposition.

3. Solution: Enter modes of presentation; since each of the names presents the referent under a distinct mode of presentation, a competent speaker who says "Hesperus is Phosphorus" may not realize that there is a single referent; nevertheless he expresses a singular proposition of the form $a = a$. He thus may understand the sentence—grasp the operative modes of presentation, etc.—without taking it to express a trivial truth; he may not even know that it's true. So the distinct ways of determining reference associated with the different names constitute the sought-after cognitive difference between the co-referential names.

It's worth noting, as I point out in chapter 1, that Frege himself supplies the inspiration for this solution. I'm thinking here of the *Begriffsschrift*—its quasi-direct reference approach (references as the contents of names) and its recognizing modes of presentation. Given that the *Begriffsschrift* has all this equipment lying around, Frege could have offered what I'm calling the classical direct reference solution. In fact, he never mentions it and goes on to advance the questionable metalinguistic solution.

Perhaps the reason is this: According to the proposed solution, one might understand the sentence "Hesperus is Phosphorus" and not know that what is asserted—the content—is of the form $a = a$. Such separation between what the speaker understands and the proposition expressed may well have been foreign to Frege's thinking, as it certainly was later.

A second and more striking reason is that the proposed solution—the classical direct reference approach—does not really work. *One cannot solve Frege's puzzle by incorporating modes of presentation within a direct reference framework.* The modes of presentation do make for a solution to *a* problem of informativeness, but not to the problem in which Frege was interested, the classical puzzle. I discussed the matter in chapter 1; let me review what I said there.

One who thinks of Hesperus in a very different way than he thinks of Phosphorus may be surprised, informed, when he is told that Hesperus is Phosphorus. But the explanation of this kind of informativeness was not Frege's concern. Focused on thought, the common treasure of mankind, Frege wanted to understand how the thought content of such a sentence—the proposition it expresses, what it says—could be nontrivial. Remember that on Frege's *Begriffsschrift* view, the proposition expressed is constituted not by senses, but rather by referents. So even with different ways of determining reference associated with the co-referring names, "Hesperus is Phosphorus" still expresses the trivial $a = a$ proposition. The classical puzzle remains unaddressed.

Modes of presentation can help with Frege's official puzzle only if one can find a way to get them into the proposition. Frege eventually found such a way—in "On Sense and Reference." But the advocate of direct reference *cum* modes of presentation does not want modes of presentation in the proposition. He wishes to separate the issue of propositional content from that of cognitive significance and to use the Fregean apparatus only for the latter. As we will see, some anti-Fregeans who adopt the classical solution are almost aware that their solution does not resolve the classical puzzle; their remarks implicitly acknowledge this. Nevertheless they proceed to explain "informativeness" in terms of modes of presentation. We will of course need to explore the matter, as well as the question of what kind of sanitized modes of presentation are in the offing.

3. The Kaplan-Perry Implementation:
Direct Reference with Modes of Presentation

I turn now to a striking and influential attempt by David Kaplan and John Perry to advance just such a classical direct reference solution to Frege's puzzle. The Kaplan-Perry solution takes advantage of Kaplan's original contribution concerning the semantics of indexical expressions. In what follows, I will focus upon Kaplan's treatment of these ideas in "Demonstratives."[11]

As I reconstruct Kaplan's approach[12], it begins with an important and largely uncontroversial distinction between proper names and indexicals. Proper names are distinctive in that they are *given* to individuals and later applied to those very individuals. Our ability to make things subjects of discourse by using names thus depends upon rather ad hoc acts of dubbing.[13] By contrast with names, indexical expressions—unambiguous expressions whose references shift with context, for example pronouns and demonstratives—stand in more systematic relations to their referents. These relations seem to be formulable by general rules, for example (and roughly), "In any context, 'I' refers to the speaker or writer." Kaplan calls such rules *character rules*.

The next step consists in the application of the notion of *linguistic meaning*. While it may not make sense to speak of the meaning of a proper name, says Kaplan, it surely makes sense to

---

[11] Perry writes about these things in a somewhat different vocabulary than does Kaplan. For simplicity of exposition I focus in the text mainly upon Kaplan's treatment in his monograph "Demonstratives." But Perry's contribution to the application of the Kaplan semantical apparatus to the problems of cognitive significance was substantial. See his seminal articles "Frege on Demonstratives," *The Philosophical Review*, 86(4): 476–97, and "The Problem of the Essential Indexical" *Noûs*, 13(1): 3–21 (1979).

[12] Kaplan's work on indexicals consists of philosophical and formal components. Some sections of the work are largely if not wholly philosophical, some largely if not wholly formal, some have both components. Some take the formal development to represent the official Kaplan theory, the informal and philosophical remarks to be the accompanying music. I have always read Kaplan the opposite way: The formal development is meant to capture the driving philosophical ideas as much as one can in a formal treatment. In conversation, Kaplan has agreed with my characterization, and I so interpret him here in the text. For example, *characters* are here understood as rules—sometimes as meanings—as Kaplan often suggests, rather than as functions in the mathematical sense, as the formal side of Kaplan's work has it. But there are times, both in reading the text and in hearing Kaplan lecture on this and related subjects, that he seems of two minds on the question.

[13] Or functional equivalents, like using a name for someone as if there had been a dubbing.

speak of the meaning—even the descriptive meaning—of words such as 'I', 'you', and 'he'. Kaplan suggests that we think of the character rules as formulating the meanings of indexical expressions. But character rules, whatever else they do, determine the references of indexicals relative to contexts of utterance. Think of the rule for the first-person pronoun just cited. So, if character rules formulate the meanings of indexicals, then the meanings of indexicals determine their references relative to context. Relative to a context in which I am speaking, the character of 'I' determines me, Howard Wettstein, to be the referent.

One can detect in this second step the scent of Fregean ideas: meaning, indeed descriptive meaning, determines reference. But Kaplan does not stop with step two. He proceeds further in Frege's direction: Competence with an indexical requires that the speaker grasp the rule. (Cf. Frege: competence with a name requires that the speaker grasp the relevant sense.) So not only does meaning determine reference; these reference determiners, the meanings, are grasped by the mind. Still further toward Frege: The meaning, in addition to determining reference, provides the speaker's mode of presentation of the referent. When I tell you that "I am happy to see you," I am conceiving and presenting the referent of 'I' as *the speaker or writer.*

Kaplan thus finds the spirit of Frege's approach to be congenial.[14] Yet his seminal writings, especially "Demonstratives," are rightly seen as having a prominent place in the anti-Frege literature. How is this? There are two crucial points of divergence with Frege: Kaplan's modification of Frege's modes of presentation and his starkly non-Fregean explication of propositions. First Kaplan and

---

[14] Think of Kaplan as proposing a friendly amendment to Frege's view. (As I indicate in this paragraph in the text, Kaplan is at the same time critical of Frege.) Frege regrets that the senses of proper names are assigned ad hoc; they are up to the speaker and not a matter of linguistic convention. Indeed the same speaker can associate different senses with the same name according to how she happens to be thinking of the referent. What Frege thinks about indexicals is more difficult to say. Clearly, their senses, i.e., what they contribute to the thought, are not assigned ad hoc as in the case of proper names. But equally clearly their senses are not formulable by general rules that apply across cases, as Frege suggests with his remark (in "The Thought") that the speaker (of an indexical-containing sentence) relies on the context to complete the thought. Think of Kaplan as supplying a Frege-friendly view of the systematicity of indexicals. 'I' always means, roughly, the person speaking or writing. This is a matter of linguistic convention; not at all ad hoc. Of course, such *characters*, unlike standard Fregean senses, only determine a reference relative to context. They do not enter into the content of thought. Still characters are very much like context-sensitive senses.

especially Perry make important and telling criticisms of Frege's treatment of modes of presentation, which they see as embodying a mistaken picture of our cognitive situation. We would be able to say and think very little, they argue, if such talk and thought required Fregean senses, concepts that uniquely apply, that select the referent from everything else in the universe. We simply do not carry around such purely qualitative individuating conceptions. Nor are our concepts always accurate renderings of the things to which we refer. One can refer to oneself with the first-person pronoun even in the absence of a purely qualitative conception that distinguishes oneself from everyone else. One can also refer to oneself by 'I' even if one has a plainly false self-concept, even if one believes oneself to be Napoleon, for example.

One can avoid these pitfalls, thinks Kaplan, if one reins in modes of presentation. Don't think of the mode of presentation associated with 'I' as formulating the speaker's self-concept. Rather, that mode of presentation is nothing more than the conventional meaning of the first-person pronoun, roughly "the present speaker." Kaplan's modes of presentation, unlike Frege's, thus select referents only relative to contexts of utterance. The character of 'I' selects me in a context in which I am speaking, but that same character selects you in a context in which you are speaking. Thus Kaplan (and Perry emphasizes this) sees modes of presentation as doing more limited work than did Frege; context does crucial work, unappreciated by Frege.[15] As Perry notes, Frege, *per impossibile*, tries to absorb the work of the context into the sense. Kaplan and Perry, you might say, bring modes of presentation down to earth. This is a good thing, all else equal.

Kaplan and Perry also take issue with Frege's idea that modes of presentation are propositional constituents; this is their second major anti-Fregean innovation.[16] Kaplan famously champions *singular propositions*. With Russell and against Frege, he allows that objects—you and me, tables, and mountains—can be constituents

---

[15] Frege recognizes that the speaker makes use of the context in the expression of his thought. But this is not necessarily to give context a semantic role, as opposed to a communication-facilitating role. The speaker uses the context to allow the listener to ascertain what thought the speaker is thinking and expressing. Needless to say, the interpretation of the relevant passages in "The Thought" is a disputed matter.

[16] I am avoiding discussion of a question that would take us too far afield: that of Kaplan's motivation for replacing Fregean thoughts with the more Russellian conception of proposition. Briefly, it is at least in part a response to the Kripke-Kaplan modal argument. In section IX of "Demonstratives," Kaplan argues that modal con-

of propositions.[17] The characters of indexicals, their meanings, are not, for Kaplan, constituents of the propositions expressed. When I say, "I am happy," and, addressing me, you say, "You are happy," the indexicals we use have different characters. Yet we say the same thing, assert the same proposition, a proposition constituted by me and the property[18] of being happy.

Kaplan thus departs from Frege in these two ways: non-Fregean modes of presentation and singular propositions. Kaplan's substitution of singular propositions for Frege's thoughts represents a radical departure from Frege. Not so for Kaplan's idea that character rules capture modes of presentation. Kaplan's modes of presentation—despite their non-Fregean elaboration—represent the Fregean side of his thought.

Let's turn to the Kaplan-Perry approach to Frege's puzzle. Someone suddenly comes to realize that he is looking into a mirror. "God, that must be me," he says, or "I am he." This is an indexical version of "Hesperus is Phosphorus." What is asserted by "I am he" is, according to Kaplan, the singular proposition that has me twice over, so to speak, as a constituent. Nevertheless, say Kaplan and Perry, the utterance can still convey news. Its propositional content is indeed of $a = a$ form, but the two pronouns present the (single) referent under two different Kaplanian characters, that is, under two different modes of presentation. The informativeness of which Kaplan and Perry speak is thus not a matter of a nontrivial propositional content. An utterance, albeit one whose content is of the $a = a$ form, can still inform. It can bring one to see that there is a single referent where one had supposed otherwise.

---

siderations show that Frege's classical conception leads to anomalies. Kripke advances a similar argument against Frege in Lecture I of *Naming and Necessity*, but it is somewhat less developed there, and also is aimed not so much at Frege's conception of proposition as at the idea that the reference of a name is determined by a definite description. The singular propositions idea may also reflect a number of the other anti-Fregean points, as it does in my earlier work—the essays in *Has Semantics Rested on Mistake?and Other Essays*—as well as, for example, in Lecture II of *Naming and Necessity* and also in "A Puzzle About Belief," where Kripke says that perhaps the strongest argument against Frege is that speakers commonly have available no adequate full-blown Fregean senses when referring by the use of a name. Kripke's focus is again not the topic of propositions, but what he says cuts against Frege's explication of propositional content and is congenial to singular propositions.

[17] Unlike Russell, he at least sometimes seems to suggest that the predicate constituents of propositions are senses.

[18] I use "property" here just to avoid the issue mentioned in note 17.

But what of the substantial intuition that fuels Frege's approach, that what is said, the proposition expressed, by sentences like "God, that must be me" are nontrivial? Isn't it just plain implausible to suppose that the proposition expressed by "I am he"—expressed for example in a moment of surprise—is of the form $a = a$? Moreover, isn't there something strange about having propositions as part of one's picture but not having the propositions figure in the explanation of informativeness?

I will suggest answers to these questions, but I want to do so in the context of another query about Kaplan-Perry-Russell propositions. Singular propositions are often thought to be weird and unintuitive in contrast to Frege's more natural explication of the contents of thought. It's difficult to wrap one's mind around a way of thinking about propositions that has them contain things such as tables and chairs, you and me, as opposed to representational entities such as concepts, senses, and the like. Kaplan himself reports that early on he thought that Russell's propositions-that-contain-objects conception involved some sort of category mistake. What's going on?

I think that the way to make the best intuitive sense of the Kaplan-Perry conception is to think of propositions not as Frege did, that is, not as contents of thought, entities with which the mind has a kind of special access. Instead think of propositions as worldly correlates of sentences, roughly along the lines of facts or states of affairs. Then much of what Kaplan and Perry say falls into place. For example, both $a = a$ and $a = b$ sentences express the same proposition—something like the same fact. The informativeness of the $a = b$ utterance pertains not to the factual side of the matter; on the factual side the $a = b$ utterance is no different from that of $a = a$. Informativeness is a reflection instead of the cognitive properties of the names, the way the names present their references.

Frege thought, and Kaplan and Perry agree, that one aspect of significance lies on the side of the world and one on the side of the mind. Kaplan agrees with Frege that a speaker enjoys special cognitive intimacy with the mode of presentation; it's on the side of the mind. The mind enjoys no such intimacy with references, items that lie on the side of the world.

However, unlike in Frege's view, the representation that lies on the side of the mind is for Kaplan no full-blown Fregean sense; it is not something that determines reference in an absolute, or context-independent, way. The context of utterance, external to the mind, has much to say about the determination of reference. Also unlike in Frege's view, the propositions are constituted by what lies on the side of the world. But if such worldly propositions seem almost oxymoronic, let's stop calling them propositions—and especially let's stop calling them "thoughts," as Kaplan and Perry sometimes misleadingly do. They are the worldly correlates of sentences, the constituents of which are not representations of things and properties but the things and properties themselves.

If we think of propositions, called whatever-you-like, in this way, then it is perfectly reasonable to think that the $a = a$ and $a = b$ sentences express the same one of these items, one in which the same referent appears twice. On such a view, the categories of the trivial and nontrivial no longer apply to "propositions" *simpliciter.* What the mind directly grasps are not the (worldly) propositions but their representational correlates. Kaplan and Perry can hardly be faulted then for not providing a solution to the classical puzzle, for the classical puzzle assumes that the proposition expressed by, for example, "I am he" is nontrivial. Nor can they be faulted for creating distance between what the speaker understands and the proposition expressed. That they countenance such distance is no oversight.

Kaplan and Perry thus reject Frege's classical puzzle. But they remain exercised about informativeness. On their view, Frege has directed our attention to a crucial datum that he proceeds to misidentify, or to identify in terms of his own theoretical perspective. Nontriviality of propositional content is not the real datum. The real datum is the fact that $a = b$ sentences can inform, surprise, convey news, as $a = a$ sentences do not. (From here on, except where indicated, I will use 'informativeness' for the Kaplan-Perry version of the datum; 'informativeness', as I will use it, should not suggest nontrivial propositional content.)

4. Criticism of Kaplan: Failure to Generalize

Imagine that we are observing a rock singer who is so outfitted and made up that when one glances at his right profile and then his left, one may easily miss the fact that the same person is in question. You observe him first from a small window in a door on one side of the auditorium and then walk to another doorway and see what you take to be an entirely different performer, performing in what you take to be a different auditorium. I know what you don't know, and I say, "He [dragging you down the hall] is the same person as he is," or "That one is none other than that one." (There are Kap-

lanesque examples in which one points to the Evening Star. "That,"
he says, and speaking very slowly, savors his words until the Morning Star appears, "is that.")

These are informative identity statements, distinctive only in
that they involve identity sentences with the same singular term
occurring twice. As with other informative identity statements, the
two singular terms play different cognitive roles. But a distinct cognitive role for each occurrence of 'he' (or 'that one') presents a problem for the Kaplan-Perry approach. Indexical expressions are supposed to be unambiguous expressions that nonetheless refer to
different things in different contexts. To say that indexicals are unambiguous is to say that their characters remain constant from context to context. If so, 'he' would always present its referent under
the same mode of presentation. How then to explain the informativeness of "He = he"?[19]

Lest this look too hokey or artificial—"He is he" is not something one says everyday—let me give another example. In this
chapter I have discussed Frege's puzzle as Frege himself does, in
terms of identity sentences. But in chapter 1 I generalized the problem, pointing out that Frege's fundamental concern is the different
cognitive roles that co-referential expressions can play. Frege worries about identity sentences, but the same concern exists for pairs
of subject–predicate sentences, for example, "Cicero was an orator"
and "Tully was an orator." Clearly 'Cicero' and 'Tully' play different cognitive roles; a competent speaker might take one sentence
of the pair to express a truth, the other a falsehood. Parallel to the
Cicero-Tully pair of sentences but utilizing indexicals rather than
names, is "He has a booming voice" (said about the rock singer in
the last example) and (looking through the other window) "He has
a booming voice." The classical Fregean challenge, particularized
to this last example, is to explain what Frege would certainly take
to be the two sentences' obvious difference in propositional content; they say different things. Eschewing Frege's classical puzzle,
Kaplan and Perry take the propositions to be the same but seek to
explain the cognitive difference between the two occurrences of
'he'. Their approach dictates that such a cognitive difference reflects different modes of presentation. But since the linguistic

---

[19] Kaplan tries—unsuccessfully in my view—to address these sorts of examples
in section IX of "Demonstratives." See his discussion there. I remark further on
this in the article "Has Semantics Rested on a Mistake?"; see esp. notes 16 and 17.

meaning of 'he' does not shift from occurrence to occurrence, Kaplan and Perry are up the proverbial creek.

Examples that involve proper names rather than indexicals, such as the Cicero-Tully pair of sentences, raise even more difficult problems for Kaplan and Perry. We can begin with the thought that the notion of the meaning of a name is, to put it mildly, an undeveloped one in the anti-Fregean literature. This is not to say that we anti-Fregeans have incurred a debt. Indeed, it has always seemed to me that the most natural Millian thing to say on this topic, as I suggested in chapter 5, is that names do not possess meanings—which is of course not to say that they lack significance. If one wants some notion of a name's meaning on a Millian approach, one will likely appeal to the referent as the name's meaning, as Russell did. But then all co-referential names will be synonymous. So much for distinguishing the cognitive roles of co-referential names such as 'Cicero' and 'Tully' in terms of their respective meanings. All, however, is not lost for Kaplan.

One way to proceed is to forget about "meaning," a concept that is anyway more at home with indexicals than with names. Perhaps we should stick with the notion of a semantic rule. For the case of indexicals, the rules yield or capture the meanings, according to Kaplan. For proper names, perhaps we can peel off modes of presentation directly from the rules and skip the meanings.

But even here there is trouble. As is noted earlier, proper names do not exhibit the sort of semantic regularity exhibited by indexicals. That a name applies to an individual is a matter not of the individual's satisfying a condition associated with the name—the contrast is with indexicals such as 'I'—but rather of the individual's being so dubbed.

This of course is not to suggest that there are no regular practices with proper names, in which case some of us would need to look for another line of work. The question is whether those practices are governed by rules that are anything like the ones Kaplan suggests for indexicals, rules that apply to proper names one by one. Indeed, intuitively, what is semantically interesting about names, what will seize the theorist's attention, is not that someone was dubbed by a particular name, but rather that proper names as a kind of expression get applied in this ad hoc way. This fact suggests that the rule operates, so to speak, at the kind-of-expression level—proper names—rather than at the individual expression level.

This doesn't prove that there is nothing that can count as a semantic rule at the individual name level. One hears it said that there is such a rule, something like "'Aristotle' refers to Aristotle." Putting aside questions of disambiguation—the old problem that there have been lots of Aristotles—it's far from clear that anything like this would help Kaplan. To help with his project, the name-specific characterizations would need to be plausible formulations of the modes of presentation associated with the names. And such rules do not yield any obvious candidates for modes of presentation. (I'll say more about this in the next section.) Kaplan muses, in the concluding section of "Demonstratives," "The problem is that proper names do not seem to fit into the whole semantical and epistemological scheme as I have developed it."[20]

5. The Kaplan-Perry Approach: What Has Gone Wrong?

Kaplan and Perry posit a kind of preestablished harmony: When we use indexicals, the ways we conceptualize referents are very tightly connected with the meanings of or rules that govern the expressions used. This idea—I used to think of it as attractive, I'd now say seductive, with regard to certain examples—misses the mark generally. This is not only a matter of counterexamples, of a promising and plausible idea that does not quite work out in practice. The harmony thesis is, as I will now argue, implausible. (This implausibility is independent of my general gripes about modes of presentation, to which I return in the next section. For now, I am still in retrogression: Modes of presentation are the key to informativeness.)

Why does one choose to refer with a certain indexical expression, say 'he', over another one or over some other sort of singular term? Is it in general because that expression best captures how the speaker is thinking of the referent? Clearly not. It's rather a matter of convenience, of expected utility in directing attention to the intended object, even of stylistic considerations. That alone should give us pause about the harmony thesis. This is even more dramatic for demonstratives, 'that', for example." To what extent does 'that', in typical examples, provide a window on the speaker's mind? How much can we infer about how the speaker is thinking of the object, about the operative mode of presentation? The same question is revealing for many uses of proper names, even for some uses of definite descriptions.

[20] p. 562.

It would be wrong to insist that one can never tell anything about the cognitive side from the linguistic. Perhaps when a speaker uses the second-person pronoun, she is thinking of the referent at least roughly as "the addressee." But in general, linguistic expression chosen is a poor guide to cognitive perspective. Indeed, especially on the approach I am currently exploring, one that puts great weight on the mode of presentation, the way the speaker is thinking of the referent will be seen as typically much richer and more complicated than what the linguistic expression suggests. And it is just that substantial additional information that will be seen as relevant to the cognitive significance of the term. When we think about an informative utterance of "that = that," for example, what is revealed by the words is certainly not the key to informativeness. Informativeness is rather a matter of representational aspects that go beyond what is revealed by the words.

More trouble for the Kaplan-Perry harmony thesis: If Kaplan and Perry were correct, the semanticist, by exploring the semantic rules, would throw much light on the mind, on the ways we think about referents. Indeed, the harmony thesis suggests a Fregean-spirited adequacy condition for a correct semantic account of linguistic expressions: that it yield a plausible story about modes of presentation. But no such adequacy condition plays a role in the actual debate, at least not on the anti-Fregean side of the street. Here's what I mean.

A few years ago there was much interest in the semantics of demonstratives. Various proposals emerged in the spirit of direct reference;[21] one emphasized the role of pointing gestures, others stressed such factors as causal ties between speaker and referent, referential intentions, or contextual salience.[22] Most of the proposed rules were on the face of it bad candidates for capturing speakers' modes of presentation. It is highly implausible, for example, to suppose that speakers think of their referents in causal terms, say, as "the individual who stands in the appropriate causal relation. . . . " But this was not seen as a problem by causal theorists of reference, nor by their opponents. To turn to the proper names debate, the various approaches—say my Millian approach,

---

[21] That is to say, these proposals were accounts of what, other than descriptions or senses, might determine the reference of demonstratives. See my article mentioned in the next note for references to the various proposals.

[22] I argued, in the context of that debate, for something like contextual salience in "How to Bridge the Gap between Meaning and Reference," in *Has Semantics Rested on a Mistake? and Other Essays.*

or the Donnellan-Kripke's historical chain conception—have no implications for characterization of speakers' cognitive perspectives on the references of names. Nor have participants in the debate—at least on the anti-Fregean side—taken them to have such implications. Accordingly, no such adequacy condition surfaced in this debate, as it should have on the harmony thesis.

Even the expressions that seemed to furnish models of the Kaplan-Perry harmony idea—'I', for example—are problematic. When one begins to think about the first-person pronoun, the rule seems more or less obvious, something like "the referent is the speaker or writer." But by the time Kaplan finishes his exploration of 'I' in "Demonstratives," he formulates the rule in terms of an arcane notion, that of "the agent of the context," a notion that applies even to contexts in which no one is speaking or writing. Whatever the virtues of Kaplan's rule as a characterization of linguistic practice, it seems out of the question as an account of the mode of presentation associated with the first person pronoun. 'I' would be a much less useful expression if it were appropriate only when the speaker apprehended himself as the agent of the context, in Kaplan's sense.

Linguistic meaning/semantic rules thus have little to do with modes of presentation. Intuitively, this makes good sense. Semantics, at least as practiced by the anti-Fregean, has an anthropological flavor. Its target is a social practice, or a system of them. Why would anyone suppose that such an anthropological project would yield an understanding of how people conceptualize referents? The latter is a matter of what's going on with us individually. It varies from person to person, from case to case.

The anthropological picture has another significant implication that is violated by the Kaplan-Perry picture. Contrary to Kaplan's idea that the rules are known to the competent speaker, the anti-Fregean anthropological project is in fact one of charting unknown waters, of uncovering features of our practice. The semanticist will not get far by asking the competent speaker for the rule governing 'that'; how should she know? Even for the case of the first person pronoun, where the practice seems more easily penetrable, the competent speaker cannot formulate the character of the practice at any serious level of detail. And this is so even if the actual rule is not as remote from ordinary thinking as Kaplan's agent-of-the-context idea. As Kaplan himself later writes in "Afterthoughts,"[23]

---

[23] Published with "Demonstratives," in *Themes From Kaplan.*" See p. 577, "A Generic Argument for Transparency."

"If one could articulate all the cultural rules one conformed to, anthropology would be a much easier discipline."

Proficiency in practice, here as elsewhere, co-exists quite comfortably with theoretical innocence. Nor is the competent speaker in the dark only in the sense that he could not, on his own, formulate the rule. Give him a list of alternatives, as in the previous example of 'that', and he cannot even select the correct rule. Even the theorists, and even at this late date, don't know; we are still arguing about so much of this. The semanticist, as Walker Percy suggested and as Kaplan himself later independently emphasized, is like a Martian anthropologist of linguistic practice. He characterizes our practices in ways that we could not, sometimes in ways that we would find very difficult to understand.

Kaplan and Perry fail to maintain semantic rules at an appropriate epistemic distance; they move the rules too close in, so to speak. This tendency reveals itself in Kaplan's making knowledge of the rules a requirement for linguistic competence in "Demonstratives." But more important, it reveals itself in the Kaplan-Perry thesis that the rules capture the way speakers think about their referents. The correct characterization of linguistic practice is cognitively remote, but if Kaplan and Perry were correct, this would be much less so. For modes of presentation—I'm still in retrogression, suppressing doubts about the mode-of-presentation idea—are close in, cognitively immediate.[24]

6. Modes of Presentation?

Neither the counterexamples of section 4 nor the more theoretical criticisms of the previous section call into question the very idea of modes of presentation, or their explanatory utility. It is now time—the wait has not been easy—to question the classical direct reference approach at the most fundamental level.

The thesis that modes of presentation are the key to informativeness—whether one thinks of informativeness as Frege does or

[24] Perhaps one defending the Kaplan-Perry position could find a way to make modes of presentation less cognitively immediate. But this course seems epicyclical and in any case it's difficult to see how it would go. More plausibly (but still implausibly, I think) one might maintain that the rule, although itself not in the intellectual purview of the speaker, still captures the cognitively immediate mode of presentation. Kaplan seems to be moving in the latter direction in his "Afterthoughts." Both the general considerations I've mentioned and the actual semantic work noted suggests considerably more distance between the semantic and the cognitive. It certainly seems that in "Demonstratives," Kaplan's taking the rules to be known by speakers was important to his seeing them as capturing the modes of presentation.

rather as does Kaplan—can appear unassailable. For a long time I and, so far as I could tell, everyone else thought in such terms. Accordingly, in "Has Semantics Rested on a Mistake?" I didn't fault Kaplan and Perry for championing modes of presentation. But the Kaplan-Perry identification of modes of presentation with linguistic meanings was a distinct thesis and quite another matter. Given the failure of this identification, I concluded that one needs to go back to the drawing board; one needs to think hard about the proper characterization of modes of presentation.

But it was not clear where the anti-Fregean was to turn. It was not only that semantic rules and linguistic meanings seemed like the wrong ideas for explicating speakers' cognitive perspectives and that, as if to emphasize this point, actual work in semantics had thrown no light on modes of presentation. It was not easy to see how anything in the purview of anti-Fregean semantics might be of help. The anthropological semanticist aims to unearth a characterization of social practice; an individual's cognitive perspectives on referents seems like quite another matter. It is one thing to explicate the character of our practices with, for example, proper names; it's quite another to explore how someone is thinking of 'Aristotle' when he uses the name.

Either this is a big problem for direct reference or it's a ticket to freedom. If, as Frege and Russell supposed, semantics needs to explicate Frege's favorite phenomena, then we have arrived at the end of the road for direct reference. On the other hand, is it any longer so clear that an account of modes of presentation is something that we can reasonably assign to the semanticist? Focused as the anti-Fregean is on social practice, perhaps he should bequeath modes of presentation to those more directly concerned with the mind. Perhaps we have been unfairly burdening the anti-Fregean with cognitive significance. This was my conclusion in "Has Semantics Rested on a Mistake?"

That semantics is not and should not be responsible for the explanation of informativeness was a startling, unanticipated result, one that many philosophers of language found very troubling. I was, after all, taking bread off their tables. (I'm joking.) But we were closer than they, or I, supposed. I was agreeing at the most fundamental level: Modes of presentation are the key to informativeness.

Had Kaplan not seen the rules as available to speakers, it would not have been very tempting to see them as capturing modes of presentation.

As I now see the matter, the conclusion I reached in "Has Semantics Rested on a Mistake?" should be put in conditional form: *If* one takes modes of presentation to be focal to informativeness, *then* one should bequeath the explanation of informativeness to the philosopher of mind (or somebody). What needs further scrutiny is the antecedent of this conditional. If, as I believe, modes of presentation are a bad idea, then we will need another look at the consequent of the conditional. Perhaps the anti-Fregean conception will have something to say about informativeness after all.

While the direct reference literature has generally been upbeat about modes of presentation and their explanatory utility, there is a subversive tendency. The seeds of this subversive line of thought were sown by Putnam and Kripke, but for the most part in connection with semantic issues, not cognitive significance. Hilary Putnam, in his well-known 1973 "Meaning and Reference,"[25] after admitting that he cannot tell an elm from a beech tree, writes: "Is it really credible that this difference in extension ['beech' applies to beech trees, 'elm' to a very different sort of tree] is brought about by some difference in our *concepts?* My *concept* of an elm tree is exactly the same as my concept of a beech tree (I blush to confess)."

Someone might object that there is a sense in which Putnam's concepts of elm and beech must be different since he doesn't think that elms are beeches. There is, of course, a harmless use of "concept" in which we can say that Putnam has different concepts of elm and beech simply in virtue of thinking that elms are different from beeches. But that's beside the point. Putnam's point is that insofar as he associates properties with these words, he associates the same properties, say, that these trees are "large deciduous trees that grow in the east." If someone is looking for associated modes of presentation, he will find only one. And yet the references, or extensions, are not the same. "Meanings"—Putnam uses the term somewhat ironically for whatever it is that determines reference— "just ain't in the head."

Think of this as Step One in the assault on Frege's fundamental notion: The reference of expressions is not determined by modes of presentation.[26] But Putnam's elm-beech example seems to me even

---

[25] *The Journal of Philosophy* 70 (1973).

[26] Putnam restricts his discussion to some key examples but if he is on the right track, the same phenomenon will no doubt show up much more widely. And it's not that Frege's picture permits of exceptions. To return to the analogy I used in chapter 2, admitting an exception here is not unlike a perceptual dualist saying that most of the time we don't perceive material objects directly.

more exciting for its "cognitive significance" implications. Imagine that you, like Putnam, think of both elms and beeches in such terms as "large deciduous trees that grow in the east." Further imagine that you are taxonomically even less developed than Putnam. You are not sure whether elms are beeches or not, whether there is really one species here or two.[27] Were someone to tell you that elms are beeches—or that elms are not beeches—you would become informed of something new. And this is so despite the fact that there is only a single mode of presentation here. The elm-beech example thus suggests that *informativeness does not require two different modes of presentation.*

This thought is worth repeating: Expressions can differ in cognitive value or significance without being associated with different modes of presentation.[28] This violates the Fregean outlook at the deepest level. Indeed, by now the semantic moral of Putnam's story has been quite widely assimilated—this is always pleasantly surprising to me, since early along it was often shrugged off. But the cognitive moral is another matter.

Kripke, in Lecture II of *Naming and Necessity*, conducts something of a frontal assault on modes of presentation. He notes that, in general, competence with a proper name requires very little in the way of information about the referent. The man in the street, asked to identify the famous physicist Richard Feynman, may reply that "he is a physicist or something." Such a person typically does not know enough to differentiate him from Murray Gell-Mann, if indeed he has heard of the latter. Insofar as there is a concept here, a mode of presentation, there is a single one, something like "a famous physicist." So here too, the information associated with the expression is not what determines reference.

In his later article, "A Puzzle About Belief," Kripke goes further and addresses the cognitive dimension. At the same time, he doesn't, as one might say, make a big deal of it. Or, as I would say, he

[27] Notice that such ignorance would not make one linguistically incompetent with respect to the relevant expressions. Were such a person to speculate about elms, for example, he would be judged correct or incorrect according to the properties of elms. That is, he uses 'elm' to speak of elms, despite his not knowing whether they are the same as beeches.

[28] The elm-beech example is a bit different from Cicero-Tully/Hesperus-Phosphorus, since in fact elms are not beeches and we have nothing here like a true and informative identity sentence. But the example suffices to show that expressions can play different cognitive roles without the association of different modes of presentation.

doesn't seem to underscore appropriately the big deal that it is, given the dominance of modes of presentation even in anti-Fregean work on cognitive significance. He rather notes the point in passing.

> individuals who "define 'Cicero'" by such phrases as "the Catiline denouncer," "the author of *De Fato,*" etc., are relatively rare: their prevalence in the philosophical literature is the product of the excessive classical learning of some philosophers. Common men who clearly use 'Cicero' as a name for Cicero may be able to give no better answer to "Who was Cicero?" than "a famous Roman orator," and they probably would say the same (if anything!) for 'Tully'. . . . Similarly, many people who have heard of both Feynman and Gell-Mann, would identify each as "a leading contemporary theoretical physicist." Such people do not assign "senses" of the usual type [that uniquely identify the referent] to the names (even though they use the names with a determinate reference). But to the extent that the *indefinite* descriptions attached or associated can be called "senses," the "senses" assigned to 'Cicero' and 'Tully', or to 'Feynman' and 'Gell-Mann' are *identical.* Yet clearly speakers of this type can ask, "Were Cicero and Tully one Roman orator, or two different ones?" or "Are Feynman and Gell-Mann two different physicists, or one?" without knowing the answer to either question by inspecting "senses" alone. Some such speaker might even conjecture, or be under the false impression, that, as he would say, "Cicero was bald but Tully was not' [even though he associates the same "sense" with the names]. [I have added the bracketed remarks—HW.]

These well-taken remarks of Putnam and Kripke do not conclusively prove that modes of presentation are not the key to cognitive significance. Someone might argue that they are the key, that cognitive differences are in general to be cashed in terms of mode-of-presentational differences, but that something special is going on in the sorts of cases cited. Or that Putnam and Kripke are wrong and somehow 'Cicero' and 'Tully', 'Elm' and 'Beech' really are—must be—associated with different modes of presentation. Some of the moves are well known. It has been argued, beginning with Russell himself, that the concept (or part of the concept) associated with 'Cicero' is "person called Cicero." I will not here attempt to refute such moves. But given the Fregean flavor of the classical direct reference account of informativeness, I am interested in the Putnam-Kripke examples for their enticing suggestion of a radically different way to proceed. Actually Putnam and Kripke don't tell us much about how to proceed so much as they suggest that the old way won't do.[29] Not only is meaning (read: the determination of reference) not in the head, neither is cognitive significance. Don't look to modes of presentation—don't look to our concepts—either to determine reference or to serve as cognitive differentiators. How to proceed with the explanation of informativeness is the subject of my next section.

As I speculate in chapter 3, Frege is a "conceptual dualist": Thinking about a thing *just is* entertaining a concept that selects it. If one so begins, then modes of presentation will be a central theoretical device, a natural and crucial part of the apparatus for understanding language and thought. My own view is that modes of presentation are dispensable artifacts of a misconceived theory.

To see modes of presentation as dispensable is not to deny that when we are asked, for example, "Who is Aristotle?" we typically have things to say. However, the traditionalist is apt to put an unnecessary spin on this question, to hear "Who is Aristotle?" as a request for a specification of the mode of presentation, of the way Aristotle is being presented to the mind. I don't hear it as a query about the contents of the mind, but rather as a request for information about the world, specifically about the properties of the individual just mentioned by name. Indeed, I hear even the question "How are you thinking of Aristotle?" as a similar request for information about the world, not for a specification of a mental link to the world, of the way Aristotle is represented to the mind.

"But," the Fregean might reply, "that's all I mean by mode of presentation, the fact that the original speaker can supply the requisite information." We should remember, however, that while a name user might reply to the question, "Who was Aristotle?" with information available to her, if she has such information that would prove useful to the listener, she may not have such information. Indeed, when what she has to say is not helpful, she may well consult another, or an encyclopedia. Her aim is to provide information about the referent. It is neither here nor there that, in some cases, she had the information available to her in making the original reference.

The real problem with modes of presentation is not just that we can't provide a systematic treatment of them by means of se-

---

[29] This is a bit reminiscent of Kripke's remark in Part One of *Naming and Necessity* (Cambridge, Mass.: Harvard University Press, 1972), that although he doesn't know how to work out the answers to all the puzzles, surely Frege was on the wrong track.

mantic rules. The very idea that we apprehend things by means of modes of presentation seems a misleading characterization of our mental lives.

7. Starting Over

I propose to take a fresh look at Frege's puzzle. The first order of business is to say exactly what it is that we wish to explain. If one is thinking about propositions as Kaplan does, then, as I've argued, it's natural to reject Frege's original puzzle. The real datum for Kaplan does not concern propositional content; it's that (despite *a = a*-ish content) true identity sentences can surprise, inform, and so on. Similarly, if one were to do without propositions—this is my suggestion, to be explored further in chapter 9—one still needs to account for Kaplan-informativeness, as it were. So I am with Kaplan on this rejection of the original Frege puzzle and the remaining crucial task. When I speak in this section of Frege's puzzle or of informativeness, I mean the newsworthiness of utterances such as "Hesperus is Phosphorus," and not Frege's original puzzle.

I said before that neither I nor the critics of "Has Semantics Rested on a Mistake"—those who didn't much care for my relegating cognitive significance to some other philosophical domain—appreciated how close we were. I was, after all, merely redrawing the lines of responsibility, not questioning the basic picture. What remained intact was the Fregean idea—accepted by the classical direct reference approach—that modes of presentation are the key to cognitive significance.

Now that I have rejected modes of presentation outright, I need to say how exactly we are to do without them. If modes of presentation will not serve as cognitive differentiators, what will? My idea is that nothing will, and nothing should. That we feel puzzled about the informativeness of "Hesperus is Phosphorus" is a tribute to the power and influence of traditional, Cartesian-inspired ways of thinking about language, framed in chapter 3. My strategy is dissolution of the puzzle.

Notice that Kaplan and Perry are themselves dissolutionists with respect to Frege's classical puzzle. I want to return the favor, sort of. Unlike their dissolution with its rejection of Frege's putative datum about non-trivial contents of thought, mine does not involve invalidating a datum. Indeed, their datum is my datum: that "Hesperus is Phosphorus" can inform, that expressions can be referentially on a par but can differ cognitively.

What I want to dispel is the sense that there is something puzzling here, something that shouldn't be as it appears to be, the sense that we are faced with several ideas that seem at once correct and incompatible. One would have a genuine puzzle if, with Frege, one were to take the propositional content of "Hesperus is Phosphorus" to be nontrivial while assuming that the contribution of a name to the proposition is just its referent. Similarly, to anticipate the problem of the next chapter, if one were to take the meaning of a name to be its referent, one would have a puzzle—a crushing headache— with proper names that fail to refer but that surely are significant (since we use empty names to say things). I will argue that informative identities present no such puzzle. In subsequent chapters I will so argue for the other famous puzzles, empty names and belief sentences.[30]

I have repeatedly contrasted the traditional, individualistic, thought-oriented approach with my favored public language conception. That contrast is at issue here again. To see why informative identities are not surprising, that they are just what we should have expected—to see why the Kaplan-Perry informativeness puzzle dissolves—one needs a clear view of both perspectives plus the ability to look at things in the traditional way and then flip perspectives, a duck-rabbit Gestalt-like thing. If one begins with the traditional idea that reference is driven by the mind's grip on the referent, informative identities will constitute a thought-provoking phenomenon. To fix ideas, let's begin with an extreme view: Russell's idea that reference supervenes on the mind's direct acquaintance with the referent. The name is hardly in the driver's seat— it's a sort of external mark of the mind's virtually supernatural grip on the referent. Can you see why, on such a perspective, it would be very puzzling indeed if a true identity sentence between co-referring names were newsworthy? One must be in perfect touch with the referent to use a name; thus one must be in perfect touch with it twice in order to have two names for it. How can one then be in doubt that it's the same thing?[31] Indeed, Russell concluded that there could not be such informative identity statements. If a state-

---

[30] See my remarks on puzzle-dissolution as a philosophical strategy in section 3 of the introduction to this book.

[31] One might well want to think more about this. Is it conceivable, for example, that one could be in this sort of perfect touch with something and yet not discern all its properties? Given the vagaries of "perfect touch," perhaps one could find a way to make such identities informative. But Russell himself doesn't go this way. His view is that such identity statements cannot be informative.

ment of grammatical form $a = b$ is informative, this can be so only because the "names" are disguised descriptions and the relevant sentence is not really of the form $a = b$.

Russell's conception of the required cognitive fix is so strong that in the end it precludes informative identities. But the very requirement of a cognitive fix—the picture of reference as supervening on the mind's apprehension—yields the need for an explanation of informative identities. If one is in touch with the same thing twice over, how doesn't one know this?

Since Frege endorses a cognitive fix requirement, his view yields the same puzzlement.[32] But Frege's view of the appropriate cognitive fix is more modest than Russell's. One who refers is, as it were, staring at a thing but (analogous to what perceptual dualists would say about the perceptual case) is directly apprehending only a representation of the thing. This idea permits Frege, unlike Russell, to admit the phenomenon of informative identity and, equally important, to explain how one can be in touch with the same thing twice over without knowing this fact.

So much for the duck; now for the rabbit. Fix firmly in your mind the public language picture with its rejection of the cognitive fix requirement. Not only do names not require a prior cognitive fix; sometimes they provide the cognitive relation. It may be the mere presence of 'Cicero' in the student's vocabulary—he doesn't know who Cicero is—that allows him to think about Cicero, to ask or speculate (correctly or incorrectly) about him. And similarly for the name 'Tully'. The student, we will assume, has picked up both names.

The names 'Cicero' and 'Tully' are co-referential. How, we want to know, can we explain the cognitive difference between the names, the fact that it may be news to the student that Cicero is Tully. But wait—why is this a question? Why isn't it plain that this may be news, a simple consequence of the basic picture of the functioning of names? One doesn't need to know much to become competent with a name, to acquire it as in the example just given. *So* it's very easy to see how one might pick up two names that, unbeknownst to one, name the same thing. Nothing about the conditions for acquiring names mandates or even suggests that if names co-refer they should be cognitively on a par.

---

[32] Remember, my concern here is not Frege's original puzzle. When I say that Frege's outlook makes it puzzling how identity can be informative, I am speaking of Kaplan-informativeness. Of course, Frege's outlook also yields the original puzzle, but that's not relevant now.

I've agreed with Kaplan and Perry that there is a datum to which Frege pointed us. But my idea is that we don't really need to render the datum intelligible; it's intelligible, unproblematic, on the face of it. The only resource we need is a firm grip on the social practice conception I've been developing since chapter 3. Frege's classical puzzle is of course quite another thing. If one starts with the nontriviality of propositional content as a datum, then nothing I've said will explicate that. But once one has rejected this conception and has identified the real datum as the potential newsiness of true $a = b$ sentences, then my Millian conception renders it perfectly clear how co-referential names can figure in informative identity sentences. Competence requires very little identifying information, and so cognitive differences between co-referential expressions are no surprise at all.

We have now arrived at a more thoroughgoing anti-representationalism than earlier in this book. By the time I had rejected the Kaplan-Perry approach—Kaplan's characters as formulating modes of presentation—I had freed myself from representationalism in the philosophy of language. Not only are proper names Millian, competence with indexicals as well involve no mental intermediaries, no grasping of meanings, senses, characters. The thesis of direct reference—contra Kaplan—is analogous to that of direct perception: no mental intermediaries. Rules like Kaplan's characters play a role in the semantic story, but only as "anthropological" characterizations of our practice, from the outside, as it were.

Nevertheless, I was still mired in representationalism. I couldn't get past the Fregean idea that if "Hesperus is Phosphorus" is informative, this must reflect distinct associated representations, distinct "cognitive contents." Even if such contents had no role in my direct reference semantic story, they were necessary to explain the cognitive datum, the cognitive differences between co-referential names. What I needed, or so I thought, was a new way to think about representational cognitive content. But this is to pursue a Frege-style solution, even if a number of Fregean theses had been shed along the way. Why, I began to wonder, are we still dealing in Fregean goods?[33]

The Kripke-Putnam examples were powerful. They suggested that even cognitive significance was not, as it were, in the head.

[33] More accurately, my wonder was occasioned by a question posed forcefully by Arthur Collins.

But they did not suggest a positive story. Where should we look for such a story, if not to the representations? In earlier chapters, I have addressed the parallel question for the case of reference. In impressionistic terms, the answer was that we should look to our practices rather than to our representations. But it was not easy to see how the sort of answer I proposed might help with the cognitive dimension. That was my job here.

7

Essentialism about Meaning: Empty Names

God must exist; he has a name, doesn't he?

Jonathan Wettstein, age 5

anticipated (sort of) by Russell:
What does not name anything is not a name, and therefore, if intended to be a name, is a symbol devoid of meaning.

Introduction to Mathematical Philosophy

1. Names without Bearers: Several Puzzles

Empty names—names that lack bearers—have puzzled philosophers for millennia. Negative existentials—"Zeus does not exist"—constitute the most famous and time-honored of the conundra. Such statements are sometimes true, they are coherent even when not true, and they are of course important. But how are they possible? They seem to involve reference—to Zeus for example—and predication. But if there is no Zeus—nothing corresponding to the grammatical subject of the sentence—what is it about which one speaks, about which one says that it fails to exist?

I'll make some suggestions about negative existentials at the end of this chapter, but they are not my central concern here, for what is puzzling about them has nothing special to do with direct reference. To see this point, imagine that the name 'Zeus' has a Fregean sense—or change the example to one involving a definite description instead of a name. It remains puzzling how we can say of something that it does not exist.[1] The problem is the absence of a subject of predication, not the directness of reference.[2]

Here's another issue I will set aside: the truth value of statements that contain empty referring expressions. Consider "Santa Claus arrives tonight," "Vulcan is . . . miles from the earth," or, for an example that involves a definite description, "The present king of France is bald." Are such statements false, as Russell supposed, or are they lacking in truth value, as Strawson argued? This problem, like the last, is not specific to direct reference.

My concern is at once more basic than these and specific to direct reference: Direct reference appears to threaten the significance, the very meaningfulness, of empty names and of the sentences that contain such expressions.

2. The Significance of Empty Expressions

If direct reference yields the consequence that empty names are without significance, this doesn't bode well for the view. For we would not naturally, pre-philosophically, suppose that in general empty expressions are meaningless.

To fix intuitions, let's first consider definite descriptions that fail to apply. Someone says, "Our most senior colleague voted for her," forgetting for a moment that there are two colleagues equally most senior. Intuitively there is no question here about significance. That is, it goes without saying that

1. the definite description is a meaningful English expression,
2. the containing sentence is a meaningful sentence of English, and
3. the speaker makes a significant assertion in uttering the sentence.

---

[1] Russell's theory of descriptions can handle the problem. Thus it might be thought that this shows the problem to be one of proper names; when the names are analyzed à la Russell, the problem disappears. This conclusion is mistaken. Russell's solution not only changes the names to descriptions, it advances the idea that the grammatical form of the original statement is misleading and that there is no straightforward predication here. This is not the place to discuss the virtues and vices of Russell's approach. My point is that substituting descriptions for names does not resolve the problem.

[2] As is well known but sometimes forgotten, it does no good to, as it were, change the subject and posit the existence of a concept or some such thing to be the referent in such contexts. Since the concept does exist, the negative existence statement would turn out to be false. This is no solution to the question of how we can ever manage to say (truly) of what does not exist that it does not.

Think of these as three dimensions or levels of significance, at the individual expression level, at the sentential level, and at that of the utterance. I will return to these levels throughout this chapter.

Let's turn from definite descriptions to proper names. If we think with the vulgar, then empty names seem on a par with empty descriptions. Imagine for a moment that 'God' is a proper name. (Or consider the use of some name of a god, perhaps 'Zeus' as used by an ancient Greek believer, or the Tetragrammaton name as used by a High Priest of ancient Israel). Intuitively, atheists need not be positivists, as it were; that is, they need not deny that the name 'God' (level 1) or sentences such as "God created the heaven and the earth" (level 2) are meaningful. Nor need they deny that utterances of such sentences express significant claims (level 3). Similarly, if someone has mistakenly hypothesized a planet Vulcan and goes on to say that "Vulcan is 97 million miles from the earth," all three dimensions of significance are intact.

That we ordinarily treat empty names as significant is also clear from the way we talk about their referential deficit. When someone points out that, contrary to what the speaker presumes, there is no such planet or deity, the critic does not hesitate to use the names in question. Moreover, when one recognizes that a name one has been using, say 'Vulcan', fails to apply, one will not suppose that there was something radically wrong with his former utterances (other than, of course, their incorrectness); he will not suppose, for example, that they were not even meaningful or that they did not really claim anything. The ability of empty names to function in discourse is to all appearances not compromised by their striking deficiency.

It is a great virtue of Frege's view in "On Sense and Reference" that it provides a natural account of these actual practices and ordinary intuitions. Worldly vicissitudes—like the failure of the world to provide an entity corresponding to a linguistic expression—can of course affect the truth value of a proposition.[3] But these vicissitudes cannot affect the significance of a word or sentence, or the integrity of a thought expressed. Let's call this the autonomy of linguistic significance from worldly vicissitudes.[4] As I read Frege

---

[3] Whether to render it false or lacking in truth value is of course another question, one I don't address.

[4] A very different side of Frege's mind emerges in various places, e.g., in H. Hermes, F. Kambartel, and F. Kaulback, eds., *Posthumous Writings* trans. P. Long and R. White (Oxford: Basil Blackwell, 1979), according to which senses are seen as object dependent. Various writers have made much of this Frege, e.g., Gareth Evans in *Varieties of Reference* (Oxford: Oxford University Press, 1982).

in "On Sense and Reference," all singular terms are descriptional. Accordingly, there is no threat to the significance of empty singular terms, including proper names—no more than to "our senior colleague" in the example above. If you read "On Sense and Reference" in some nondescriptional way, the sense of a singular term—and so the Fregean thought—is still intact even when the referent fails to show up.

3. The Millian's Problem

So much for ordinary intuitions and Frege's exemplary account that needs to bite no bullets. Pivotal to Frege's account of the autonomy of linguistic significance is his notion of sense. This doesn't augur well for the Millian. It's difficult to see how the sense-less Millian can avoid letting worldly vicissitudes affect significance. The problem becomes dramatic for Millians who maintain with Russell that the meaning of a proper name is its bearer. Such a Millian will have to work much too hard to avoid (or neutralize) the conclusion that names that lack bearers lack meaning. In earlier chapters I expressed skepticism about the desirability of seeing names as possessing meanings. My skepticism was not motivated by the present problem, but empty names certainly dramatize the undesirability of seeing referents as meanings.

This is not to say that my preferred Millianism—without meaning-as-reference—has no problem with empty names. I will eventually say just that. But it's not easy to see how or why. Given that I reject the category of sense, given that along with Millians generally I'm given to remarks like "The semantic significance of a name is exhausted by its reference," there is certainly a striking prima facie problem with names that lack reference.

Kaplan's conception of propositional content makes the problem dramatic. Imagine that one suffering from delusions states that Harvey (there is no such person) is a spy. There is, as we have seen, an immediate threat to the significance of 'Harvey' (level 1) and thus to the significance of the sentence "Harvey is a spy" (level 2). Kaplan's classical direct reference explication of what-is-said—propositions that contain objects like me and you—faces an equally immediate problem. Indeed, imagine that we could somehow provide a direct reference-friendly account according to which even empty names, and their containing sentences, are meaningful. (I will do so, or try to, shortly.) Kaplan's explication of what-is-said would still be in trouble. For in the "Harvey" example, the subject position of the Kaplanian singular proposition is empty: Even if

'Harvey' is (somehow) meaningful, since there is no Harvey, there is nothing to fill the subject position of the singular proposition.

Early along I felt the force of these problems for direct reference, an approach that, as I saw it, takes pride in its faithfulness with actual linguistic practice. What an embarrassment that when it comes to empty names, everyday talk becomes problematic.

This is one of those places where the going gets rough for the Millian, and it becomes tempting to force things a little. Kaplan suggested to me some years ago a couple of bullet-biting ways one could proceed. First, one might deny semantic significance to empty names in accordance with the apparent theoretical dictates of Millianism and might insist that indeed there is no proposition expressed by such empty-name – containing utterances. A second way, a bit more accommodating to ordinary practice, would be to maintain that the proposition is intact: There is something said, but the proposition has a hole in it at the subject position; it's gappy.

I remember the conversation with Kaplan vividly. If this is what it takes to defend direct reference, I thought, we are in trouble. These moves seem strained. One finds oneself saying things "one could say," things that one would never say except under theoretical pressure. It seems very implausible that the truth about a domain might include such theoretically motivated "one could say's." This is like nature accommodating itself to our theoretical quirks.

Moreover, each of Kaplan's ideas has special problems. Most philosophers would be loath to deny outright what we ordinarily assume, that in assertively uttering sentences with empty names, something gets said. If the no-propositions approach is to be taken seriously, more needs to be said on its behalf. (I'll return to this subject momentarily.) With regard to the other strategy—gappy propositions—do we really have a grip on the idea of a proposition with an empty slot? Moreover, even if we were to admit gappy propositions as a coherent idea, all sorts of anomalies ensue. For example, "Zeus sits on Mt. Olympus" and "Odysseus sits on Mt. Olympus" express the same thing, the same gappy proposition.

One might try to soften these blows in various ways. One way, with respect to the no propositions idea, is what I'll call the pragmatic[5] maneuver. A pragmatic theorist can argue that while a sen-

---

[5] The word "pragmatic" hearkens back to Carnap's distinction between syntax, semantics, and pragmatics. The inspiration for the "pragmatic maneuver" is the work of H. P. Grice. *Studies in the Ways of Words* (Cambridge, Mass.: Harvard University Press, 1989).

tence with an empty name fails to formulate semantically a proposition—this is the no-propositions thesis—nevertheless the speaker may manage to convey (pragmatically) a proposition to the audience. But what then is the proposition conveyed pragmatically by "Zeus sits on Mt. Olympus"? It can't be the proposition that Zeus sits on Mt. Olympus, since by hypothesis there isn't any such proposition. It might be suggested at this point that it's a closely related one, perhaps the proposition that the name, 'Zeus', names something that sits on Mt. Olympus.

One problem with this sort of blow-softener is that the proposition identified as the one pragmatically conveyed—a metalinguistic proposition concerning the name 'Zeus'—is not the proposition that intuition suggested. Another problem concerns the general sort of move involved. The pragmatic maneuver is grounded in the truism that linguistic communication is not limited to what our words strictly formulate. Indeed, as ironic speech makes manifest, we sometimes communicate just the reverse of what our words say. But such natural examples are one thing, and philosophers' theoretically motivated extensions of the idea are quite another. In cases like empty names—and we will see other examples in the next chapter—the pragmatic maneuver is not recommended by intuition, as even its friends sometimes admit. It rather represents a theoretical fallback position, a way to explain an otherwise embarrassing gap between theory and fact. I am skeptical.[6]

We would do better to save our teeth and stick with the altogether wholesome sense that the significance of empty expressions and of the utterances that contain them is not dependent upon worldly vicissitudes. That 'Zeus' or 'God' or 'Vulcan' is a meaningful expression—and that "God exists" expresses something significant[7]—is not contingent upon the existence of the things so-called.

---

[6] An alternative to the pragmatic maneuver—another way to soften the blow of either the no-propositions or the gappy propositions defense—is to insist again that the sentences in question are meaningless but to maintain that such semantically insignificant expressions can still figure in the expression of genuine belief. This method is different from the pragmatic strategy, since no propositions figure in this story, not even ones "pragmatically communicated." David Braun provides an excellent exploration of some of the moves here in his article, "Empty Names" *Noûs* 93; 274(4): 449–69. In the end, Braun finds ways to soften a number of the bullets, but not all of them.

[7] Unless of course one makes a specific case that, e.g., "God" is an incoherent concept and not just because there is no such thing.

So Frege insisted in "On Sense and Reference." At the same time, Frege's way has its own costs. Frege seals off significance from worldly vicissitudes but does so by positing a nonworldly thing to be the significance. Russell also (sort of) seals off significance from worldly vicissitudes. Indeed he manages to do so within the realm of the worldly; his genuine names name (and have as their meanings) particulars.[8] The enormous cost is Russell's Cartesian epistemology of direct acquaintance: Something is a name if and only if it stands for a particular with which the thinker is immediately acquainted. Still, both Frege and Russell seem better off than one who with Russell sees the bearer of the name as the name's meaning but who sees ordinary things (nonsubjects of direct acquaintance) as bearers. This view gives the world all too much power over significance.

4. What to Do?

I want to suggest an innovation in our understanding of direct reference, one that emphasizes the role of linguistic practice even more than I have until now. (After all my propaganda about epicycles, I had better be careful. If my innovation feels like an epicycle, the reader should conclude that I have failed with empty names. In fact, I think the problem of the significance of empty names points us to a real insight about the Millian perspective I have been developing.)

In some of Kaplan's early discussions of direct reference, it is not communal practice that gets underscored—not our giving names and passing them along—but rather the occurrence in mathematical and logical contexts of a variable under an assignment. I don't doubt the utility of images like Kaplan's for certain purposes; in the case of a variable under an assignment there are nothing like senses that intervene between linguistic item and referent. But exclusive attention to such images is costly. Stay focused on Kaplan's idea and you will worry about how a term without a referent can be significant. There is another way, however.

Direct reference insists that

Names are tags; their semantic significance is exhausted by reference.

Let's distinguish two ways of taking these slogans. The first way, the conventional wisdom, sees in them an essential condition for

---

[8] I'm leaving aside his treatment of universals.

being a proper name of the language, namely having a bearer. Empty names—intuitively significant—are then a problem. My alternative idea is to decline to posit any such essential feature. Our practice with proper names, as with other social and linguistic practices, is not a uniform affair. Characteristic of social practices is the existence of central cases. These illustrate the way it goes for the most part and highlight features of the practice that are at its heart. And then there are less central instances that trail off in various directions, in one way or another lacking important features of the central cases.

I think of the Millian slogans as characterizing the central or paradigmatic instances. The slogans thus reflect one important point of the practice, to allow people to tag things and thus be able to speak and think about them. But people are fallible. One may think that one is naming something and the universe may fail to cooperate—thus empty names, one important class of noncentral instances.

The orthodox, essentialist[9] reading of the Millian slogans makes empty names a problem. My preferred nonessentialist reading, by contrast, dissolves that problem. I don't mean that it is somehow a logical consequence of my way of taking the slogans that empty names are significant. Given that the Millian slogans identify a key feature of the practice, it's hardly a priori that empty names are significant. And a tag that fails to tag anything is a weird bird. Still, my picture makes the verdict of significance an overwhelmingly natural one. Here's why: Orthodox Millianism provides a theoretical reason why empty names must (on pain of fancy footwork) lack significance. Absent this theoretically induced problem, we are left with all sorts of ordinary intuitive considerations that make plain the verdict of significance.

Consider first how extreme is the charge of insignificance. One has to travel pretty far to find examples of linguistic items that quite clearly, uncontroversially, deserve the extreme judgment. Here's a sentence that may provide an example: "Green ideas sleep furiously." (I'm not sure that even here there isn't a bit of reluctance to declare insignificance.) Second, notice that with respect to examples such as "Green ideas sleep furiously," the judgment of insignificance is not theoretically motivated. Rather the charge of

---

[9] Please note (what I hope goes without saying): My "anti-essentialism" here has nothing to do with the general question of the significance or correctness of essential attribution. I am speaking only of a particular reading of the Millian slogan.

insignificance reflects the fact that the sentence makes no sense to competent speakers. One can't comprehend its import.

"Green ideas sleep furiously" is arguably a meaningless sentence. Meaningless terms are much more difficult to find. Examples that spring to mind are likely to be nonsense terms that a philosopher or linguist might make up as an illustration. In actual practice, when someone uses a strange term, we inquire what she is doing with it, the assumption being that perhaps she is hereby introducing it or is using an exotic term we haven't heard in order to do some actual linguistic work.

We can usefully enlist the Martian anthropologist here. Imagine her scrutinizing our linguistic practices, specifically competent speakers' reactions to (1) radically ungrammatical utterances, (2) semantically dysfunctional ones, such as the "green ideas" sentence, and (3) sentences that contain empty names. With respect to (1) and (2) she might well conclude that competent speakers typically take such sentences to be meaningless. But empty names, no way! Everything about the ways we correct each other and correct ourselves upon learning our mistakes suggests otherwise.

One can imagine other ways in which our practices might have developed, ways that would make it more natural (for us or for the Martian) to conclude that empty names lack significance. Imagine that people regularly accused those who used empty names of "having said nothing." Atheists, in our imagined scenario, typically maintain that theistic "believers" not only are mistaken, even radically mistaken, but are not really advancing theses at all; since there is no *God*, their sincere utterances fail to count as significant assertions. Furthermore, imagine it commonplace that when one is apprised of the fact that one used a name that lacked a bearer, one not only acknowledged one's mistake but took oneself to have uttered insignificant noises.

These imagined scenarios are confusing, no doubt because we have no sense of how to fill in the surroundings of the envisaged practice so as to make sense of the verdicts of insignificance. We understand the words in question and so it's confusing how they could be lacking in significance. Such imaginings serve to emphasize that nothing about actual practice suggests the extreme verdict—quite the contrary.

No one but a philosopher with a contrary theory, so the expression goes, would deny the meaningful character of empty names. I have been arguing that there is no reason for the Millian to deny this. An empty name is significant because it is a linguistic expression that is being used as a name; its use, while not paradigmatic, is certainly closely enough related to the central and more typical instances to count as significant.

It is instructive here to compare empty names with other directly referential expressions—indexicals, for example. Someone says, "I want that," hallucinating a Maserati. Is the demonstrative rendered meaningless by the absence of a car? Surely not. Why not?

There is a traditional, Fregean-spirited answer: Kaplan, in "Demonstratives," says that indexical expressions, as opposed to names, have descriptive meanings. These meanings—Kaplan's "characters"—are both context sensitive and context invariant: That is, the meanings don't change across contexts, but they do determine different referents in different contexts. An empty occurrence of 'that' would then be guaranteed significance, à la Frege, for a demonstrative, even an empty one, possesses its usual linguistic meaning. Character—just like Frege's sense[10]—remains intact no matter whether the universe cooperates.

One could proceed in such a way. But one need not. As I've argued, one can understand the significance of indexicals without employing the apparatus of descriptive meanings that competent speakers associate with the expressions. If one proceeds in my way, the significance of empty indexicals is not in question any more than empty names: There is no reason to suppose that an empty indexical—'that' in the Maserati example earlier—that is properly used in other respects, is meaningless. The Maserati's failure to exist, while disqualifying the example as a paradigm use of indexicals, does not render it insignificant. Neither empty indexicals nor empty names require meaning entities to account for their significance.

I'll close this section with a brief comment about propositions. Sentences with empty names, as was seen in the last section, make big trouble for Kaplan's explication of propositional content. My idea is to drop the propositions, to avoid theorizing in such terms. As with my proposal to reject the idea of meaning-as-reference, making do without propositions is by no means motivated by the desire to avoid these problems. But it sure helps: no more worries about no proposition expressed by "Zeus sits on Mt. Olympus," no temptation to posit gappy propositions. We will see similar dividends when we explore belief sentences in chapters 8 and 9. The topic of propositions, and their lack of role in my approach, is the focus of chapter 10.

---

[10] Again, it is the Frege of "On Sense and Reference" to whom I refer here.

5. Other Benefits of the Paradigm-Based Picture

The shift to the paradigm-centered picture, as opposed to what I called the orthodox, essentialist way, confers other benefits in connection with other kinds of nonparadigmatic occurrences of names.

5.1. Names in Fiction

Once the practice with proper names is in place, empty names are inevitable; it is only a matter of time until someone introduces a name mistakenly thinking that there is an object to name.[11] Almost as inevitably, given human nature, the existence of the practice engenders another significance-inheriting phenomenon, the use of names in pretense, as in a child's game or in fiction.

Before we proceed, a word about my use of *pretense*. There is a growing literature on the subject,[12] the central idea of which is the use of a name not to refer but in a mere pretense of reference. On this approach a child playing a game of make-believe or an author of fiction does not refer to the made-up characters; she uses the name as if she were referring. An alternative in such cases would be to allow reference—real reference—but to locate the pretense elsewhere: The child or the author refers, but to something that exists only in pretense. My tentative preference is for the latter. In general—in cases of empty names, fictional names, and the like—I prefer to speak as we ordinarily do, that is, to ascribe reference even when we don't believe in the entities referred to. "He was referring to Zeus," we say, "not to Odysseus."[13] However, I don't believe that anything currently under discussion hinges on this question, so I won't pursue it further.

---

[11] I here employ a sort of mythology, somewhat reminiscent of social contract mythologies. I speak as if the sorts of cases that are in some sense logically central are historically the originals. This seems in fact unlikely. This issue becomes especially dramatic in one's thinking about the examples in this section, names in stories. Who is to say that our linguistic ancestors sharply distinguished these cases or even had a "naming actual objects" practice in place before they told stories about the ancestors or the gods? Perhaps these were more confused and intermixed, the way they may be for young children. The subject requires further thought.

[12] Seminal work was done by Kendall Walton. See his *Mimesis as Make-Believe: On the Foundations of the Representational Arts* (Cambridge, Mass.: Harvard University Press, 1990).

[13] When in the next section I argue that the pretense is not "internal to the name-using practice" (in a sense to be explained there), this thesis further militates toward speaking of reference even where the name is empty, fictional, and the like. I argued for a pretended reference view in my 1984 article, "Did the Greeks Really

To return to fictional names and similar phenomena, their significance should go without saying, for the same reasons as with empty names: They are nonparadigmatic uses, but surely close enough to the more standard cases to count as significant. Accordingly, no metaphysical posits of "fictional characters"—as referents of names in fiction—are needed to secure significance.

However, avoiding such posits becomes considerably more difficult when we turn our attention from the literary work itself to remarks about the characters whom we meet in fiction. A student taking an exam says that Hamlet was a prince. The student—as opposed to the Hamlet-sentences in Shakespeare's work[14]—said something true; he gets full credit. But for there to be a truth here, we seem to need a correct predication and a subject for the predication to be about: What he said was true just in case *Hamlet* has the appropriate property. Here it's hard to see how one might avoid some sort of metaphysics of fictional characters.

Enter the original philosophical temptation concerning fiction: Posit a "fictional object" to be the referent of the name 'Hamlet' in the student's mouth. Accordingly Kripke supposes that Shakespeare, in writing the play, creates a fictional object, Hamlet—Kripke takes this to be an abstract entity[15]—subsequently available for reference. You don't need the fictional object, says Kripke, to make sense of the original writing; a pretense view (pretended reference) would be preferable. But without the fictional entity, we could not make sense of the truth or falsity of the subsequent discourse.

It's often assumed that once one has posited such fictional abstract entities, one has taken care of the problem of truth and falsity. But, Kripke points out, this may not be correct. For the predication "is a prince,"—that is, is a real, flesh-and-blood, prince—is not true of any fictional entity. No entity that fails to exist could be a prince. In response to this problem, Kripke posits a systematic

---

Worship Zeus?" reprinted in *Has Semantics Rested on a Mistake? and Other Essays* (Palo Alto, Cal.: Stanford University Press, 1995).

[14] Sentences in the fictional work are, plausibly, neither true nor false. One could insist, I suppose, that they are true automatically, as it were. But what the point of such insistence would be is not clear.

[15] When Kripke claims that the fictional character is an abstract entity, I'm supposing that his point is only that it's not concrete the way that, say, Shakespeare is. I say this because abstract entities of the usual kind—like redness, even the number 7—seem related to the world in a different way than is Hamlet. One doesn't arrive, so to speak, at Hamlet by abstraction.

ambiguity for predicates. "Is a prince" can thus function as a "straight" or a "fictional" predicate; the latter presumably has a distinctive sense, something like "is written of—fictionally spoken of—as a prince."

But isn't the original temptation, the reifying impulse, considerably weakened or made more costly, by the need to introduce such a systematic ambiguity? As Kripke emphasizes elsewhere, positing ambiguities to resolve philosophical quandaries is to be avoided.[16] Even more important, the move to reify fictional characters has the wrong aroma; it has the virtue of—to paraphrase Russell—theft over honest toil. Indeed, the reifying move seems like a mythological rendering of the author's creativity, almost a pun on "creativity."

To be fair to Kripke, perhaps there is an intuition to which one might appeal in favor of reifying fictional characters. When we speak of an author's creating people and places, we are using language metaphorically. But when we speak of an author's creating a fictional character, this is less clearly metaphorical. Shakespeare, one might say, really did create the character Hamlet. But the matter is confusing. What are we to make of this in terms of ontology? We can say at least this much: A universe with a Hamlet character is not just like one without such a character. The former includes certain modes of thought and talk that are absent in the latter.

Suitably developed, this intuition might support Kripke. It might even improve upon Kripke's presentation of the reification move (if I'm remembering his presentation correctly). Notice that Kripke motivates that move by noting that it will help us to resolve a philosophical problem—ascriptions of truth and falsity. This seems like one of those things "one could say." Whereas the intuition that I mentioned has the virtue of motivating reification directly, it tries to make sense of the core idea.

I propose a nonreification approach to truth and falsity. Let's return to the student who is quizzed on the Hamlet story. Don't think of the student's use of 'Hamlet' as a reference to an abstract Hamlet character. Instead she is merely carrying on Shakespeare's pretense, continuing the name-using practice Shakespeare intro-

---

[16] See his remarks on Donnellan's referential-attributive distinction—in Kripke's view, just such an unfortunate posited ambiguity. See Kripke's "Speaker's Reference and Semantic Reference," in *Contemporary Perspectives in the Philosophy of Language* (Minneapolis: University of Minnesota Press, 1979),

duced.[17] Truth and falsity enter the picture since the original text provides a model against which we can judge the student's rendition as correct or incorrect. My idea, then, is that the truth and falsity of "Hamlet was a prince" amounts to no more than this: Did the student get the story right?

It will be objected that "right" and "wrong," in whatever loose sense I am using these concepts, is not truth and falsity. The former pair does not require that the terms in question make real reference, merely a kind of coherence between the original story and the retelling. But perhaps we should conclude, on the contrary, that the Hamlet example shows something important about the concepts of truth and falsity, about our actual practices with these terms. The truth and falsity of common currency are significantly broader in application than the notions with which we in philosophy typically work. "The cat is on the mat"—with its almost picture-like relation to the fact that makes it true—plays too important a role in philosophical thinking about truth.

My idea is that "is true," as applied either to "The cat is on the mat" or to "Hamlet is a prince," involves "getting it right."[18] Of course, "getting it right" applies quite differently to these different cases. With respect to "The cat is on the mat," getting it right plausibly involves something like the sort of correspondence between words and the world that has been the philosophical focus. In the Hamlet case no such story seems apt. Perhaps there is no very precise specification of "getting it right" that extends across the different sorts of cases. Perhaps something like Wittgenstein's family resemblance idea is at work here, with different kinds of cases importantly related.

Actual practice with 'true' probably extends considerably beyond the broadening I have been suggesting. A novel—itself quite false if taken as a description of reality—might express deep *truths* about the human condition. People use the notions of truth and falsity in extremely broad ways for poetry, mythology, even music.

---

[17] In the next section I distinguish between two sorts of talk about name-using practices. First, my talk throughout the book about *our practice with proper names*, meaning the general practice under discussion throughout, about which, for example, Fregeans and anti-Fregeans argue. But second, and new in this discussion, is the conception of a particular name-using practice. In the text here, when I speak of the name-using practice that Shakespeare introduced when he wrote of Hamlet, I mean the particular name-using practice. See the next section for details.

[18] Thanks to Joseph Almog for suggesting this formulation of my idea.

We need not see such speakers as unduly sloppy with their language. Perhaps such broad talk of truth and falsity embodies subtle but significant coherences with the philosophically more familiar talk of truth and falsity. An important project would then be to scrutinize the broader practice, the idea of "getting it right" in areas as far-flung as mathematics and poetry.

I have used the term "coherence" to characterize the relation between the original Hamlet story and the student's rendition that "gets the story right." I mean "coherence" in some intuitive sense that may or may not be related to coherence theories of truth. So I'm not suggesting that in the context of discourse about fiction the coherence theory of truth is applicable while the correspondence conception is at work in talk about factual matters. What is even more clear is that coherence provides no general formula for the sorts of cases not emphasized by analytic philosophy. Think about the examples of novels, poetry, and mythology. One could, I suppose, stretch and find coherence at work in such contexts: One could see truth as involving coherence, say with experience. But it seems more promising to focus on the literature's facilitating or expressing a recognition of important aspects of reality. Perhaps we speak of truth in such domains when the literature points us to what's real and important. The full story here, of course, awaits, among other things, an account of metaphor and figurative usage more generally. I mention it only to allude to a future agenda item and to suggest a further broadening of analytic philosophical thinking about truth and falsity.

5.2. Negative Existentials

I conclude this chapter with this giant slayer of a problem. My remarks will be brief and speculative, hopefully suggestive for further work. As I see it, there are at least two issues here. One concerns the fact that nothing in the world answers to, corresponds to, an empty name. What is it, then, that we are claiming not to exist? The other concerns the existence predicate. What exactly is the force of the predicate—what are we saying—when we say that something does not exist?

I begin by sketching a distinction that will be useful in answering the first question, the problem posed by the fact that a negative existential involves a name that has no bearer. Throughout this book I have spoken of *our practice with proper names* (in the singular); that is the practice of using these devices, as Mill says, to make something the subject of discourse. Now I want to speak of *name-using practices* (in the plural).[19] When someone names a baby, one is in this latter sense initiating *a name-using practice,* a particular name-using practice. (Of course, the parent is also participating in *our practice with proper names.*)

If the parent who gives a name is initiating a particular name-using practice, so is the author of fiction.[20] So far this is uncontroversial. More controversial is this idea: The author's pretense is not, as I'll say, "internal" to the name-using practice. To see what I mean, consider this example: Someone mistakenly takes Shakespeare's *Hamlet* to be historically accurate. In his subsequent discourse about Hamlet, he is joining the particular name-using practice Shakespeare initiated. However, since he thinks he is speaking about a real person, he uses the name "seriously," that is, not in the mode of pretense.[21] So the name-using practice is one thing; the question of pretense is quite another.

My point about pretense not being internal to the name-using practice can also be made using an opposite sort of example: The name initiator really believes in the thing and the name-using practice is continued by a nonbeliever. For example, an atheist anthropologist wants to speak about the local gods. The anthropologist uses the gods' names when communicating with native informants and indeed with her colleagues. Thus the anthropologist need not share the natives' views about the existence of things named in order to engage in their name-using practice.

In both the Shakespeare case (in which the earlier pretense-use is continuous with a later nonpretense use of the name) and the anthropologist case (which represents the reverse), the name-using practice is one thing, but the question of pretense—yes or no—is quite another.

Armed with these ideas about particular name-using practices, I return to negative existentials, for example "Vulcan does not exist." The classical puzzle pivots on the idea that an empty name fails to supply a subject matter, a something about which one can go on and say that it does not exist. It is here that the conception of name-using practices just adumbrated gets into the action. The

---

[19] I spoke this way briefly in the last section, but in the text I didn't call attention to it or differentiate it from talk of *our name-using practice.* Cf. note 17.

[20] Sometimes, of course, authors merely spin stories about really existing items, but that's not important or relevant at the moment.

[21] This seems more natural than saying that the person uses the name in the pretend mode but doesn't know he is doing so.

introducer of the name 'Vulcan', we will assume, fully intended to be speaking of a real planet. We, on the other hand, mean to deny that there is such a thing. In so denying we join in the name-introducer's practice with 'Vulcan', albeit not joining in her pretense. Accordingly, we do have a subject matter in place, one as definite as required, one fixed by the name-using practice.

By itself, this approach hardly solves the problem. We still need to know how the existence predicate functions, and specifically how it supplements an empty or fictional name—albeit a name in use, one associated with a definite subject matter.

What I have not discussed so far in this book—a big enough topic for another book—is how to think about the significance, the linguistic function, of predicates. Here is my suggestion: Think of predicates not as bearers of descriptive concepts—the sorts of things formulable by definitions—but rather as categorizers.

Crucial to our thinking and speaking is our ability to see disparate things as going together. This is not to suggest that similarity is something that we create, that it is somehow all a matter of social construction, whatever exactly that means. But given the similarities between things, we still have all sorts of latitude in categorization. And our actual categorizations reflect social and linguistic history, interests, and the like. Sometimes (as in some of Wittgenstein's favorite examples) the groupings are rough and ready; sometimes they are quite closely knit, perhaps even precisely definable.

One dimension along which categorizations differ is that of generality. The category "blue" is less general, more specific, than "color." Generality and specificity are related to what—how much—the categories include and exclude. "Blue" excludes differently—it excludes more—than does "color." "Blue" excludes everything "color" excludes, but it also excludes colors that are not blue. Generality of categorization is sometimes said to be related to "content."[22] The more specific—the more excluded—the more content. One could thus say that blue has more content than color.

Consider now the existence predicate and the category of existents. The existence predicate seems like a kind of limiting case of a categorizer. It applies to everything. What is its utility, then, given that it applies to everything and so it apparently fails to distinguish anything from anything else?

---

[22] The metaphor of "content" seems more benign here than some in some of the other contexts I have been and will be exploring.

My suggestion is that the utility of the existence predicate at least in part concerns phenomena like empty names, such as 'Vulcan', as well as fictional names such as 'Hamlet'. Because of such phenomena, it is important to be able to exclude things from this broadest—most contentless—category.

But still, when we point out the Vulcan-believer's mistake, what exactly is the item that we exclude from this most general category? This is the old problem of a lack of subject matter. My suggestion from earlier in this section is that there can be a definite subject matter even if it's not one we can get our hands around. The definiteness is provided by the particular name-using practice, the use of 'Vulcan', for example. That being in place, I carry on the Vulcan-believer's name-using practice and say in effect, "not among these things," where these things include the heaven and earth and all therein.

8

*Bringing Belief Down
to Earth: Part I*

Or
God Wouldn't Be That Vicious

We come now to the final and thorniest puzzle in the traditionalists' arsenal.[1] The issues here—they concern belief and the other
propositional attitudes[2]—are intrinsically difficult; they touch upon
vexed questions in the philosophy of mind, metaphysics, and the
philosophy of language. And it's difficult to keep all these things
appropriately separate and appropriately related. So hold on.

The puzzle is a classical one. It is highlighted by Russell in "On

---

An early version of chapters 8 and 9 was presented orally at the Kaplan Conference in Tel Aviv and Jerusalem in 1990.

[1] It would be best not to read the current chapter out of sequence. If one does
read it out of sequence, it may help to bear the following in mind. Direct reference
means different things to different people. What I take to be at its heart is often
ignored or implicitly rejected by direct reference advocates, for example, what I have
called cognitively innocent reference. Conversely, what I take to be dispensable is
often seen as essential: My version of direct reference is not committed to propositions, singular or otherwise. Nor, on my view, do the fundamental ideas of direct
reference lead us very directly to an account of the semantics of belief reports. It
would be strange, of course, for a Millian of my (or any) stripe to switch suddenly
to, say, a Fregean story about names in belief reports. Names are still names in such
contexts, and my account will preserve that idea. But this does not take us to what
is often thought of as the paradigmatically direct reference thesis about belief reports, that they formulate relations between persons and singular propositions.

[2] Belief, assertion, and related phenomena are often referred to as attitudes to
propositions. In the end, I will reject the Fregean picture that underlies this nomen-
clature, but I'll stick with the customary terminology for want of anything better.

Denoting" when he remarks that puzzles in philosophy play the role of experiments in science and that one should stock one's mind with puzzles. Russell thought that his own approach nicely handled the puzzle, and it's easy to suppose—and often supposed—that Frege's does so as well. Indeed, it has been widely assumed that the phenomena we will be discussing are problematic exclusively for direct reference. As we will see, that is not so. Indeed, the phenomena put extreme pressure on both Fregean and direct reference approaches. In this chapter I lay out the problem and provide a critical overview of the Fregean way in which both Fregeans and direct reference advocates have approached it. In the next chapter I will present my own account.

1. Belief: A Topic in the Philosophy of Mind; Belief Reports: A Topic in the Philosophy of Language

Frege, in "On Sense and Reference," expounded a (probably *the*) dominant picture of belief, the history of which extends, no doubt, to the ancients. The idea is that to have a belief, to believe something, is to stand in a certain relation—roughly, the "accepting as true" relation—to a representation. Not just any representation will do here. Concepts are representational entities, but they are not of the sort that possess truth values; they don't tell us how things stand. So the sort of representation in question must have propositional form. Let's say that to believe something is to stand in a relation to a proposition, or to a propositional content.[3]

It is worth focusing on this core idea—*belief: a relation between a person and a propositional content*—since this is *the* focal idea in an increasingly large and confusing literature. The "relation to a content" idea, moreover, can get lost in its very different implementations, that is, in the different conceptions of propositional content. In Frege's own realization of the core idea, propositional contents are *thoughts*, thoroughly conceptual entities constituted by senses. On the direct reference alternative, propositional contents are typically constituted (at least partially) by references. (As was noted before, Kaplan dubbed such propositions *singular propositions*.) Propositional contents have also been identified with sets of possible worlds and even with linguistic entities: sentence types,

---

[3] This latter expression, "propositional content," should not be taken to suggest that the propositions themselves possess contents. Indeed, a proposition is the same thing as a propositional content. "Propositional content," then, should not be taken as "the content *of* a proposition" but rather as "a content of the propositional kind."

or tokens, of a natural language or of a hypothesized language of thought. Whatever one does with the notion of propositional content, the core idea is that to believe is to stand in a relation to a propositional representation.

That believing is so constituted is a thesis in the philosophy of mind, not in the philosophy of language. That is, it is a thesis about the character of the mental or psychological phenomenon of believing; it does not address the character of our discourse concerning those phenomena. Frege also advanced a closely related thesis about this discourse, a natural correlate to his philosophy of mind picture of believing, a second core idea. A belief report is, for Frege, a relational statement. When we say "John believes that Cicero is an orator," we refer to John (the believer), to the belief relation (by means of the verb), and (by way of "that Cicero is an orator") to the proposition believed.[4] And, as we will see, just as Frege's philosophy of mind idea has proved generally attractive, so too has his semantic idea about belief reports.

It's easy to suppose that the two core ideas—believing as a relation to a content and belief reports as formulating that relation— are more than closely connected. The philosophy of mind idea, it might be supposed, entails its mirror image in the philosophy of language; or at least it does so on minimal, uncontroversial assumptions. But no such tight connection exists. Even granting the first core idea, it may well be that ordinary belief sentences are not aimed, so to speak, at what philosophers may be most interested in, propositional content. Our belief reporting practices have evolved to serve social, communicative ends that, for all one knows ahead of time, do not include getting the propositional content well formulated—philosophically apt as doing so would be. The gods who were responsible for our practices might well have had, to mix metaphors, other fish to fry. More naturalistically, evolution does not always keep its eye on our favorite ideas.

Accordingly, there is no simple route from the first core idea to the second; from the philosophical account of believing to a seman-

---

[4] On Frege's approach, *that p* not only designates the proposition believed, in an important sense the *that p* it also articulates the proposition believed. That is, one can read off the propositional content believed from the *that p* phrase. (I am idealizing a bit. When the embedded sentence *p* contains indexicals or other sources of context sensitivity the articulation will be less than perfect.) This is not true of all ways of designating propositions, e.g., naming a proposition, say, "Elizabeth," or designating it by means of a description, e.g., "the last proposition enunciated by Schneerson."

tics of belief reports. Here as elsewhere, there is no substitute for a sustained look at linguistic practice. In fact, given that belief is one of those phenomena that in the idiom of chapter 3 is hardly out in the open, perhaps scrutiny of our reporting practices might usefully come first and might help with our thinking about belief, the psychological phenomenon.[5] This suggests that perhaps traditional philosophy of language/mind gets things exactly backwards in this domain.[6] But I'm getting ahead of myself.

2. Enter Direct Reference

Frege's two core ideas have been more than influential. Details aside, they have seemed to go almost without saying, the proverbial only game in town. But we should remember that Frege's general orientation in the philosophy of language, his sense-reference approach, appeared in the same light some years ago.[7] Nevertheless, one finds in the early direct reference literature radical criticisms of the Fregean general orientation. Indeed, as I've argued in earlier chapters, one finds something of Wittgenstein's "look, don't think" approach. In the domain of belief and belief reports, however, direct reference has come to mean a mere implementation of Frege's approach. That this is so is not easy to discern from the present state of the debate; it is late in the day and the implementations, responsive to a myriad of counterexamples, have become increasingly complex. A look at the early history will again assist us, as it did in earlier chapters. It was at first suggested by direct reference advocates that to believe is to stand in the *accepting as true* relation to a *singular* proposition. And, turning from philosophy of mind to semantics, to report a belief is to refer to the believer, to the belief relation, and to the *singular* proposition believed. Frege's structure

---

[5] This is not to suggest that an account of the semantics of belief sentences entails an account of believing.

[6] This is not to suggest that Frege *et al.* have given little thought to our practices of reporting belief. That is not so. At the same time, the counterexamples on both sides of the debate show that actual linguistic practice does not fit very well with how the tradition has construed belief reports. In what follows, I will present the counterexamples and then argue that our practices suggest an entirely different picture of belief, of believing.

[7] In both of these cases, the sense-reference distinction and Frege's approach to belief, Frege's views are not, and were not, the only game in town, strictly speaking. But they had the status of *the* received view and thus probably felt to many philosophers like the only viable game in town.

is thus left intact; singular propositions are substituted for Fregean thoughts.[8]

The project for direct reference in the domain of the "propositional attitudes" has thus been a rather conservative one. But from the outset, that project has been troubled. The problems begin with a powerful class of counterexamples from actual linguistic practice offered early along by neo-Fregean critics. There is irony here. Direct reference, virtually born of Frege's difficulties with actual practice, ends up taking Frege's lead in the domain of the attitudes. Suddenly, actual practice is the problem, a problem pointed out no less by Fregeans. What's more, Frege's own implementation of the core ideas seems to sit much better at least locally—concerning attitude sentences—with actual practice. Revenge of the Fregeans!

In the end a very large literature of counterexamples and responses was born, a new Gettierology, as I quipped earlier. In the next section I will come to the famous counterexamples, but first I will consider something more basic: the implications of taking singular propositions to be the objects of belief. Much of the subsequent literature is concerned, explicitly or implicitly, with the implications of the shift from Fregean thoughts to singular propositions. And despite the fact that the shift occurs in the service of a mere implementation of Frege's core ideas, it is quite startling.

On Frege's own realization of the core ideas, propositions—the things believed—are meaning-like entities. Direct reference philosophers reject Frege's conception in favor of a Russell-inspired one: Objects, particulars, things like you and me can be constituents of propositions. But what they accept is not Russell's approach; it is Russell-without-acquaintance. Russell insisted that for a thing to be a constituent of a proposition that one can entertain, the thing needs to stand in a particularly close relation to the mind, the relation of direct acquaintance.[9] For contemporary direct reference advocates, however, the propositions believed may include ordinary "external" objects. The move from Fregean thoughts to singular propositions is thus no mere move from Frege to Russell. It represents a very significant departure from tradition, the sort that breeds incredulity and talking at cross-purposes.

---

[8] Kripke's views are another story. His seminal article, "A Puzzle About Belief" (in A. Margalit, ed., *Meaning and Use* [Dordrecht: D. Reidel, 1979]), although it does not articulate a positive picture, clearly distinguishes him from most direct reference advocates—and from the position I'm now discussing on the question at issue.

[9] Interestingly, the epistemological intimacy in question is, for Russell, something like that enjoyed by the mind with respect to senses for Frege.

To Frege and his followers, of course, the very idea that singular propositions could be belief contents seemed bizarre, even incoherent. The direct reference twist also seemed wacky to orthodox Russellians, since the propositions believed were alleged to contain external things like Aristotle, tables, and chairs. For traditionalists generally, the direct reference outlook on the objects of belief was as bad as, if not worse than, its outlook on cognitively unmediated reference. That's pretty bad.

The move to singular propositions was so radical that even its advocates were not quite prepared for it. How, for example, was one to understand our cognitive/epistemic relation to the new sorts of belief contents? Might one still talk in traditional ways about grasping concepts and propositions? What indeed is it to *grasp* a singular proposition? It just isn't self-evident what's going on here.

One might proceed, as some did, by taming the radical idea, bringing it into the orbit of traditional philosophical thought. Inspired by the Fregean side of Kaplan,[10] one might posit modes of presentation that connect the mind with the externally constituted propositions. One would thus see the mind's grasp of such propositions as mediated; *ways of apprehending* the propositions now become the immediate and direct objects of thought.[11] This, as was noted earlier, is not of a piece with the anti-Cartesian tendency in direct reference that I prize, its sometime radical denial of modes of presentation, for example.

But there is another way, even if it was rarely if ever considered. It is not, in the end, my preferred way, but it is one that will prepare the ground. Why not give up on grasping propositions? I don't mean give up on grasping propositions because what we grasp is something else, closer in. Rather, why not give up the grasping picture altogether, as I suggested in regard to reference? When one refers to, say, Boethius, one may lack acquaintance not only with Boethius himself but also with anything closer in, for example a sense

---

[10] I've argued in earlier writings and in chapter 6 of this book that Kaplan, in "Demonstratives," provides a kind of conservative approach to direct reference, one that pays great respect to Frege's sense-reference picture.

[11] As David Braun points out in his "Understanding Belief Reports," *The Philosophical Review* (1998): 555–95, there are many alternatives for filling out the picture of the intermediate entities. One might take them to be linguistic meanings, or (if this is different) Kaplan's characters, or sentences of a natural language, or mental representations, or mental states. Approaching believing in terms of such intermediate entities has implications for, and may be at least in part motivated by, the famous puzzle cases. I will return to this issue later.

or body of information that might constitute a cognitive connection to Boethius. I can talk and think about him because I am a member of a linguistic community that has a name for him.

So the singular propositions theorist, implementing Frege's core ideas about belief, need not adopt the "taming" strategy. If one is with me on cognitively unmediated reference, singular propositions can function as objects of belief without the agent grasping either them or their associated modes of presentation. Belief in externally constituted propositions is thus no more of a special problem than is cognitively unmediated reference. That is, it is no special problem at all.

In the end I will reject Frege's core ideas and their implementations, Fregean and direct reference. Indeed, singular propositions will play no role in my account, and so I won't explore the current proposal further.[12]

3. The Famous Puzzle

The famous puzzle I'm about to present, and many related conundra, pivot on Frege's relational conception of belief reports. In a bit more detail, Frege's idea is this. "Sam believes *that p*" formulates a relation between Sam and the proposition he believes. This proposition is the referent of the phrase "that *p*." "That *p*" is thus seen as a referring expression; it designates the proposition that the sentence *p* ordinarily[13] expresses. For example, if I say, "Sam believes that John Wayne was an actor," the phrase "that John Wayne was an actor" designates the same proposition that the sentence "John Wayne was an actor" ordinarily expresses. It is this proposition that I'm claiming is believed by Sam.

As I've said, there are Fregean and direct reference implementations[14] of this relational conception. For the moment, let's stick

---

[12] In chapter 4 I defend cognitively unmediated reference, but there the discussion does not involve propositions. A question to be further explored: Does the introduction of propositions make the "no-grasping" approach problematic? I will comment on closely related questions in chapter 10. If propositions make a "grasping" account virtually inevitable, then what I have been proposing in the name of the singular propositions theorist will not do.

[13] The Fregean idea I'm exploring—about the designation of *that p*—has both a Fregean and a direct reference implementation. The insertion of the word 'ordinarily' is crucial on the Fregean implementation. More on this shortly.

[14] Throughout this discussion I will be discussing the direct reference implementation of the core Fregean ideas. Sometimes I will simply speak of direct reference, but I mean to refer only to this turn that direct reference took, its (according to me) ultimately inadvisable Fregean way of treating belief and belief reports.

with the direct reference version. I'll return to make trouble for the other side soon.

The singular propositions theorist maintains that the phrase "that John Wayne was an actor" names the singular proposition expressed by the contained sentence "John Wayne was an actor." What proposition is that? It is the singular proposition consisting of the person, Wayne, and the property of being an actor. Notice that it does not matter by what name one refers to Wayne; one could use the actor's actual given name, "Marion Morrison." "Marion Morrison was an actor" and "John Wayne was an actor" express the same singular proposition. But then "Sam believes that Marion Morrison was an actor" attributes to Sam precisely the same belief—that is, belief in the same proposition—as does the "John Wayne" belief sentence. The new report still says that Sam stands in the belief relation to the same singular proposition, the one that consists of this particular person—Wayne, Morrison—and this property—being an actor. To use a liturgical flourish, substituting co-referring proper names in the embedded sentence of an attitude report can never alter the belief ascribed—according to the singular propositions theorist. But if the same belief is ascribed, then the two reports must of course have the same truth values.

This is nothing but trouble. It can't be that switching the name is so insignificant that there is no difference in the belief ascribed, no difference in the truth values. For it's easy to generate examples in which, intuitively speaking, the following reports have different truth values and so would have to express different propositions:

a. Sam believes that Wayne was an actor.
b. Sam believes that Morrison was an actor.

For example, imagine that Sam doesn't know that the famous John Wayne was none other than his boyhood friend, Marion Morrison. He assumes that Marion spent his life back in Winterset, Iowa, pumping gas or some such thing. Marion Morrison, he tells us, was certainly no famous actor; he even failed to make the cut in various high school productions.[15]

Direct reference looks to be refuted, for contrary to its dictates, substitution of one proper name for another with which it co-refers can turn a true report into a false one.[16] Moreover, Frege's own im-

---

[15] This last, about Wayne's high school career, is fast and loose with thespian history.

[16] There are two contexts in which talk of substitution arises in discussions of these topics. First, there is the question of inference from one report to another, the

plementation is supported. The example suggests that substituting co-referring names can change the propositional content, something that fits well with Frege's approach.

This difficulty for direct reference is not specific to belief; it arises for the attitudes generally. If Sam uttered, "John Wayne was a famous actor," one could correctly report not only that Sam believed that John Wayne was a famous actor but also that Sam *said* this. But for Sam to have said this, according to direct reference, is for him to have asserted the singular proposition that John Wayne was a famous actor, that is, the singular proposition that Marion Morrison was a famous actor, these being the same singular proposition. But—here again is the rub for direct reference—it is (perhaps even more obviously) false that Sam said that Marion Morrison was a famous actor.

I am ready to accept this criticism of direct reference—its unfaithfulness to ordinary linguistic practice. But it is important that we pinpoint the source of the difficulty. It is not direct reference per se—for example, the Millian thesis that names are purely denotative—that causes the trouble. This Millian idea, as I'll try to convince you in the next chapter, can comport well with what I agree is the plain fact that Sam can believe that Wayne is an actor without believing that Morrison is. When I say that direct reference is in trouble, I should be understood as speaking about the singular propositions implementation of the basic Fregean picture.

The criticism of the singular propositions approach that I've been considering seems to me very powerful. This is a function of its directness and simplicity. Notice that the sort of counterexample considered does not involve philosophical exotica—no puzzle cases, not even a modal context—just ordinary garden-variety reports of belief.

The recalcitrance of actual practice should have signaled that we were on the wrong track. What it did instead was to engender defensiveness, as in the unfortunate tendency among direct reference theorists to deny the data, to insist that if Sam believes that

---

question of which substitutions preserve truth. Second, and equally important, there is the question of the latitude enjoyed by the reporter in substituting another name (or other singular term) for the name (or other singular term) uttered by the original speaker, the believer. I am not being careful to discriminate these different kinds of substitution since in much of the discussion it doesn't matter of which we are speaking. Similar considerations apply to both. I will be careful about the distinction only where it makes a difference.

Wayne was an actor, then it's just plain true that he believes that Morrison was as well, no matter what Sam says on the topic, and no matter what we, in our nontheoretical moments, would ordinarily say on the question of Sam's belief. Later, when for many the stubbornness of actual practice began to outrun such theoretical stubbornness, what ensued was not a thorough reevaluation but rather many new rounds of increasingly sophisticated theoretical refinement. The subtitle of this chapter, "God Would Not Be That Vicious," is borrowed from a remark by linguist Tanya Reinhart at the 1990 conference in Tel Aviv and Jerusalem in honor of David Kaplan. Reinhart was reacting to an especially sophisticated and baroque proposal about the semantics of belief reports. Her reaction is to be prized more than the most ingenious counterexample.

In contrast to the notorious difficulties for direct reference, Frege's approach to belief reports seemed unproblematic, at least early along. Indeed, had we only belief (or attitude) sentences to explore, or so it was supposed, Frege's semantical outlook would have been the approach of choice. This does not mean that Frege's was actually the approach of choice. For many, the old problems with Frege remained decisive. Frege's view fell far short, long before we came to belief sentences; it could not provide an adequate account of "Aristotle was wise." Frege's account of belief sentences seemed exemplary, as did his account of empty names. The only problem was that it was wrong.

4. Frege Upschlugged

Like some movies that initially receive rave reviews, Frege's approach to belief reports didn't hold up well. That the approach seemed successful, even exemplary, seems in retrospect a matter of focusing upon a limited range of examples.

The singular propositions view doesn't sit well with actual linguistic practice: True belief reports don't always remain true when a name in the embedded sentence is replaced by another co-referring name. There are examples, however, that comport well with direct reference but not with Frege, examples in which substitutions of co-referring names indeed preserve truth.

Imagine two communities each of which uses a different name for the same individual. In America, let's imagine, we always refer to the famous Roman as "Cicero"; in England, he is known only as "Tully." Further assume that while there is considerable overlap among the respective communities' characteristic beliefs about the man Cicero/Tully, their beliefs are different enough to constitute a difference in the sense of the names. Sam, an American, says "Cicero was an orator"—to pick an especially juicy example. I travel to England, where Sam's views are of great interest, and I report Sam as having said or as believing *that Tully was an orator.* In many such examples, truth is preserved, and this fact does not sit well with Fregean scruples.[17]

We often correctly report a person's remarks or beliefs in very different terms from those in which the agent expressed, or would express, herself. Nor, in many such contexts, contrary to the dictates of Fregean theory, need we concern ourselves with the question of whether the new expressions are associated with the same information as the old. Fregeans were quick to point out that the latitudinarian approach of direct reference to substitution of co-referring names was inconsistent with actual practice. We now see that the more restrictive Fregean view is not much better off.

Here's a second sort of difficulty for Frege. Frege maintains that ordinary proper names often, perhaps usually, do not have community-wide senses. Even individual speakers will often associate different senses with the same name in different contexts, presumably depending upon the salient properties of the referent in the context. Given the lack of shared senses, a listener often will not be able to tell which sense the speaker attaches to a name. Practical problems do not ensue, Frege tells us, so long as we use the same names with the same references. I imagine what Frege had in mind was that as long as we use the names with the same references, our practices of applying the names remain coordinated. But if a listener cannot tell which sense a speaker attaches to a name, then the listener's understanding of the speaker's thought is incomplete—even if their uses of the name are coordinated in practice. How then can the listener report the speaker's remarks in an indirect discourse, "*S* said that *p*," report; how can the listener report the speaker's belief? Remember that for Frege, such reports require getting the proposition—the Fregean thought—right. Moreover, if someone does report Sam as having said (believed) that John Wayne was an actor—surely a true report—the report will, on Frege's theory, probably turn out false: If the reporter uses his own preferred sense for 'John

[17] Whether or not the substitution intuitively preserves truth may depend upon subtleties of the context. But there are many such contexts in which truth is indeed preserved, e.g., where what is important in the context is whether Sam takes the individual in question, i.e., Cicero/Tully, to be an orator (rather than how Sam refers to or conceptualizes this individual).

Wayne', then his utterance of "Sam said (or believes) that John Wayne was an actor" attributes to Sam the assertion of or belief in a Fregean thought that may well be not the thought expressed by Sam.

So far, two problems for Frege:

1. the substitution of co-referring names often does preserve truth, and
2. on Frege's theory it's mysterious how we ordinarily correctly report the sayings and beliefs of another (when names are involved).

Notice that both difficulties suggest that in reporting speech or belief, what is often important are the references of the names used by the speaker, not the senses. So it's not only that the highlighted examples pose problems for Frege. It's also that they support the intuitions of the singular propositions theorist.

Still another problem for Frege is created by his own implantation of the relational conception of belief reports. Here is the idea. On Frege's view, when I say, "Sam believes that John Wayne was an actor," I refer with the clause *that John Wayne was an actor* to a Fregean thought. Specifically I refer to the thought that this embedded sentence would ordinarily express as its sense—that is, when the sentence occurs unembedded in a belief (or other attitude) report. So the ordinary sense of "John Wayne was an actor" becomes the referent of 'that John Wayne was an actor' when the latter clause occurs in a belief report.

Furthermore, in such a report, the linguistic constituents of the embedded sentence (the name 'John Wayne', for example) refer not to the person, Wayne, but to the constituents of the ascribed thought. This makes sense; for if "that John Wayne was an actor" refers to a proposition, then the name 'John Wayne' (in that context) refers to a part of that proposition.

This is Frege's doctrine of indirect sense and reference. One arrives at this doctrine in reasonable enough ways, but one may look up a bit astonished when one arrives. One potential problem is that according to this doctrine of Frege, singular terms and predicates are systematically ambiguous. An expression, when embedded in a "that *p*" clause refers to something altogether different than is usual, to a sense. Here is Davidson's reaction:

> Since Frege philosophers have become hardened to the idea that content-sentences in talk about propositional attitudes may strangely refer to such entities as intensions, propositions, sentences, utterances

and inscriptions. What is strange is not the entities, which are all right in their place (if they have one), but the notion that ordinary words for planets, people, tables and hippopotami in indirect discourse may give up these pedestrian references for the exotica. *If we could recover our pre-Fregean semantic innocence, I think it would seem to us plainly incredible that the words "The earth moves," uttered after the words "Galileo said that," mean anything different, or refer to anything else, than is their wont when they come in other environments.* [Italics added.] No doubt their role in *oratio obliqua* is in some sense special; but that is another story. Language is the instrument it is because the same expression, with the semantic features (meaning) unchanged, can serve countless purposes.[18]

Davidson emphasizes ambiguity: For Frege the words when embedded have new meanings and references. As Kripke quips in "Speaker's Reference and Semantic Reference,"[19] "positing ambiguities is the lazy man's way in philosophy." Surely Frege's posit of such systematic ambiguities is a theoretical liability.

But there is also the suggestion in Davidson's remarks of another Fregean offense here. Perhaps even worse than the ambiguity per se is the unnaturalness of the new semantic properties, especially the unnaturalness of the new references. Imagine that I say, "Jonathan thinks that Eve [here I point to Eve] acts like a *pezzonevante*.*" Intuitively, I refer to two people, a believer and the person I point to, the person the belief is about. On Frege's theory, however, I never refer to Eve; I rather use her name to refer to its ordinary sense.[20]

Embedded sentences with indexical expressions provide maybe an even more striking example of the same phenomenon. I say, "Jonathan thinks that she [again pointing to Eve] acts like a *pezzonevante*.*" Again, on Frege's proposal, I am referring not to Eve but to a sense. This seems altogether unacceptable.[21]

---

[18] Donald Davidson, "On Saying That," in D. Davidson and J. Hintikka, eds., *Words and Objections* (Dordecht: Reidel, 1969), pp. 172–73.

[19] In *Contemporary Perspectives in the Philosophy of Language* (Minneapolis: University of Minnesota Press, 1979).

[20] My point is not that senses per se are unnatural, although that's so also. As Davidson says, "What is strange is not the entities, which are all right in their place (if they have one), but the notion that ordinary words for planets, people, tables and hippopotami in indirect discourse may give up these pedestrian references for the exotica." Donald Davidson, "On Saying That," in D. Davidson and J. Hintikka, eds., *Words and Objections* (Dordecht: Reidel, 1969), pp. 172–73.

[21] There is the additional problem of what to make of the idea of the ordinary sense when indexicals are at issue. I assume that Frege would say that the relevant sense is not the native (incomplete) sense of 'she', what 'she' expresses in every

I've explored a number of reasons why Frege's own implementation of the core ideas does not hold up—and there are more in the literature. I say this not in defense of the at least equally troubled direct reference implementation. In fact let me mention an additional issue for direct reference, a problem that surfaced in the last chapter but that is especially relevant now. Emma believes, we correctly say, that Dentor (the tooth fairy) is coming this very night. When Emma uses the name, Dentor, she fails to refer. Accordingly, as I noted in the last chapter, it seems plausible to maintain that she fails to assert a singular proposition. Nevertheless our report of Emma's belief can be true. This is another severe problem for the direct reference implementation of Frege's view of belief and belief reports. We just do not seem to be reporting a relation between a person and a singular proposition.[22]

5. The Real Problem

Frege's basic picture of the attitudes has proven very difficult to implement adequately. Could it be that the problem is not with this or that realization, but with the Fregean core?

The idea that there may be trouble at the core receives support from additional counterexamples. These counterexamples are directed not at one implementation or the other, but rather at what they share, what they agree upon. Both sides agree that when the contents of two expressions are the same (read "content" here as what gets contributed to the proposition),[23] then those expressions may be substituted (in the embedded sentences), preserving truth. The idea is that such content-equivalent substitutions can affect only the linguistic surface, not the propositional essence. That the two approaches disagree about substitutivity of proper names reflects their disagreement about the content of names. However, both sides agree about the content of definite descriptions; a definite description, even according to the direct reference advocate,

---

context, but the complete sense that the indexical obtains in a particular context. This is an idea that has it own problems that are independent of our concerns here.

[22] As I noted in the last chapter, David Braun explores some ways in which one could still maintain the singular propositions conception here. But this doesn't look plausible on the face of it, and there are problems that remain on Braun's view.

[23] As I keep saying, "content" is an expression that deserves scrutiny. For now, I'm using the term as a traditionalist would, in explicating a problem for the traditional views, Fregean and direct reference.

contributes to the proposition not its denotation but rather descriptive information.[24] So they agree that when a definite description is substituted (for a name or another description), co-reference is not enough to preserve truth.[25]

There are, however, plenty of examples in which even this sort of substitution is unproblematic; truth is indeed preserved. You say to me that Bill (our dean and former colleague) is a jerk, something that you firmly believe. I say to my wife that you mentioned to me, or that you believe, that Joan's husband is a jerk. (My wife, let's assume, doesn't know Bill but knows Joan.) This report will often be a perfectly acceptable, correct one. But it shouldn't be acceptable and may well turn out false, not only according to Frege but even according to direct reference. For according to both of those approaches, the proposition I'm attributing to you is one in which Joan (according to direct reference), or some description of Joan (according to Frege), figures. This proposition will be false if Joan fails to figure in your thinking. Intuitively, however, the truth of the report does not require any such figuring of Joan in your thought. Similar remarks apply to a report based on Sam's remark that John Wayne was a great actor, that Sam believes that the son of Mary Morrison was a great actor. In the right context, for example said to someone in Winterset, Iowa, such a report is unproblematically true.

The suggestion of this sort of counterexample is that both approaches—even direct reference—fail to appreciate just how latitudinarian our practices are. There is another sort of counterexample that militates in the opposite direction: Our practices can be even more restrictive than the Fregean appreciates or can easily accommodate. Take any two expressions that share the same associated information, perhaps "doctor" and "physician," or "fortnight" and "period of two weeks." There are well-known examples—adduced many years ago, and much discussed[26]—that suggest that even such

---

[24] Donnellan's referentially used descriptions function in many ways like names and so possibly substitution of co-referential ones would preserve truth. What I say, then, in the text may not apply to referential uses, for those who accept Donnellan's distinction.

[25] More fully stated, when a definite description is substituted in the embedded sentence of an attitude report, say for another definite description that denotes the same thing, truth value is not necessarily preserved. Similarly when a definite description is substituted for a name that refers to the same thing that that the description denotes, the two approaches agree that truth is not necessarily preserved.

[26] The discussion begins with Benson Mates, "Synonymity," *University of California Publications in Philosophy*, reprinted in *Semantics and the Philosophy of Language*, L. Linsky (ed.) (Urbana: University of Illinois Press, 1952). Saul Kripke

synonyms are not always intersubstitutable: Someone can wonder whether a fortnight is a period of two weeks while being certain that a fortnight is a fortnight, someone can be certain that all (medical) doctors are (medical) doctors without being certain that all (medical) doctors are physicians.

This is of course not to say that these last or in fact any of the counterexamples are decisive. There is a substantial literature, about which I will comment in the next section, that explores a great variety of moves made in response to just such examples. My aim so far has been to display the significant pressure that many ordinary examples exert on the Fregean core. I would hardly be disappointed, though, if the reader were to begin to suspect that perhaps something other than what Frege supposed is going on with our practice of reporting belief. Could it be that ordinary reports of belief do not formulate relations between persons and propositional contents?

Another way to focus this pressure on Frege's relational conception of belief reports is to attend to the role of the context of the belief report. In some kinds of reporting situations, Frege's construction of propositional content seems to yield the right substitution patterns. In others, those intuitions produce just the wrong results and direct reference intuitions are just the ticket. In still other situations, both sorts of explications of propositional content, both sorts of implementation of Frege's picture, seem to miss the mark. It seems to be a matter of context. Indeed, the very same belief attribution can be true in one context and false in another. Consider "Sam believes that Marion Morrison is a great actor." If we are reflecting on Sam's remarks about famous actors and his subsequent response to queries about his high school classmates, we will judge this sentence false. Clearly he would deny that Morrison was a great actor. If we are speaking to Morrison's relatives in Iowa, trying to encourage pride in Morrison's achievement, it will be natural and correct to quote the famous Sam as having said, or as believing, that Marion made the grade.

Context sensitivity looms large. But this is not something that Frege's relational picture suggests. Whether a report is true should depend upon, and just upon, whether it gets the content believed

---

mentions Mates's essay in this connection in "A Puzzle About Belief," in A. Margalit (ed.), *Meaning and Use* (Dordrecht: D. Reidel, 1979), pp. 239–83. See note 15 and the text thereto.

right, whether it accurately depicts what's going on in the head of the believer. But even if Frege's picture does not suggest contextual dependence, perhaps there is a way for that picture to accommodate the data. I turn to this in the next section.

First I want to explore briefly a natural way of thinking about the character of the contextual dependence. Let's begin with contexts in which substitution of co-referring names preserves truth. Think about the true report issued to Marion Morrison's relatives, that Sam believes that Marion—or that Mary's son—was a great actor. The communicative aim of the report was to inform that a certain person was taken by Sam to be a great actor. The way the believer was thinking about Marion is not important given the communicative end; all important is that it was Morrison—that is, Wayne—under discussion. In such contexts, truth is preserved by substitution, presumably since substitution preserves what is crucial, that this individual is in question. On the other hand, it is sometimes quite important for purposes at hand how the believer is thinking of her referent, as "John Wayne" or as "Marion Morrison." Perhaps we have been discussing the fact that some people know of this identity and some don't, and someone says "Sam doesn't believe that Marion Morrison is an actor." Such contexts are very sensitive to the substitution of one name for the other. In short, sometimes it's important for us to get into the believer's head more deeply than at other times. And our intuitive judgments track this factor, perhaps among other factors.

This sounds plausible enough, but how are we to assimilate it theoretically? Are such observations compatible with the Fregean basic picture, or are they suggestive of another?

6. Traditionalist Response: The Pragmatic Strategy

Logical space is sizable. When sufficient attention is given to such puzzles, many modes of response are liable to surface. In the case of the attitudes, the attention has been intense and extensive. Although I won't canvas the field with its many variations and epicycles, I will explore two central patterns of response, one in this section, another in the next. This exploration will be instructive for how we might proceed.

The mode of response I'll explore in this section—biting the bullet, resolutely maintaining the intuitively troubling consequences of one's view—is available to both Fregeans and direct reference theorists. In the present case, however, and to the credit of Fregeans, it has found prominent expression only among defenders of direct reference. Direct reference bullet biters have insisted that if Sam believes that John Wayne was a great actor, then he ipso facto believes the same of Marion Morrison. What then of our powerful contrary sense? How exactly is that intuition to be explained away? Here the distinction between semantics and pragmatics has been pressed into service. Let me take a moment to review the distinction and explain its application here.[27]

Here's an uncontroversial, and uncontroversially important, linguistic phenomenon. Someone says, "Aristotle wrote *The Nicomachean Ethics.*" In addition to what is straightforwardly stated, that Aristotle wrote *The Ethics*, there is all sorts of collateral information that a listener might glean from the speech act. For example, that the speaker is competent with English and with certain specific expressions, (perhaps) that the speaker is an American, that she knows something about Greek philosophy, and so on. Indeed, as Grice emphasized, sometimes one utters a sentence intending for the listener to infer just such collateral information. Nor do such conversational or pragmatic "implicatures" need to be informational in the sense of propositional. Kripke mentions this example: Someone says "The cops are coming," intending to communicate "Let's get out of here."

This distinction between what is explicitly stated and collateral information is one that might get past an ordinary speaker, at least some of the time. Imagine that someone says something that is strictly speaking true but that his utterance of that truth conveys false collateral information. In such a case, a listener might issue a verdict of falsity, actually attending to false collateral information and not being focused on the truth of what was strictly speaking asserted.

That this is theoretically possible goes without saying. But whether it actually happens, whether people often confuse things in this way—taking an utterance to be false just because it is misleading—is another question. The most plausible, uncontroversial examples of the implicature phenomenon, like those mentioned two paragraphs above, typically involve no such confusion between

---

[27] See chapter 7, esp. note 5, for my earlier mention of pragmatic strategies. On Grice's emphasis discussed in the next paragraph, see *Studies in the Ways of Words* (Cambridge, Mass.: Harvard University Press, 1989).

what is asserted and what is conveyed. But let's press on to the use of this train of thought to insulate direct reference or Frege from the recalcitrant data about attitude reports.

The problem for the singular propositions approach was that substitution of co-referring names in the embedded sentences—which should according to direct reference always preserve truth—sometimes actually produced falsehoods. Sam says, "John Wayne was an actor," and in many actual speech situations it would be false to report Sam as saying or believing "that Morrison was an actor." Could it be that in such cases the apparently false reports, such as "Sam believes that Marion Morrison was an actor," are really true strictly speaking? Maybe there is a falsehood in the neighborhood, but it's the falsehood of some collateral bit of information. Perhaps it is the lack of acuity with the distinction between collateral information and what the sentence actually formulates that accounts for the ordinary blanket judgment of falsity. That's the idea, the defensive move on behalf of direct reference.

One big question, of course, is this: What precisely is this false collateral information, say in the example just considered? There are in the recent literature on belief sentences many accounts, increasingly sophisticated, about the collateral information conveyed by utterances of attitude reports. Here's a simple one just to fix ideas: Perhaps the speaker collaterally conveys that Sam would assent to "Marion Morrison was an actor." If so, the collateral information would be false.

A singular propositions theorist might try another such "pragmatic" move for the problem of nondenoting names. It is intuitively *true* to say that Emma believes that Dentor (the tooth fairy) will arrive this evening, since she said so. But there is no true singular proposition in the vicinity, for there is no Dentor to function as a propositional constituent. Biting the bullet, the pragmatic strategist might insist that no proposition was expressed by Emma; therefore to report Emma as believing *that Dentor would arrive* would be strictly speaking false, or without truth value. But such untrue reports can serve important communicational needs; there may well be correct collateral information. The ordinary judgment that the report is true is thus seen as the product of a lack of care or lack of clarity, of confusing the untrue report with the correct collateral information, perhaps about what Emma takes to be real, what words she takes to denote, what properties she takes to hold of the things she takes to populate the world.

It is important to see that a parallel pragmatic strategy is available to the Fregean. Let's begin with the problem, for Frege, of the listener's incomplete understanding of the speaker's comments. True enough, the listener may not know which sense the speaker attaches to the name. And so the said-that and belief reports the listener issues are possibly, even likely, wrong by Frege's lights. This consequence of course conflicts with the ordinary sense that we often report people's remarks and beliefs correctly, truly. The "pragmatic" Fregean might say, however, that while the reports are strictly speaking wrong—the Fregean thought, the semantic content, is false—still they convey correct collateral information. And when ordinarily folks take such reports to be true, this reflects a lack of care with the distinction between what is stated and collateral material.

There is a quite natural way a Fregean might flesh out the collateral information. Let's imagine that although the speaker and the listener associate different senses with 'John Wayne', they are coordinated with respect to the reference of the name. Then when the one says "Sam believes that John Wayne was an actor," one will (collaterally) convey something correct, albeit not the (official Fregean) semantic content of the report: The speaker in effect singles out Wayne for the listener—just in virtue of his use of the name and the shared reference—and says of the referent, Wayne, that he was an actor. One thus conveys a kind of correct partial sketch of what Sam believes, that Sam believes concerning this person that he was an actor. How Sam is thinking of him we are not told.[28]

A Fregean pragmatist can also use this strategy, fleshed out similarly, for those cases favorable to direct reference but problematic for Frege in which substitutions preserve truth. Such substitutions, she might insist, are false strictly speaking;[29] it's the collateral information that is true. For example, in contexts in which one can substitute "Morrison" for "Wayne," what is collaterally conveyed is that a certain individual—the one pointed out by the speaker in one way and by the reporter in another—is a great actor. Again, the full propositional content, the Fregean thought, is left underspecified.

---

[28] One could call what is thus conveyed a *de re* sketch. This is not to say that the Fregean admits to some new kind of belief, *de re* belief, but only that one can provide a *de re* sketch of someone's doxastic situation.

[29] Unless, of course, the believer, Sam, who said "John Wayne was an actor" happens also to believe the Fregean thought expressed by "Marion Morrison was an actor."

A pragmatic defensive strategy also might be employed with respect to the counterexamples that affect areas of agreement between direct reference advocates and Fregeans. For example, one might bite the bullet with regard to the truth-preserving substitution of definite descriptions—a problem for both sides. One might insist that the theoretically troublesome reports, adjudicated as true in actual practice, are really false—but communicationally felicitous. One might try to flesh out this assertion roughly along the lines of the suggestion that I have attributed to the Fregean pragmatist.

I don't know that all the problems can be treated in this way. Certainly many of them can. But the pragmatic strategy raises many questions—both general questions and ones that are specific to singular-propositions theorists' employment of the strategy— and to my mind it is unacceptable. That someone can convey something that is collateral to what her words formulate is not at issue. Simple, uncontroversial examples have been mentioned. But there is reason to be suspicious of the extension of a plain distinction to an arena where intuitions are much less clear, when that extension is motivated by the need to shore up a philosophical theory. In the end, I can't get away from the sense that these moves are all too easy, a classic case of "what you could say" instead of what it's natural to say.

To turn to more specific problems with the strategy, let's remember first that the plainest, least controversial examples of the distinction between semantic content and collateral information are not ones in which it's easy to confuse the two and attribute properties of one to the other. A reasonable person would not attribute falsity to "Aristotle wrote the *Nicomachean Ethics*" just because she took it to be false that the speaker was an authority on Greek thought.[30] That said, let's turn to a case in which just such a confusion is often supposed in the philosophical literature.

The semantics of English is considerably simplified if one supposes that various English sentential connectives mean the same as their sentential logic counterparts. Thus it is often said that the ordinary English sentential connective 'and' means, strictly speaking, just what '&' does in sentential logic. But there are immediate

---

[30] She might suspend judgment on the original statement. But that's another matter. Or to return to Kripke's nonpropositional example, one wouldn't reject "The cops are coming" only because one rejected the advice that was collaterally conveyed—that we should get out of here (that is, in case one thought that the wisest policy was to sit still and hide from the cops).

counterexamples: "He turned the ignition key and the car started" seems to say something very different from "The car started and he turned the ignition key." When one uses 'and', the order of the events is often significant; 'and' in many contexts seems to convey "and then." With '&', order is irrelevant. But one can defend the synonymy claim in the face of such counterexamples by arguing that while 'and' means exactly what '&' means—semantically they are on a par—pragmatically they (or their typical contexts) are not on a par. Ordinary English conjunctions often convey temporal succession. But that's a comment about pragmatics, about collateral information.

This is the simplest application of the pragmatic strategy, one that raises relatively few questions. But even here things are less than obvious. The thesis that 'and' in ordinary English means, or can mean, or sometimes means "and then" is not an obvious falsehood. Or to put the point even more strongly, it is surely not obvious that "The car started and he turned the ignition key" is, strictly speaking, true. Surely linguistic intuition doesn't make this at all obvious; it may suggest the opposite. To trust one's ear is to go a good distance toward rejecting the identity-of-meaning assumption. Perhaps there are methodological grounds relating to simplicity that trump here. Still, the move is not one that should go unquestioned. An explanation is needed, one that is strong enough to overcome one's initial trust in one's ear.

So even applied to sentential conjunction the pragmatic strategy hardly goes without saying. But the application to belief sentences is much more daring, much less naturally motivated. How plausible is it that even when Sam forcefully denies that Marion Morrison was an actor, we should nevertheless count "Sam believes that Marion Morrison was an actor" as true?[31,32] Or to take another, perhaps even more damaging case, consider "Sam believes that John Wayne is Marion Morrison," when Sam forcefully denies this is so. The belief attribution should be true according to the singular propositions view, the product of substituting 'Marion Morrison' for 'John Wayne' in "Sam believes that John Wayne is John Wayne."

---

[31] It seems relatively clear that this can be true in some of the contexts mentioned earlier, as when one speaks to Morrison's mother. But that's not to the point. The bite-the-bullet direct reference idea is that it's true in the more usual contexts as well, or even true independent of context.

[32] I here adapt some remarks of David Braun, "Understanding Belief Reports," pp. 570 ff. Braun there gives credit to Mark Richard's 1990 book, *Propositional Attitudes* (Cambridge: Cambridge University Press, pp. 125–26).

In this case, it is completely implausible that our intuition of falsity really pertains to collateral information.[33]

The pragmatic strategy, as was noted, is available to both direct reference advocates and Fregeans. Moreover, it's out of character for each, because each side has previously taken intuitive judgments about truth and falsity very seriously. Such ordinary judgments play a central role in the original direct reference counterexamples to Frege's idea that the reference of names is determined by associated senses. And they also occupy a key role in the Fregean critique of the singular propositions approach to belief reports. How strange then not to take such judgments at face value when they go against one. Is this why Fregeans have not availed themselves of the move, or is it rather because the move I will consider in the next section is more attractive to them?

A final source of concern about the direct reference/pragmatic strategy is the specific content of the collateral information. To take the example just mentioned, what exactly is this false collateral information conveyed by the utterance of "Sam believes Marion Morrison was an actor"? To fix ideas, I provided a simple way of construing the collateral information: The utterance conveys collaterally that Sam would assent to "Marion Morrison was an actor." But that won't do, for one thing since Sam, or another in a parallel case, might have been speaking a foreign language and wouldn't or couldn't assent to the English sentence, "Marion Morrison was an actor." For this and other reasons, quite sophisticated stories come into play as direct reference theorists' suggestions for the collateral information. But these accounts often involve the implausible attribution to ordinary speakers of sophisticated philosophical ideas supposedly conveyed as collateral information.[34] The more philo-

---

[33] Why is this case "perhaps even more damaging"? When in the past I approached these matters from the perspective of singular propositions theory, it was tempting to hear in "Sam believes that Wayne is an actor" the same claim, i.e., the same singular proposition expressed as in the corresponding "Morrison" sentence. And this makes it almost acceptable to insist on the counterintuitive idea that Sam indeed believes that Morrison was an actor, no matter what Sam says. But to insist that Sam believes even that Wayne *is* Morrison requires an almost supernatural hardening of the heart (or of intuition).

[34] See David Braun, "Understanding Belief Reports," pp. 567 ff., in which he criticizes several variants due to Nathan Salmon and Scott Soames. In one variant, sentences of the form *A believes that S* routinely pragmatically convey propositions roughly of the form *A BELs that S via W*, where the relation *BEL* is a ternary relation that holds between a person, a singular proposition, and a *way of believing*. *BEL* holds between such relata if and only if the person believes the proposition *in that*

sophically sophisticated the collateral information, the less plausible it is that this is either what speakers mean to convey or what actually gets conveyed to ordinary listeners.

While the literature abounds with sophisticated elaboration and equally sophisticated criticism of the pragmatic strategy, what seems to me most interesting and most significant about this phase of the debate—something that points the way forward—is an important concession the pragmatic strategy makes to the counterexamples. Whether or not "concession" is quite right, there is certainly something important that those examples teach, something to which philosophers had been insufficiently attentive and to which even the pragmatist must attend—even having bitten the relevant bullets. Prior to the counterexamples, one might have had a rather austere picture of our reporting practices, in fact the very picture that I sketched at the beginning of the chapter: To report belief is to assert of a person that she stands in the belief relation to a specified proposition.[35] Attention to the counterexamples—while it leaves the semantics of belief sentences intact for the pragmatist—forces upon us a considerably richer conception of the *practice* of reporting belief. For better or for worse, ordinary judgments of truth and falsity often cling, not to the semantic content of the report, but rather to the collateral information. Nor is it only for the audience that collateral information is important, but presumably for the speaker as well.[36] For both belief reporter and audience, then, semantic content can play a kind of in-practice second fiddle to collateral information. We should not forget, of course, that for the

---

way, that is, via the right mode of presentation. Braun points out that on this proposal, ordinary speakers routinely entertain and believe propositions of the sort just sketched, ternary relational propositions. But it's strange, says Braun, that speakers are unable to articulate such things at all, they never assert them explicitly, nor do they have any linguistically conventional means for expressing such things. A variant that I mentioned in the text in an oversimplified form, that the collateral information associated with a belief sentence is that the believer would assent to such a sentence (or, in a more sophisticated version, to a translation of such a sentence), involves the implausible claim, says Braun, that in uttering ordinary belief sentences, speakers routinely entertain and collaterally convey complex metalinguistic propositions.

[35] This is not to say that one would have denied that such assertions might be associated with conversational implicatures. But this is no different than in other cases of assertion and it does not suggest that the pragmatic side involves something particularly important or philosophically interesting about the practice of reporting.

[36] Typical speakers certainly would agree—if apprised of the relevant facts, etc.—to the ordinary truth evaluations that prompt the pragmatic strategy.

pragmatist, ordinary ascriptions of truth and falsity, no matter what they "cling to," are often confused ascriptions; truth and falsity properly pertain to the semantic content of the reports. Nevertheless, the semantic content of a report constitutes considerably less of the focus both for reporter and for audience than we would have supposed.

What emerges—almost against the will of the pragmatic strategist—is a new understanding of the project of reporting belief, the cooperative enterprise of reporter and audience: *keeping track of the believer's cognitive whereabouts*. It's not that the proposition that is believed, that is, the one semantically formulated by the report, plays no role in cognitively locating the believer. Sometimes it plays a major role; other times, less so. It's just that this proposition is now seen as one part in something quite rich and complex. Previously it was the almost exclusive focus of philosophical thinking about belief.

7. Traditionalist Response:
Semanticizing Collateral Information

After all is said and done, it is perhaps the brush-off that our intuitive truth/falsity evaluations receive at the hands of the pragmatic strategy that is most troubling. To deny the other's intuitively powerful data is almost always to violate sound methodology. I now turn to a strategy that respects the data.

As I said earlier, it would be natural enough, although mistaken, to suppose that Frege's first core idea, the relational picture of believing, entails the second, the relational picture of belief reports. Thus counterexamples to the latter might seem to strike at the heart of the former. Once one sees that there is no such entailment, one can contemplate the counterexamples with a new freedom. One can admit that the semantics of reports needs more work—one can be flexible on that score—while steadfastly maintaining one's philosophy of mind picture of believing.

Here's one way. I take the liberty of speaking for the Fregean:

> We Fregeans were too hasty to adopt a view of belief reports that was suggested by our favored relational conception of believing. After all, because of the lack of community-wide senses for proper names, a listener often will not know precisely which proposition was asserted. And so he is often hardly in a position to report on the details of what was asserted or is believed. Even where the listener knows precisely what was asserted, it may not be particularly germane to the contextu-

ally important aims that the precise content be formulated. What the reporter can do is to use the embedded name as she, the reporter, ordinarily uses it, associating it with her preferred sense. To say this in the context of Frege's theory of indirect reference yields an immediate problem: The wrong proposition gets attributed to the believer. So let's improve upon Frege by assuming that the reporter uses the embedded name—her own favored sense attached—to refer to its ordinary referent. The reporter thus does not formulate a relation between the believer and the Fregean thought believed, but between the believer, the referent of the embedded name—that is, the person about whom the believer believes something—and what the believer believes about that referent. If Sam says, "John Wayne was a great actor," and I say, "Sam believes that John Wayne was a great actor," I attach *my* favored sense to the name 'John Wayne'. The report thus says of Sam that he believes concerning this man, John Wayne, that he was a great actor. Such reports are only partial reports of belief; they fail to specify the Fregean thought believed. But they are often the best we can do, and other times all that is important in the context.

Such a Fregean has found a natural way to move the collateral information into the semantic content, so to speak. All to the good; there is no longer a gap between intuitive ascription of truth values and the dictates of theory. This same semanticizing strategy also seems natural in other cases that were troublesome to Frege, for example those in which substitution does preserve truth. On the new strategy such embedded names refer to the person, John Wayne, not to a sense, and again, the content of belief is only partially represented. In contexts in which substitution does not preserve truth—the contexts that are friendlier to Frege's original conception—the name occurs as in the orthodox Fregean treatment of belief sentences, referring to its ordinary sense and so on.[37] In such cases the report indeed formulates the proposition, the Fregean thought, that is believed, and it states that the person in question stands in the belief relation to that proposition.

I asked earlier why only direct reference advocates employ the pragmatic strategy; it is, after all, available to both sides. The answer is perhaps that the post-pragmatic strategy just adumbrated is supe-

---

[37] To use the jargon, if substitution preserves truth, the report is a *de re* report. In that case, it formulates a relation between a believer, another individual whom the belief is about, and the sense of a predicate. Where substitution does not preserve truth, the report is *de dicto*. But for the Fregean the *de re/de dicto* distinction applies only to the reports. There is no *de re* belief. The propositions expressed by the original speaker is always a Fregean thought. Indeed the proposition expressed by the belief sentence is itself a Fregean thought.

rior. There are no bullets to bite; what is sacrificed, or amended, is the second core idea, the relational theory of belief reports.

While such a neo-Fregean view has virtues, there are still difficulties. According to the new approach, embedded names do sometimes refer in their ordinary ways, thus bypassing Davidson's problems, but only sometimes. In a way the problem has gotten worse, since belief sentences now exhibit a kind of general ambiguity. They sometimes report relations to propositions, sometimes not. And as always, there are the problems that attach to any Fregean views, the basic difficulties inherent in a sense-reference approach.

How about the other side, that of direct reference? It's clear that a structurally similar post-pragmatic move is available. One would begin by admitting theoretical hastiness, moving too quickly from a conception of believing—as a relation to a singular proposition—to a semantics of reports. Where substitution intuitively fails to preserve truth, the direct reference advocate will now admit that the belief report really is false. If Sam denies that Marion Morrison was an actor, then at least in some contexts it would be false to report him as believing that Marion Morrison was an actor, even though this report gets the content believed exactly right. In such contexts, clearly, the truth of a report is dependent on more than just capturing the singular proposition believed. What it is dependent upon—this is the semanticizing move—is what the pragmatist thought of as the collateral information. The idea then is to bring this information in from the cold, from information that is merely collateral to part and parcel of the semantic content of the report.

But how is this formerly collateral information to be brought in from the cold? Here's an idea (borrowed from earlier Fregean maneuvers)[38]: In the troublesome contexts in which substitution fails to preserve truth, the embedded sentence is doing double duty, specifying the correct singular proposition, the one believed, but also specifying the other (incorrect) information. How does the embedded sentence do all that? Perhaps the presence of the embedded sentence indicates (incorrectly in the cases about which we are thinking) the sentence by means of which the proposition in question is believed—or to which the believer would assent. Perhaps one will have to make room here for implicit references to ways of believing. In some such way the direct reference advocate can ac-

---

[38] In the work, e.g., of Hector-Neri Castañeda. Notice that we are speaking of borrowing the opponents' intellectual apparatus, a mark of philosophy-as-epicycles.

count for cases in which substitution fails: The new report, the one that contains the substituted name, correctly captures the singular proposition believed—so far so good. But it fails to capture the correct sentence used by the believer or the believer's mode of presentation, and so on.

So it's clear that the semanticizing strategy is available on the direct reference side.[39] This is not to say that the going will be smooth, even aside from the question of overall naturalness. The latter is immediately compromised simply by building in a new parameter; what looked to be a simple and natural analysis—albeit subject to counterexample—has become quite complicated. In addition, there are the Davidson problems. It's not clear that such a double-duty story for the embedded sentence can escape without violating semantic innocence, ambiguity, and the like. More difficult still will be accounting for the problem posed by empty names. One will need to admit that "Emma believes that Dentor is on his way" is true and will need to build into the semantics what the pragmatist saw as the correct collateral information. It is difficult to see how this is to be done. These difficulties perhaps explain the emphasis on biting bullets among direct reference theorists, that is, opting for the pragmatic option. Fregeans, by and large, have been more interested in the strategy explored in this section.

Our practice of reporting belief serves ends that would remain unserved were we limited to commenting upon propositional content believed. Even the pragmatic theorist would agree. The new strategy gives those communicational ends a central, semantic role. Semantically speaking, belief sentences formulate the believer's cognitive whereabouts, where this activity is not limited to, and may not even involve, articulating propositions believed.

We have here another step forward, one that advances the discussion by making focal the project of cognitively locating agents and by respecting what ought to be inviolable, ordinary truth evaluations.

8. Starting Over

Here's an overview of the situation. Ordinary linguistic practice renders incorrect, or at least problematic, Frege's second core idea—

---

[39] I have been emphasizing the cases in which substitution fails. But this semanticizing strategy will of course see its semantic proposal—e.g., the double duty of the embedded sentence—as present in all belief reports, not just the problematic ones.

his relational conception of belief sentences. But there are ways to save the theory from the appearances—pragmatic ways and, as we have lately seen, even semantic ways. At the same time, one has to work quite hard to make it all come out right. The real question, though, is not whether some version can be made to work, but whether the fit is natural. The almost geometrically increasing complexity of the various proposals, Fregean and direct reference, makes it tempting to look for another way to think about the whole business. That's what I am about to propose.

Frege's first core idea—the philosophy-of-mind picture of believing propositions, while it suggests the relational semantic picture, does not entail the latter. And so the semantic story's failure does not quite sink the original philosophy-of-mind idea. Still it makes one wonder. It remains to be seen what a more satisfying story about our reporting practices would look like. And whether such a story would cohere with Frege's philosophy-of-mind picture.

Frege took thought to be transparent, relatively (maybe absolutely) clear and distinct, and linguistic practice to be a muddy domain, about which it is difficult to theorize. There was at least in the early days of direct reference a tendency to go at things the other way around, to suppose that the body, as it were, is better known than the mind.[40] It is that tendency I want to bring back into play here. Believing, after all, is, in Percy's idiom, not one of those things that is out in the open. Instead of starting with Frege's or some other philosophical conception of the psychological phenomenon, let's start with the anthropology, as it were, of our reporting practices.

---

[40] See chapter 3.

9

Bringing Belief Down to Earth: Part II

Most of the last chapter was taken with the semantic face of belief, with the semantics of sentences that ascribe belief. What we saw was largely negative, that Frege's relational conception of belief sentences—his second core idea—faces considerable difficulty. At the same time constructive ideas emerged, desiderata for any positive account. Here I will follow those up, proposing a different way of thinking about what we are up to when we ascribe belief.

Frege's first core idea—the relational conception of believing— is not a thesis about ascriptions of belief, about language. It is rather about the mind, about the phenomenon of belief. Perhaps even more than Frege's semantic ideas, his picture of believing has seemed to go without saying. But the more one reflects on the foibles of the second core idea—we just don't seem to be reporting propositional contents believed—the more one may find oneself wondering about the underlying philosophy-of-mind picture of believing. Here I'll be developing an alternative semantic account that will, I hope, further encourage that wonder. At the end of this chapter, I will sketch an alternative conception of believing, one that is suggestive/ reflective of a very different way in the philosophy of mind.

To begin with the reports, here are the desiderata. First, there is Davidson's *semantic innocence:* One would naively suppose— Davidson argues, and I agree, that we should suppose—that linguistic expressions in the embedded sentences function as they normally do. We should not posit ambiguities here, attributing new meanings to expressions when so embedded. Names, for example, are in ordinary contexts Millian; they remain so in belief sentences. 'John Wayne' directly refers to John Wayne whether I use the name to attribute to him a certain height or to say that you believe that he held certain political views.

This requirement has seemed to conflict with another that seems equally correct: *No fudging on truth values*. We should insist on the truth values provided by ordinary intuitive judgments. What we want is an account that not only accommodates these ordinary intuitive judgments but one to which these judgments are congenial. The truth values provided by ordinary judgments should seem like what we would have expected from the core ideas of the account. The account should not seem gerrymandered, engineered to avoid the counterexamples.

This second constraint yields a closely related one that is worth enumerating as a third. Belief sentences are highly context sensitive. Indeed, the same sentence—for example, "Sam believes that Marion Morrison was a great actor"—can be true in one context and false in another. *Context cannot be an afterthought in our thinking about the linguistic function of reports, any more than context can be an afterthought in our thinking about indexicals.*

How does one accommodate these constraints? Or more to the point here, how might a Millian accommodate them? One possibility, the only one so far explored, is last chapter's Millian version of the semanticizing strategy. But that seems like the kind of epicycle I have been railing about, not to speak of its apparent violation of semantic innocence. I will proceed in a very different direction.

Kripke, in *Naming and Necessity*, effected an elemental change in our thinking about reference and proper names. True, it was only a picture, one that needed further development. But it represented a radical departure from the received view and pointed the way forward. I believe that nothing less is needed in the domain of the attitudes. My aim is to provide a conception that is semantically innocent and thoroughly Millian, that is to say, it utilizes no Fregean or neo-Fregean notions: no senses, modes of presentation, or the like. Moreover, it is one to which the data from actual practice are congenial.

1. Quine as Martian Anthropologist: Reports of Speech

Quine, in §45 of *Word and Object*, provides what I see as a master key to the domain. But Quine's ideas on the subject are embedded in his complex and controversial overall outlook. To distill Quine's insights and to render the resulting picture as natural as I believe it to be, I'll present the material in my own way. Quine treats belief reports not in isolation, but in their connections with reports of sayings, direct ("John said '*p*'") and indirect ("John said that *p*"). In this section, I will say a word about direct discourse and then explore indirect at more length. In section 2 I will turn to belief reports.

What follows is a kind of philosophical or armchair history of our practices, treating the more sophisticated forms as developing from the simpler. Indirect discourse is thus the child of direct, and belief reports the grandchild. While I intend no serious developmental claims, such plausible schemes—like imagined social contracts—can illuminate the phenomena and help break the hold of received views.[1]

Imagine then a primitive linguistic culture, one in which language has nevertheless progressed quite far. Speakers here are sophisticated relative to those in, say, Wittgenstein's primordial situations. They refer to all sorts of things—people, places, events, and the like—and predicate all sorts of things of the items to which they refer. Perhaps they even have devices of quantification. (It won't matter for what follows.) But they are, you might say, attitudinally impoverished; their practices do not include reporting on the speech or mental lives of their fellows, or indeed of themselves. They can say "The cat is on mat," but not that John said such a thing or that he believes it.

1.1. Direct and Indirect Discourse

Imagine now a simple enhancement of their practice developed by a linguistic engineer or, less mythically, by his natural counterpart—linguistic evolution: the ability to quote someone. Quine says:

> When we quote a man's utterance directly we report it almost as we might a bird call. However significant the utterance, direct quotation merely reports the physical incident and leaves any implications to us.[2]

[1] See Martha Burns, "Beyond 'Dartmouth': J. S. Mill's Commonsensical Approach to Singular, General, Abstract, Connotative, and Kind Terms," Ph.D. dissertation, University of California, Riverside, 2001. See esp. chapter 7. Burns is attracted to eighteenth-century stories about the development of language, stories that illuminate linguistic practice in general and help to break the hold of the sort of traditional picture of language of which in our time Frege has become the classical spokesman.

[2] W. V. O. Quine, *Word and Object* (Cambridge Mass.: MIT, 1960), p. 219.

Driving Quine's remark is the idea that in quoting a person's words, our business is not interpretation. The reporter has no real latitude with respect to the sentence that she embeds in the quotation marks. For the most part, one's direct discourse report is true just in case one gets the sentence uttered just right. Still, matters may be slightly less stark than Quine suggests. We might allow, say, the substitution of words in our own language for a foreigner's words, enclosing what we attribute to him in quotation marks. Similarly for grammatical and other trivial corrections.[3]

Direct quotation represents an important advance for the linguistically impoverished culture. But even on my liberal rendering, it is subject to severe limitations. It puts great demands on memory, indeed a kind of eidetic memory. And its limiting the reporter to the exact words of the speaker cramps communication. If, say, the reporter's audience has trouble with the original speaker's vocabulary, or if they are unaware of relevant features of the original speaker's context or his culture, audience uptake may fail. The reporter's ability to convey the speaker's point would be increased substantially were we to allow her to alter her formulation dynamically.

Thus arises the next developmental stage, that of "indirect discourse," relating that someone *said that p.* We don't use quotation marks, perhaps to signal that we may not be providing the speaker's words, even more or less. The reporter chooses a sentence that in the current context conveys the original speaker's point and, as it were, puts this sentence into the original speaker's mouth.

Putting a sentence in the speaker's mouth—this is Quine's master key. Suitably developed, it will furnish a natural way of making intelligible our reporting of speech and belief. To those familiar with Quine's skepticism about propositional content it will come as no surprise that Quine's attention is focused on the sentence that the reporter embeds and not on an associated proposition. At the same time, the embedded sentence, I just said, must

---

[3] Of course, the minute one allows any corrections to the original words, one starts down a slippery slope. How much difference is there between the sort of corrections I'm envisaging in the text and, say, correcting for the use of indexicals in the speaker's original context—the reporter can "update" the speaker's use of "I" by using the speaker's name in the quoted report? Quine's policy apparently is to allow no variation at all in direct quotation. Thus the bird-call remark. The distinction between direct and indirect is a distinction of art—or philosophy—since in actual practice we use quotation marks with varying degrees of correction. And so lines need to be drawn; there will be intermediate cases in which a decision rather than a discovery will be required.

"convey the original speaker's point." And this might seem like propositional content in another guise. As we will see shortly, that is not so.

1.2. Translation and Indirect Discourse

Quine associates indirect discourse with translation: Putting words in someone's mouth is like translating his words for the current context. I want to reflect on translation with an eye to what it might reveal about indirect discourse. In philosophy we often oversimplify both of these practices. We think of translation—I'll return to indirect discourse shortly—on the model of "capturing literal meaning in different words." For a more adequate conception, don't think of translating a single sentence, as in an exercise for a student. Reflect instead on translating the Bible or some great work of literature, literature that needs to be retranslated from time to time and from culture to culture. While different vocabularies separate cultures, the divide inevitably goes deeper. To make the original work available, a translator often needs to do more than or other than simply finding words that get the literal meaning right.

In such actual translation, maintaining the integrity of the original is of course paramount. But there is a second goal—bringing the original into contact with the new culture. And as was noted, the gap to be overcome is not merely one of vocabulary. These two objectives—two constraints on translation—stand in tension with one another. The first militates toward using words very close in literal meaning to the original. The second encourages variation. How exactly are these to be balanced, integrated?

As if it were not difficult enough for a translator to discern the product of these two vectors, there are further complications. First, these aren't exactly vectors and there may not be a unique product. There may be several different ways of balancing the two constraints—perhaps each with drawbacks—and there may be no obvious choice. Moreover, the fit between the old language and the new is almost always imperfect. For example, the language of the original may not go quietly into the new language—there may be some unwanted implications in the various available formulations or some remainder from the original that the new language does not quite capture. Making this all explicit, even if one could do so, would be a major undertaking. But such a long-winded explanatory discourse would not be a translation. Instead a translator will often need to decide which features of the original she wants to preserve.

And independent of these complications, our practices give the translator considerable latitude over which aspects of the original to stress or to play down.

I'm betting that the rules for such subtle business have never been written. Reflection on translation can indeed inspire awe at cultural/linguistic evolution, at the fact that something so elaborate and functional has found its way into our practice. It's not only the fact of inheritance that is arresting; think about what it must take to learn such a complex business, or to teach it.

Just as translation, real translation, is no simple matter of capturing anything like literal meaning, neither is indirect discourse. In the last chapter I explored substitution patterns in the embedded clauses of belief sentences. The same sorts of patterns occur in indirect discourse reports and are similarly not explicable in terms of literal meaning, nor of propositional content. Whatever your favorite explication of propositional content, it produces the wrong expectations of what we can and cannot substitute. But those substitution patterns—for both indirect discourse and, as we will see, belief—make much more sense when one is thinking in terms of real translation. The reporter picks a sentence to embed that, in contextually appropriate ways, counts as a good *paraphrase* of the original. To so paraphrase is not—certainly not necessarily and not even typically—to capture literal meaning or propositional content. Indeed, the term "paraphrase" is even better here than "translation," since the former is less suggestive of anything like capturing literal meaning.

There are striking further parallels between translation/paraphrase and indirect discourse. The two primary and often divergent goals of translation are also primary and often divergent goals of indirect reports. The reporter must be faithful to the original speaker's remark. At the same time the reporter needs to choose a sentence that in the current context conveys the original speaker's point. And there may well be no uniquely correct way to satisfy both desiderata. Moreover, there is the problem of fit: No way of putting the matter in the current context may get the original remark just right. And the reporter's latitude—which features of the original to highlight or downplay—seems just like that of the translator. Finally, as with translation, the rules for how to balance all of these factors, how to report speech correctly, have never been written.

If reflection on translation can inspire awe, indirect discourse is in a way more amazing. Only the highly qualified translate great works of literature, but we all report one another's speech. Do we actually manage to learn to do this, to teach it?

1.3. Quotational Latitude and Truth Values

To return to my fanciful history—we are at the stage of indirect discourse—the ability to quote roughly and appropriately to current context represents an impressive gain. But there is a cost. It is much less clear with indirect discourse than with direct quotation what counts as getting it right.[4] Consider the all-important faithful rendering of the original speaker's remark. What about that remark's subtleties; what if it encapsulates a number of related points? What exactly does the truth of the reporter's rendition require? Moreover, given that the reporter will want to update the original speaker's sentence to facilitate communication, how much deviation do we allow, and of what sorts? At what point does acceptable deviation deform into misrepresentation, a false report?

It begins to seem almost miraculous how effortlessly we judge indirect discourse reports true or false, at least most of the time. But to what standards do we appeal? Let's deepen this difficulty before trying to resolve it. When one thinks of translation as a model, truth and falsity can begin to seem inapplicable to indirect discourse. Although we sometimes judge translations as correct or incorrect, more usual categories are better and worse, more or less nuanced, more or less sensitive. Why then don't we evaluate indirect discourse in such terms, on such a sliding scale?

That we actually evaluate indirect discourse as true or false should not incline us to suppose that real translation is the wrong model. Nor should we suppose that truth and falsity are, in the context of indirect discourse, anything less than real truth and falsity. It is helpful here to reflect on the claim that a certain expression translates another, or that a certain translation is a good one. Despite the vagaries of translation, such claims are true or false. If the translation counts as good enough for present purposes, then the claim that it's good—or the claim that a certain expression translates another—counts as true in the current context. Analogously, while a reporter's choice of a sentence to embed is better or

---

[4] Even if the contrast between the two types of reports is one of degree—I suggested above that even direct discourse is mushier than Quine supposes—still, clear cases of direct discourse are relatively straightforward to evaluate for truth and falsity.

worse, her overall report can be judged true or false, at least in the clear cases.

Here's what Quine says—he is an astute if unlikely anthropologist of linguistic practice—about evaluating indirect discourse reports:

> Commonly the degree of allowable deviation [from the original utterance] depends on why we are quoting. It is a question of what traits of the quoted speaker's remark we want to make something of; those are the traits that must be kept straight if indirect quotation is to count as true.[5]

He continues:

> Evidently we must recognize in indirect quotation and other idioms of propositional attitude a source of truth-value variation comparable to the indicator words.[6]

The idea is that an indirect discourse report counts as true just in case the embedded sentence paraphrases the original remark in a way that is satisfactory, good enough, for present purposes. All manner of substitutions are in principle allowed; the limits are set by contextual considerations.

What sorts of contextual purposes come into play? Here's an example from the last chapter, when I was doing a bit of linguistic anthropology myself.[7] Where what is important in the context is the individual to whom the original speaker refers—and it is not contextually important how the speaker refers, what terms or concepts he uses—then substitution of co-referential expressions, and not only names, is proper; it preserves truth. Imagine that the famous orator is called "Cicero" in America but in England he is called "Tully." Sam, an American, says "Cicero was an orator"; let's assume he is unfamiliar with the name "Tully." To an English audience I can report Sam as having said that Tully was an orator. Turning to a case that involves descriptions, if my English audience is up on Tully's accomplishments, I could also report Sam as having said that the author of *De Fato* was an orator. Similarly, to return to an example of the last chapter, imagine that you say to me that Bill (our dean and former colleague) is a jerk. I can say, truly, to my wife that you mentioned to me that Joan's husband is a jerk. (My wife, let's assume, doesn't know Bill but knows Joan.) Such substi-

---

[5] Quine, *Word and Object*, p. 218.
[6] Ibid.
[7] See chapter 8, esp. the end of Section 5.

tutions preserve truth; the reference of the original speaker is, as Quine says, what we wanted to make something of.

By contrast, consider this case: I report Sam's remark to other Americans who are interested in whether Sam knows that Cicero and Tully are one. In such a context, "Sam said that Tully was an orator" would be false. The context mandates, as it were, that we don't allow this sort of variation. Where it is all important how the speaker was thinking of the referent, substitution of a co-referring name can turn a truth into a falsehood.

1.4. Some Semantical Detail

I've spoken impressionistically of putting words in the original speaker's mouth. And I've suggested translation/paraphrase as a model for the choice of words to embed. But how does it work semantically? How do we describe the semantic function of the embedded sentence and that of the sentence's constituent expressions?

Quine writes suggestively but somewhat darkly that quoting someone indirectly is "an essentially dramatic act": "[I]n indirect quotation, we project ourselves into what, from his remarks and other indications, we imagine the speaker's state of mind to have been, and then we say what, in our language, is natural and relevant for us in the state thus feigned."[8]

Indulging in some drama of his own, Quine throws a spotlight on the reporter's utterance of the embedded sentence. The function of that sentence in the mouth of the reporter is for Quine unique. No assimilation of indirect discourse sentences to ordinary subject-predicate, relational, or quantificational sentences will do. An indirect report involves a radical shift in midsentence. When the reporter utters the first part of the sentence, "Sam said," she speaks normally. But when she hits the embedded sentence, something startling happens; she speaks in a different voice.[9] She becomes an actor, feigning an utterance of the original speaker.[10]

---

[8] Quine, *Word and Object*, p. 219.

[9] What happened to 'that' in "that p? Quine doesn't address this question. And not having any good idea about it, I'm happy to let it go for now. This needs to be a future agenda item, a detail but a very important one.

[10] There is another way to read Quine, less convincing I think as a reading of the passage, but possible. Perhaps Quine intends the feigning to pertain only to the "getting into the role." Then the reporter just speaks, just uses the sentence to express (without asserting) whatever it expresses. I don't read it that way, but if one did, then my further discussion here is a matter of drawing out the implications, maybe extending them.

But there is a simpler way. For the real punch of Quine's re-mark is not his neo-fundamentalist reading of "putting words in another's mouth," the alleged theatrical performance. The real punch concerns the function of the embedded sentence. To high-light that function, think about an actor's utterance: He produces a sentence that might ordinarily be used to make an assertion. The actor himself does not, of course, assert anything. He acts as if that's what he is doing without doing it. Notice that despite the actor's slightly exotic use of the sentence, the parts of the sen-tence—proper names, predicates, etc.—do not take on anything like new meanings. What's new about the actor's utterance is at the level of the speech act. Like a *Begriffsschrift* sentence without an assertion sign, like a sentence that occurs as the antecedent of a conditional, there is a lack of assertive force. My idea, then, is to see the indirect discourse reporter's utterance of the embedded sen-tence as expressing without asserting. The embedded sentence's parts occur semantically intact.

I want to consider for a moment another context in which as-sertable sentences occur unasserted: quotation. Frege's way with quotation posits an ambiguity; in this way, it's just like his treat-ment of the embedded sentences of indirect discourse.[11] But there is a difference: Embedded in indirect discourse, expressions stand for their ordinary senses. Quoted expressions are, as he says, "signs of signs."

Quine's use-mention approach to quotation is a specification of this approach. For Quine, as for Frege, a quotation such as

Botwinnik uses the French defense

names or mentions, the sentence that is contained within the quo-tation marks. One way to achieve this result—perhaps Frege's own way—is for the words in the context of quotation to refer to them-selves. The other way—Quine's—is to view the whole quotation as indissoluble, as naming the sentence inside the quotes, but not word by word. This Quinean idea—that the word 'French' fails to have any more of an occurrence in the quotation than 'cat' has in 'category'—is on a continuum with, but further out than, ambigu-ity. You take the sentence, put it in quotes, and the words, as it were, not only don't function quite as usual, they disappear; they

---

[11] "[A] word standing between quotation marks," he writes in "On Sense and Reference," "must not be taken as having its ordinary reference." "On Sense and Ref-erence," in P. Geach and M. Black, eds., *Translations from the Philosophical Writ-ings of Gottlob Frege* (Oxford: Blackwell, 1966), pp. 58–59.

yield to a complex name of a linguistic expression. Ambiguity and its cousins are one way to go with quotation. But as Kripke quips, ambiguity is "the lazy man's way in philosophy."[12] How else might we proceed? Consider another sort of quotation-device, *display*—by which one sets off a sentence on a new line in order to speak about it. While it is perhaps customary to assimilate display to quotation—as does, for example Quine—it seems more natural to assimilate quotation to display. Here's what I mean.

First, think about display this way: When one sets off a sentence on its own line, one draws attention to the sentence. That is not to say that one refers to the sentence. One makes it a subject of discourse without linguistic reference to it. One does not need an expression to refer to it, for one has something better, the item itself.[13] One can just, as it were, hold it up. The displayed sentence—appearing on the stage, as it were—need not be seen as having anything but its ordinary semantics, including truth value, references and meanings of the parts, and so on.

Now for quotation, assimilated to display: Given the story just told about display, why not think of quotation as similarly setting off a sentence—holding it up, presenting it? If so, a sentence set off by quotation marks is semantically innocent.

I have been reflecting on contexts in which sentences express without having their "normal," assertive function. Returning to indirect discourse, the first part of my idea was to adapt Quine's remarks so as to see the reporter's utterance of the embedded sentence as expressing without asserting. But the discussion of quotation and display suggests what is perhaps a further step or at least an additional perspective: indirect discourse as a context of display. Well, perhaps not exactly display.

Consider this actual practice. Someone in London asks (rhetorically), "What was Sam's point?"—assume that Sam uttered, in America, "Cicero was an orator." The rhetorical questioner, substituting for 'Cicero' the locally preferred 'Tully', answers himself, "Tully was an orator." Now imagine the following variant. One writes, "Sam's point is" and then on the next line one writes a sentence that provides a contextually appropriate paraphrase of

[12] Kripke, "Speaker's Reference and Semantic Reference" in *Contemporary Perspectives in the Philosophy of Language* (Minneapolis: University of Minnesota Press, 1979), p. 268.

[13] Cf. Searle in *Speech Acts: An Essay in the Philosophy of Language* (London: Cambridge University Press, 1969); and Wittgenstein, *Philosophical Investigations* §16.

Sam's original utterance. Or one writes, "Sam said," in a context in which it's clear that a paraphrase rather than an exact quotation is in question, and then on the next line writes the paraphrase.

My idea about indirect discourse is that "says that" creates just such a context. It's like display in that the embedded sentence occurs unasserted but with its semantics intact. It's unlike many contexts of display in that the embedded sentence is not just an object of attention, it's actually used to express something, although not to assert.

To sum up, I don't take the embedded sentence of an indirect discourse report as a device of reference,[14] nor do I take an indirect discourse sentence to be relational. "Says that" rather creates the sort of context just described—display or quasidisplay—and signals that what follows is a contextually appropriate paraphrase.[15]

1.5. The Desiderata

How does my approach fare with the desiderata? First, semantic innocence. As was noted, the embedded name in the reporter's mouth functions just as names always do. It is a Millian tag, naming what it always does. There are no senses here, no guises, no modes of presentation. Nor does the embedded sentence's semantically distinctive kind of function—it expresses without asserting—raise the specter of ambiguity. Sentences embedded in the antecedents and consequents of conditionals function similarly, and their occurrences do not prompt worries about ambiguity. Semantic innocence is thus respected.

The pragmatic strategy, championed by some direct reference advocates, is also semantically innocent. Indeed, following Grice,[16] the pragmatist is sort of fanatically anti-ambiguity. Grice assimilates 'but' to 'and', 'if, then' of ordinary English to the material

---

[14] Nor is it part of such a device as on the view that it's the expression "that *p*" that refers to the proposition asserted.

[15] My picture is a bit like Davidson's. Davidson says that the "that" in "He said that *p*" is a demonstrative, followed by a saying that is demonstrated. I don't have views about the precise function of the "that" and I want to avoid Davidson's (and the tradition's) idea that the sentence is relational. But I like the (Quinean) idea that the reporter does a distinctive kind of saying of the embedded sentence.

[16] See, for instance, H. P. Grice, *Studies in the Ways of Words* (Cambridge, Mass.: Harvard University Press, 1989); Peter Cole, ed., "Presuppositions and Conversational Implicature" in *Radical Pragmatics* (New York: Academic Press, 1997); and Grice, "Utterer's Meaning and Intentions," *The Philosophical Review* 69 (1978): 147–77.

conditional, and so on. In the current context, the pragmatist insists on the ordinary semantics of the embedded sentences. And he is willing to live with the consequent fudging on truth values. My account preserves semantic innocence without fudging. I embrace ordinary intuitions about truth values and explain substitutivity patterns by appeal to context. And I do so for the substitution of all sorts of expressions, even definite descriptions—not substitutable, preserving truth, according to both Fregeans and anti-Fregeans. Where actual practice suggests that substitution does not preserve truth, this is again a matter of context. Indeed, when the very expression used by the speaker is at issue in the context, then even synonymous expressions such as 'doctor' and 'physician' won't be intersubstitutable. Clearly, I am giving to context the central role of which I spoke.

Remember how puzzling it seemed that the same report can be true in one context and false in another? We can now make sense of this. What counts as a good paraphrase in one context can be disastrous in another. And so the claim that this is what he said can be right or wrong dependent upon context.

Let's turn to empty names. Someone says, "Vulcan is my favorite planet." The singular propositions picture renders both this assertion and the indirect discourse report of it problematic. Since there is no Vulcan, there is no singular proposition asserted, and so we can hardly report that the original speaker asserted that proposition. Nevertheless it ought to be uncontroversial that something was said and uncontroversial that it can be reported by, "She said that Vulcan is her favorite planet." On my view—without propositions—that's easy. The original occurrence of the empty name may be, in the vocabulary of chapter 7, a nonparadigm occurrence, but it is significant, Millian as ever, semantically innocent. That the report contains an empty name is also unproblematic; the reporter is not trying to capture a singular proposition asserted. She is merely paraphrasing the utterance, a project that would be considerably more difficult if one didn't use an empty name.

Quine draws attention to the fact that sometimes, he says "often": "there is just no saying whether to count an affirmation of propositional attitude as true or false, even given full knowledge of the circumstances and purposes."[17] This is also something that fits quite naturally with my picture. It's easy to imagine selecting a sentence that is and is not, so to speak, a good paraphrase. It comes

[17] Quine, *Word and Object*, p. 218.

pretty close to the original but maybe not close enough. It is somewhat attentive to what counts as contextually important to preserve, but again maybe not quite enough. These vagaries present a prima facie challenge to the traditional picture, but they fit well with my account. It would be surprising on the sort of conception I'm developing if this, as well as the substitutivity phenomena, didn't turn out quite as they do.

2. Extending the Account: Reporting Belief

2.1. Preliminary Sketch of a New Practice

The formerly primitive linguistic culture is increasingly sophisticated; indirect discourse is in place. But the linguistic engineer is hardly done. In a moment of epiphany he envisages a vastly more powerful use of putting words in people's mouths. The engineer's inspiration is this: Even when someone has not spoken on a topic, we are often in a position to speak for him, to put words in his mouth. Perhaps it never occurred to the agent to address the topic. Perhaps he has his reasons for reticence.[18] Still it may be evident to someone—or worth someone's speculating—what his verdict would be.

The new practice may begin with an eye to those who haven't spoken on a topic, but this hardly exhausts its range or significance. For even when one has spoken on a topic, one's remark may or may not be representative of one's overall view. The new sort of report may thus provide a person's all-things-considered view on a topic.

The reporter may thus have to distill a number of the agent's remarks. She may need to place those remarks in the context of the agent's behavior and of his life and culture. The embedded sentences of the new reports formulate what someone might say on the matter, whether or not one has said it.

In a word, the new reports ascribe *belief*, a term that originally connoted trust in someone or something. They do so by naming the agent, using the verb "to believe," and then adding a "that *p*" clause, embedding a sentence that formulates the view of the agent. Belief reports greatly exceed both ancestors—direct and indirect discourse—in power and utility. They are pivotal in explaining and

---

[18] The Ba'al Shem Tov, founder of Hasidism, suggested that each of us has a predetermined, quite finite number of words allotted. A person expires with his last word. A word to the wise.

predicting action and in keeping track of people's cognitive where-abouts.

To anticipate my philosophy of mind discussion in section 3, notice that my way of distinguishing indirect discourse and belief reports does not make the former merely a matter of the outer, speech; while the latter reports on the inner phenomenon, believing. Instead I'm emphasizing the wide variety of considerations—speech, behavior, and so on—to which belief reports are responsive; *said-that*-reports are responsive to something more local, more narrowly circumscribed. Certainly there are times when a person's verdict, her coming to a certain conclusion on a topic, does reflect something inner, perhaps various things that are inner in various senses. But the same can be said about a person's utterances.

2.2. Reporting Belief: A Conjuring Trick

Let's revisit Quine's "reporting as theater" idea. First, the reporter, as if she were preparing to act a part, engages the agent's perspective. Then she goes on to act the part. In her utterance of the embedded sentence she plays the agent, feigning his state of mind, speaking not only for him but as him.

I'll come to the second aspect in a moment. But the first aspect—making contact with the agent's perspective—plays a special role in reporting belief. The basis of an indirect discourse report is of course the original utterance. But with belief there may be no such generating utterance. And even where there is such an utterance, its role is less focal than with indirect discourse, as we have seen. In the absence of a generating utterance—or even in its presence—there are a variety of considerations to which the reporter may attend: the agent's remarks on related matters, his behavior, affective reactions,[19] features of his culture.

In discussing indirect discourse, I criticized the second aspect of Quine's reporting-as-theater idea. In our account of the reporter's utterance, we can settle for less than acting, less than feigning. And this is so for belief reporting as well. In both sorts of reports the embedded sentence—like a sentence in the mouth of an actor—expresses without asserting.

---

[19] When we consider the evidence for someone's believing something, we tend to emphasize the agent's behavior, verbal and other. But his affective reactions are also important, like his surprise at coming upon certain states of affairs, etc. Eric Schwitzgebel emphasizes this in his essay, "A Phenomenal, Dispositional Account of Belief," *Noûs* 36 (2002), 249–75.

I want to highlight something distinctive—different from indirect discourse—about the embedded sentence in belief reports, or about the way such embeddings are produced. The reporter then needs to engage in something of a conjuring trick. She throws into the hopper, as it were, the jumble of considerations mentioned earlier—related speech, behavior, affective reactions, culture. She factors in the reporting context. And out pops a sentence to embed.

The conjuring trick is dramatic when we are considering cases in which the believer has not spoken on the topic, but something similar is involved even when the agent has spoken. Since to report a belief is to report a verdict, the reporter's eye always needs to be ready to take in—and sometimes it will take in—a wider field than a single utterance. And so even when the agent has spoken on the topic, the conjuring abilities of the reporter may be called upon.

The magical aura is only increased when we reflect on the fact that in an important sense the reporter doesn't know what she is doing. She couldn't even begin to articulate many of the factors that go into her production of the to-be-embedded sentence. Of course this inarticulate competence is true of all of us in so many of our activities, linguistic or not. But here the level of complication seems more fantastic than usual.

There is a hint of this magical quality even in indirect discourse reporting. To digest the original utterance, the reporter may need to consider a similar miscellany: the original speaker's behavior, other things he may have said, various aspects of his culture. But in reporting speech, these factors need to be digested merely to help us interpret the agent's specific utterance, not to figure out what he thinks more generally.

The paraphrase idea from indirect discourse, although it has some purchase in the case of reporting belief, is not quite the right idea for belief. It is *as if* paraphrase were the right idea; *as if* we begin the belief reporting process with a sentence from the agent's repertoire which we then paraphrase. But we don't really do that. What we do instead is what I have been calling the conjuring trick.

The analogy with the paraphrase phenomenon of indirect discourse remains powerful, however, for there are similar constraints on the choice of a sentence to embed. First, the sentence must exhibit faithfulness to that toward which it glances backward. In the case of belief, this may include an utterance, if there was one, on the topic in question; it definitely includes the miscellany, the constellation of utterances, behavior, cultural considerations, and so on. Second, the chosen sentence must be appropriate to the current context, with all that involves.

2.3. Belief Reports as Summary Judgments and Kripke's Data

Sometimes things are simple. Someone remarks on a topic. His other utterances, behavior, and so on provide no reason not to take him at his word. And so we attribute the relevant belief to him. But not always. As I've said, attributing belief often involves distillation, summing up, an "all things considered" judgment.

Consider Kripke's example.[20] The bilingual Pierre says in Paris, *"Londres est jolie."* Back in the slums of London, speaking English and not realizing that the same city is in question, the same person denies that London is pretty. How is one to report, to distill, what Pierre believes? It seems wrong to say of him either that he believes that London is pretty or that he believes that it is not. Pierre's take on this question seems to resist formulation in the usual way.

To say that it resists formulation in the usual way is not to say that it is ineffable, that it cannot be formulated. As Kripke points out, we can tell the whole story as I have told it in the last paragraph. What Kripke emphasizes, and what I'm emphasizing, however, is the unavailability of an all-things-considered judgment, a formulation in terms of whether or not Pierre believes that London is pretty.

The problem, I think, is that Pierre's remarks in their various contexts don't fall in with one another in a way that allows a summary judgment. Nor, as Kripke says, can we put some of those remarks aside as no longer representing what he thinks. In more felicitous cases, an agent's remarks, behavior, and the rest, cohere; they feed more or less smoothly into an all-things-considered judgment. Kripke shows that such a verdict-formulating sentence is sorely lacking in Pierre's case.

Kripke's puzzle is what to say about Pierre's belief. But that there is no verdict is, I'm arguing, hardly puzzling. The ingredients of the miscellany fail to cohere with one another. Their failure, moreover, is not one that we can make good on, given our knowledge of the circumstances, people's ways, and so on. There just is no verdict.

[20] See his article, "A Puzzle About Belief" in A. Margalit, ed., *Meaning and Use* (Dordrecht; D. Reidel, 1979)

Similarly, imagine that an agent has made only one pronounce-
ment on the topic at hand: *"Londres est jolie."* But he lives in an
ugly part of London, as in the Kripke story. And although he has
never explicitly denied that London is pretty, it is obvious to his
friends that he would deny it. Again, the inputs fail to come together so as to yield an output sentence.

Somewhat similarly we might imagine a situation is which one
could not produce a correct report of speech. Think about cases in
which the goals of reporting speech cannot be simultaneously met,
in which faithful paraphrase seems to be incompatible with making
the original speaker's point accessible. Every good paraphrase seems
obscure in the new context, and every one that adequately commu-
nicates misses something important about the speaker's point.[21]

I'm not sure that in the end Kripke would disagree with any of
this. His view is that our belief-reporting practice breaks down in
cases like Pierre's. "Hard cases," he reminds us, "make bad law," a
worthwhile reminder in a time when it's fashionable in philosophy
to think of philosophical theorizing as pointedly focused on puzzle
cases. This remark of Kripke's is, I'm betting, another way of making the sort of point about reportage that I am making.

Kripke and I perhaps disagree over his principle of disquotation.
Kripke sets out this principle as having the force of necessity.[22] According to this principle, given a sincere utterance, we can infer
a corresponding belief report, obtained by embedding the uttered
sentence or a translation of it.[23] I agree that inferring belief from
sincere utterance is something we do with ease in most contexts.
But as I see the matter, such "disquotation" always involves a certain risk. This because of the "all-things-considered" character of
belief reports, the fact that they are potentially responsive to much
more than a single utterance.[24]

---

[21] Such a phenomenon seems possible also in cases of reporting belief. The problem in such a case would not be the indigestibility of the inputs, but rather the
problem of simultaneously satisfying the goals of reporting belief.

[22] Although given his resolution, perhaps that was a kind of plausible assumption Kripke advances, one that does not quite make it through Kripke's conclusion.

[23] When Kripke speaks of translation—he enunciates a "principle of translation"—my sense is that he speaks not about what I called actual translation, but of
the philosopher's ideal of capturing literal meaning in alternative words.

[24] My view thus has the consequence that a sincere utterance is not necessarily
one in accord with one's belief.

2.4. The Desiderata

My account of belief reports, like that of indirect discourse, is meant to provide a natural way to accommodate the desiderata mentioned at the beginning of the chapter. No such account was forthcoming from the traditionalists, Fregean or direct reference. The traditionalists' problem, as I see it, was not one of detail. It was rather a consequence of taking propositional content—whether explicated in terms of Fregean thoughts or singular propositions—as the master key. If one supposes that to report belief is to formulate a relation between a person and a propositional content, one makes the data from actual practice into a problem. The traditionalist is forced by that data to recognize in reporting belief something quite different than formulating the proposition believed. But such recognition is late and reluctant. The pragmatist struggles to keep whatever does not fit into the propositional content picture outside the pristine domain of semantics. The semantic defense struggles to build it into the semantics. My aim has been to accommodate the data without a struggle. In my corner has been a secret weapon. I have been unencumbered by propositional content.

Notice that the data from substitutivity patterns now fall into place. As Quine taught, the substitution patterns reflect what is important in the context. There are contexts in which the agent's mode of identifying the person about whom he has a belief may not be of great interest. In such contexts, therefore, substitution may be the rule. In terms of one of the examples I gave, when speaking to Brits the reporter may freely substitute 'Tully' for the American speaker's 'Cicero'. But where the agent's way of identifying the referent is very much in question, the same substitution may turn a truth into a falsehood.

Another desideratum is semantic innocence. As with indirect discourse, names that occur in the embedded sentence of a belief report do their regular Millian thing. The reporter just speaks the embedded sentence, expressing without asserting.

Turning to empty names, sometimes such a name seems just the ticket for a belief report. Say the agent expressed himself with a name such as 'Zeus'. If we divert our focus from propositional content and see the reporter's goal as something more like paraphrase—or finding an output sentence that properly attends to the miscellany—then the use of an empty name ceases to present a problem. This solution feels right: We do think that various people believe in gods that do not exist, and we can say so using the gods' names. We thus capture their beliefs. Singular propositions seem beside the point.

Finally, something that is not quite a desideratum: Throughout this book I have shown sympathy for Wittgenstein's idea that classic philosophical problems—according to me at least some—stand in need of dissolution. But *dissolution* is a delicate business, easily subject to misuse. So, as I have said, I don't start aiming for dissolution; it's rather something that can emerge from a sustained look at a classical problem and its classical solutions. In earlier chapters I tried to make this vivid, for example with regard to informative identities in chapter 6, the significance of empty names in 7, and earlier, in chapter 5, the problem of explaining reference. We have now seen something like dissolution with regard to the notorious puzzle about substitutivity. Direct reference, we were told, founders on the rocks of substitutivity; a Millian view cannot accommodate the obvious fact that someone can believe that Cicero was an orator without believing that Tully was. We have now seen, or I have now argued, that my sort of Millianism faces no such threat; no special help is needed with substitutivity.

3. Finally, Terra Firma

Some years ago I was discussing the subjects of this book with a colleague who shared much of the perspective for which I have been arguing. We could see our way to more adequate conceptions on many of the issues. Belief, however, stumped us. The focus of our discussion was not semantics but rather the philosophy of mind, the phenomenon of believing. Frege's first core idea—the relational conception of believing—felt very powerful, even if we were prepared to question it. But we had no idea how to proceed.

I'll turn now to a way of thinking about belief that comports both with my semantic account of belief reports and with the overall outlook I have been emphasizing. To return to intuitions I emphasized in chapter 3, I want to start with what's out in the open— not with the mind, but with linguistic practice. There is here even more reason than usual to so proceed, for believing is a very different sort of mental phenomenon than, for example, pain. A person has a grip on his own pain that is—so it seems—independent of the ways we talk of pain. This seems much less evident, even much less plausible, with believing. One has to work much harder to defend the idea that believing is something we simply notice going on within.[25] In any case, taking my cue from what is out in the open, let me ask, what does our study of belief reporting suggest about the mental phenomenon?

Here is a feature of my semantic account that is suggestive: Belief reports are—like their indirect discourse forebears—nonrelational. The verb "to believe" does not refer to a relation between an agent and a content; rather it indicates that what follows is the agent's take on the question at hand. Such a nonrelational semantic account suggests that the subject matter under discussion is, whatever else it is, not a relational phenomenon. But what is it, this phenomenon under discussion?

Traditionally, views that don't see believing as constituted by a relation between a person and a proposition tend to suppose that believing is something like a dispositional state. To believe that *p* is to be disposed to say certain things (in certain circumstances), to have certain kinds of thought episodes, to do certain things, and the like. Indeed, whether or not believing is relational, it's natural to wonder about the place of certain tendencies or dispositions. In the prior discussion I haven't spoken of dispositions. I have, however, spoken of something closely related, of a miscellany of factors to which belief ascription is responsive, including speech, behavior, and the like.

In what follows I will refer to the miscellany of factors as coherences. The idea is that associated with a particular belief will be a certain constellation of typical kinds of remarks, thought episodes, behaviors, perhaps affective reactions, and the like, in various ways keyed to circumstances.

I just spoke of an association of believing with the coherences. Certainly there is such an association. The question is how to specify that association further, to situate the coherences properly with respect to belief, neither to slight their role nor to elevate it. I'll argue in a moment that some discussions in the philosophical literature tend to do one or the other. But before plunging in, let me say a bit more by way of setting up the discussion.

I noted earlier what I hope is uncontroversial, that we look to the coherences in attributing belief, that we use as evidence for belief facts about how someone has behaved, what one has said, and

---

[25] As Wittgenstein suggests in *On Certainty*, degrees of conviction may be different.

so on. But there is a more fundamental (and nonevidential) relation between belief and the coherences: Belief-talk—certainly in its paradigm applications—presupposes such coherences. Those to whom we paradigmatically attribute belief are creatures who exhibit such coherences. Belief-talk applies with a certain strain to creatures who partially exhibit such patterns but whose equipment or development precludes the full range—for example, nonlinguistic animals or preverbal infants. Some philosophers deny belief to such creatures. This view seems excessive but its existence signals an attenuated application of belief-talk.[26]

Back to situating the coherences vis-à-vis belief. Philosophers of language influenced by Frege (or by the traditional philosophical ideas that influenced Frege) tend to slight the coherences. If one construes believing as mental assent to a grasped content, one may relegate the coherences to mere causal consequences of believing. On the other extreme, there is a tradition in the philosophy of mind which elevates the coherences. In the spirit of Ryle, one might thus identify believing with a particular range of coherences—or dispositions.

To begin with Frege's way, the assent-to-a-content idea may slight the coherences by making them inessential. For according to this idea, believing becomes not essentially embodied, something that could be going on with an unembodied Cartesian mind. Angels—who according to St. Thomas think without the use of language—might thus believe as we do; their differences from us would pertain only to the causal consequences of belief, the coherences. (This may or may not bother one. It bothers me since it presumes the ability to have some sort of grip on the mental life of a creature whose mental life is not connected with our world and our ways of making contact with the world.)

Nowadays the assent-to-a-content picture is likely to be wedded to a physiculistic reduction of the mental. Thus the charge of disembodiment looks to be mooted. But not quite. As Putnam[27] and

---

[26] Think of the application of belief-talk to animals and infants as a natural enough extension of the concept. Somewhat similarly, talk of unconscious belief can be seen as a natural—even if a late and ingenious—extension. Unconscious believers exhibit enough of the sort of coherent pattern with belief that *p* to be counted among the believers, even if their "belief" is not, in the ordinary course of things, available to them.

[27] See Putnam's "The Dewey Lectures," *The Journal of Philosophy* 91, no. 9, (1994): 445–517, for a discussion of this well-discussed but still insufficiently appreciated phenomenon.

others have pointed out, Cartesian-spirited views of the mind often find up-to-date versions in brain and neurological terms. A closer connection between believing and the coherences seems to me called for.

Now for the other extreme: To identify believing with the having of a constellation of tendencies certainly provides a more central place for the coherences. Believing becomes an essentially embodied phenomenon. This is for me congenial.

Further in its favor, this view of belief, unlike the relation-to-a-content picture, does not see believing as a mental state that explains the surface phenomena. Recall my discussion in chapter 5 of the Fregean-spirited attempt to get beneath, behind, the phenomenon of reference, to provide a substantial explanation of the connection between words and things. Also recall my contrary Wittgenstein-spirited attempt to stay at the surface. So the identification of belief with the coherences seems congenial in this way as well.

Still, this view of belief is not, in my view, correct; it gives the coherences too prominent a role. While the practice of reporting belief presupposes and gives an evidential role to the coherences and relies on them, a belief report does not have such coherences as its subject matter. It does not make a claim about the coherences. To say what someone believes is not—as the first view of belief would have it—to take a stand on a mental state that underlies the surface phenomena in question. But it's also not to assert anything about a constellation of tendencies. It is rather just to speak for the agent on the question at hand.

If what the reporter articulates in the name of the agent is in fact the agent's view, then the agent will exhibit the pattern in question. But this doesn't make the pattern the subject matter of the belief report. Compare indirect discourse. When an indirect discourse report is true—when the reporter correctly articulates something said by the agent—there may be various things that must be true about the agent, things that are involved in assertion. But that fact doesn't mean that the reporter refers to those things in her report. She merely speaks for the agent, articulates the point of his utterance (or at least a currently relevant point of that utterance).

Our belief-reporting practice represents our way of keeping track of one another with respect to such patterns, coherences. We keep track by uttering the embedded sentence and thus exemplifying the constellation of tendencies. That we do it this way is telling about us. One can imagine other ways of tracking cognitive location; for example by acting out scenes in the name of—or as—the "believer." But our practice is not like that. We are inveterate talkers, and our tracking practice writes this large, involving as it does putting words in the agent's mouth.

But what has happened to believing in all this? That was our topic, after all. It's not that which underlies the symptoms nor is it the constellation of tendencies. What's left? Here is my radical suggestion: Taking our cue from the reports, perhaps we have been looking in vain for some sort of state or process of believing. We refer to no such state or process when we report belief. We just speak for the person.

What I am proposing coheres nicely with something that Arthur Collins has been arguing for years.[28] While my concern here has been with third-person belief ascription, Collins has been largely focused upon first-person expression of belief: "I believe that *p*." He has argued forcefully that the only subject matter of such assertions is *p*, not some state, process, or condition of the agent's mind. From Collins's point of view, a dispositional account of belief is not much better than one that sees belief as a state of a Cartesian mind: both views take the subject matter of first-person belief locutions to be something about the agent. Collins sometimes expresses his view by saying that belief has no inner constitution. And that's what I'm arguing. Just as Collins sees first-person remarks as ways of asserting *that p*, I see third-person belief ascriptions as ways of putting *that p* in the agent's mouth, of expressing *that p* on behalf of the agent.

My view here certainly does not represent the way I approached this matter at first, or even long after. I said at the beginning of this section that fairly late in the day I couldn't imagine an alternative to Frege's first core idea. That's so in part because I thought of believing as, so to speak, a piece of nature, to be explained like any other. Compare the concept of *water*. There is the substance, water, and then linguistic practice evolves so as to make room for or take notice of this natural item. Similarly, I supposed that in the (relative) beginning there was believing, and our practice of reporting belief evolved to report the facts about believing. But if I am right, believing is very different. With believing, the linguistic practice of

---

[28] Collins should not get the credit for my version of it. I'm joking, since he does not agree that we agree.

belief ascription—to use J. L. Austin's happily outdated expression—wears the pants. That practice evolved as a way of keeping track of people cognitively, that is, with respect to the coherences. But the reports do not involve reference to the coherences, nor, as I have argued, to a content believed, or even to a belief relation.[29]

[29] In this chapter I have attempted something of a fundamental reorientation. It seems to be the fate of such attempts to raise questions, and sometimes to leave questions pending, that the received view seemed to accommodate en passant, questions like the following: What becomes of belief-desire explanations of action? Are they causal explanations? How can they be on such an ethereal picture of belief? What becomes of the usual philosophical idea that sincere speech is speech caused by belief? And of course many others. Some of these I have pondered and could almost write about; others await study.

10

Whither Propositions?

Propositions occupy an honored place early in this book, as they have for me since my undergraduate days. It seemed in chapter 1 that they were my central concern, the book's focal issue. Scrutiny of Frege's view of propositions, however, led naturally to a shift in focus, from propositions to Frege's basic semantic picture, the fundamental ideas of which are sense and reference. As I explored Frege's outlook and, in chapter 2, its connections and contrasts with Russell's, other topics came to the fore—the cognitive fix requirement, for example. But what began as a mere shift in attention became something very different. Propositions did not find a natural home in my developing anti-Fregean conception.

Clearly I'm advocating a different "direct reference" from that of much of the literature. Direct reference is often seen as advancing its own (Russell/Kaplan) explication of propositional content. It might even be supposed—I indeed once thought—that direct reference is all about propositions that contain objects, that this is the movement's central concern, its virtual raison d'être.[1] By my current lights much of what has been called direct reference theory,

---

[1] Kripke also doesn't appear to see the inclusion of propositions as vital to his project. Not that he ever addresses this straightaway, but in *Naming and Necessity* propositions don't show up. And when they do get mentioned in Kripke's later article, "A Puzzle About Belief," in A. Margalit, ed., *Meaning and Use* (Dordrecht: D.

216

notwithstanding its critique of Frege, is an attempt to work out Fregean ideas in the context of a new set of issues, for example, the modal problems that Kripke highlighted in Lecture I of *Naming and Necessity*. If such is the project, then propositions will figure centrally in it.

Throughout this chapter, when I speak of propositions, I have in mind the Russell/Kaplan explication; some of what I say, though, will be more generally applicable, for example to Fregean thoughts.

1. Propositions as Abstract Entities

Even at the beginning of my thinking about these matters, propositions' pivotal position was less than completely secure. I was worried about Platonism, about propositions as abstract entities, a worry that receded with time. At the same time, the philosophical turn at the heart of this book provided other reasons to be skeptical about propositions. The way I would have put it until recently is this: The emerging social practice picture suggests the rejection of the very category of *propositional content*. But this seems too rigid. The way I would put it now is what I want to explore here. I'll begin with Platonism.

There are (at least) two major objections to Platonism. A metaphysical objection concerns ontological extravagance. Quine thus speaks of his "taste for desert landscapes," his desire to make do with a minimal ontology. And Benacerraf[2] puts his finger on the epistemological issue: How can it be that we make any sort of causal contact with a realm of abstracta? And without causal contact, how can we come to know truths about them?

My qualms were much less sophisticated. (I mean this seriously and straightforwardly.) I could not wrap my mind around abstract objects. The very idea of *a thing* that was at the same time *abstract* engendered a kind of vertigo. What would it be like for an "abstract entity" to exist? If there were such things, then presumably a complete inventory of the world would include not only things like people, chairs, and tables, but also things like numbers, sets, propositions. It is not so much that I could not believe this. I couldn't quite get it.

Reidel, 1979), they get a kind of passing and slightly uncomfortable mention. Kripke is the exception, though. As powerful as the impact of his work is, his lack of attention to propositions is rarely commented upon or even noted.

[2] See Benacerraf, "Mathematical Truth," *Journal of Philosophy* (73) 1970: 661–79.

The reactions I received when I expressed such misgivings were mixed. Some people seemed of like mind. Others—I remember this vividly from graduate school—stared at me as if I was being . . . inconvenient. I do think there was something to my worry; I'll get to that in a moment. But I can understand some of what put people off, or I think I can.

Abstract vocabulary is ubiquitous, on the face of it a crucial component of our thinking on virtually every topic. That this vocabulary stimulates philosophical wonder is hardly news; the difficulties are well known and of very wide scope. Given that the philosophical issues, no matter how thorny, will never call into question the relevant cognitive abilities—abstract thinking and all that it affords—those philosophical issues will have to wait, eventually to work themselves out somehow. Why then bristle over a single case? Why not bracket the issue, say about propositions, and move on to matters of substance in the local domain? Here's an analogy from political philosophy.

Reflection on modern-day politics and political theory prompts worries like these: What sorts of things are *rights?* Are rights to be thought of as *properties?* Does taking rights seriously mean that one is committed to them ontologically? Whatever one does with these questions, it's important that they not get in the way. A political philosopher might well put these problems to the side and get on with business, exploring, say, the question of how the notion of rights integrates with other modern political ideas. Or what does the centrality of such an idea in a culture, or in the culture's philosophical expression, signal about its conception of the human being or its overall outlook. These are the sorts of matters that figure in a considered political philosophy. Political philosophies rarely founder on the rocks of ontology.[3]

---

[3] My point about priorities may be generalized. There are many contexts in which it is worth considering the bracketing of "philosophically fundamental" issues and attending first to matters of local substance. Here is a different sort of example, from the philosophy of religion. At an early (but extended) stage of reflection on religion, I took the first questions to be whether God exists, what exactly this means, and how it might ever be established. I now think that these questions—certainly fundamental—are better addressed considerably later. They may, if given too prominent a place, become obstacles to clarity.

My instincts were admittedly otherwise. Part of the transition for me was the sense that at work in the religious tradition is quite a different take on human flourishing from what is current in our culture. God-talk is both central to that different take and, by my current lights, a much more complex and subtle business than is often supposed. Its original context is not theology as practiced by philosophers and their theological cousins. Its original context—and largely its current context for

The pressing issue with propositions is thus not their abstractness. It is utility. Does the notion figure—and how centrally does it figure—in our understanding of language? Before turning to such local matters of substance, I want to suggest an additional motivation for emphasizing local concerns, for the thought that abstractness per se should not put us off. This new motivation issues not from methodological ideas about priorities, but rather from a positive intuition about abstract language and thought, one that may put to rest my original worries about abstract entities. The matter deserves much more attention than I can give it here, but let me indicate the direction of my thinking.

To think abstractly is to attend selectively, to leave unattended various aspects of the subject matter. The question is whether the explanation of selective attention involves hypostatizing the objects, as it were, of attention. That abstract vocabulary involves hypostatization is the conventional wisdom, encapsulated in the terminology of ontological commitment. The legitimacy of proposition-talk, or number-talk, or property-talk will then depend upon whether positing the relevant entities is necessary to make sense of our world. The analogy is with positing theoretical entities in physics.

That selective attention involves hypostatization seems far from obvious. One reason concerns general terms and categorization. My contention is that the naturalistic picture of our categories as rough and ready presents an obstacle to hypostatization, to seeing general terms as, for example, connoting properties. But this is a very difficult matter about which I never quite feel that I have adequately articulated the intuition. I hope that my anti-hypostatization sense will become clearer as we proceed: I discuss general terms and categorization in the second half of section 2 and in section 3 I argue for an approach to "what is said" according to which this has little to do with the idea of propositional content.

For the moment, let me glean some support from Berkeley's "Introduction" to his 1710 *Treatise Concerning The Principles Of*

---

participants—is poetry and poetic prose, as in the Bible. The implications of this linguistic turn are enormous. One is in danger of missing them, however, if one's early focus is on the questions of first philosophy.

Since I take God-talk to play a substantive role in one powerful approach to life and the world, it has for me a prima facie legitimacy. What the concept is in the end doing, what it amounts to, how it is to be understood—these really difficult and fundamental questions are better left until later. Their resolution is a subtle, delicate business.

Human Knowledge. Berkeley is no fan of abstract ideas. He thinks there are no such ideas and that none are necessary to explain the general character of thought and discourse. *Ideas* for Berkeley play many of the roles of *things* for us. So his abstract (he might prefer "general") thought and talk without abstract ideas is suggestive of abstract thought and talk without abstract entities as referents. Here is a sketch of his picture in a bit more detail:

> There are no abstract ideas. An idea is always a particular idea, a particular concrete perception.[4] For example, there cannot be an idea of a shape or a color alone, a shape or color abstracted from a shaped and colored item. One can *attend* specifically to the shape or to the color, mentally leaving behind, ignoring, the other aspects. And one can use a particular concrete image to stand for other perceptions of like color or shape. Such an idea, used to stand for other ideas, gains a kind of generality. But this is a generality of function; the idea remains concrete and particular.
>
> Similarly for linguistic expressions. Since there are no ideas that are ideas of a color alone, a color in abstraction, we cannot have a name for such an idea. But just as we can attend specifically to the color—leaving behind the rest—we can have a name that linguistically attends, as it were, only to the color. And as with functionally general ideas, names too can attain a kind of functional generality. The word 'red', for example, stands for many particular ideas, no one of which is an idea of red alone.

My Berkelean suggestion, then, is that selective attention to the greenness of a leaf does not involve a new entity, a hypostatization of the color. And just as we can selectively attend, so we can talk about the color. None of this requires the posit of a greenness entity—the sort of posit that may or may not be justified.

If my divorcing abstraction from hypostasis has merit, then my original worry about abstracta was quite beside the point, since no special abstract items, referents, are required to make sense of abstract talk. What I'm suggesting would put me at odds with Quine and much of twentieth century literature on ontological commitment, a source of both disquiet and excitement. It also may have implications for the Benacerraf problem. For if we don't have new entities, then there is no special problem about casual contact. We do, after all, have contact with colored things. Maybe that's enough

---

[4] Berkeley, like others in the empiricist tradition, takes *idea* to mean perception, image.

to generate knowledge of colors. This is, though, all too quick. And how exactly does it apply, say, to numbers? Still, I'm hoping that what I say is suggestive.

Some years ago one used to hear the injunction that philosophy ought not legislate for other branches of learning. Short of legislation, philosophers sometimes attempt to make good on philosophically troublesome ideas in other fields by proposing reductive analyses, also a perilous business. In the spirit of neither legislating nor legitimizing, my idea is to let the rather ubiquitous abstract talk speak for itself, not reduce it to anything else, not to propose meanings that seem extravagant. Abstract talk is fine as it stands, not involving ontological commitments, so called, that raise metaphysical and epistemological hackles.

2. Propositions: A Dubious Inheritance

Before turning in the next section to questions of local utility, I'll first explore my sense that the notion of propositional content, inherited from Frege and given new form by direct reference advocates, represents a theoretical burden. My first reason concerns representationalism; I'll suggest that the anti-representational tendency of direct reference and the idea of propositional content make strange bedfellows. Second, I'll turn to the clarity and distinctness of thought. In that connection I speak not for direct reference advocates generally but for myself. The framework I've been developing here makes it especially unnatural to theorize in terms of propositions.

Language is a representational medium. A crucial question is whether we need to posit further, nonlinguistic representations—in the mind, brain, or a third realm—to make sense of linguistic representation? The traditional approach—broadly Cartesian in the terminology of this book—so supposes; Frege posits arch-representational senses without which mere words could not do their work. Direct reference, as I am developing it, is radically antirepresentational. Reference is seriously direct: No senses, no modes of presentation, not even characters-as-mini-modes-of-presentation or casual chains as mediators. Millian names provide a model—they just stand for the bearers to whom they have been assigned.

Propositions, though, are representational entities. This can be confusing when one is thinking about singular propositions, for they are constituted not by the arch-representational senses but by plain things and properties.[5] As I noted in chapter 6, moreover, Kaplan sometimes speaks of his propositions as if they were more like states of affairs or even facts than like traditional propositions. Still, if propositions are to be bearers of truth and falsity, they had better be representational. For to say of something that it's true is to say that the world is the way it's represented as being.

Propositions, the "contents" of sentences, thus constitute a representational stratum between sentences and the world, one that fits perfectly with the traditional outlook. This mediating semantic layer is also the home, on the singular propositions picture, of the objects of the attitudes. Direct reference, developed in terms of singular propositions, is thus heavily representational.

Something seems out of sync here with the antirepresentational strain that looms so large for me and for much of early direct reference—the insistence in Kripke and Donnellan, for example, that there is no such mediating stratum for, say, proper names. More so if one assumes, as I do, that an important desideratum for an account of general terms—I'll sketch my view in a moment—will be a similarly unmediated connection with the world. Here is a more congenial alternative: Sentences, built out of linguistic items that represent directly, themselves directly represent the world as being a certain way—no propositional intermediaries. If one is worried about bearers of truth, it seems more natural to let the sentences themselves be the things that are right or wrong, true or false. But more about this issue in section 3.

So much for representationalism. Let's move on to the second of the anti-propositions considerations. One of the hallmarks of the broadly Cartesian outlook is its emphasis on the well-behaved character, what I'm calling the clarity and distinctness of thought. Frege's contention that a concept without sharp boundaries is no concept at all provides an illustration. The concept of a proposition is perfectly natural in such an environment. For Frege, propositions—his *thoughts*—are constituted by sharply bounded senses. They are complete in every respect and, elevated above their sometime sentential embodiments, they cannot suffer from any number of what Frege sees as maladies that affect natural language, for example, vagueness and ambiguity. What is less clear is that propositions are natural adjuncts to my more naturalistic way of thinking about language and thought. Let me explain.

---

[5] And while properties are abstract, arguably they are not representational; they are aspects of objects. I believe this point was made to me some time ago by Joseph

The Fregean and I agree that natural language falls far short of Frege's conception of a logically or scientifically appropriate language. Frege's ideal. As I see it, however, Frege's ideal supervenes on a mythology: Frege takes mathematical thought to provide a model for thought generally, and he probably mythologizes mathematical thought itself. To discern the character of thought, contrary to Frege, one cannot directly march on the castle: "Instead of starting out with such large, vexing subjects as soul, mind, ideas, consciousness, why not set forth with language, which no one denies, and see how far it takes us toward the rest."[6]

Think of the origins of natural language in prelinguistic culture: brutes bumping into each other and grunting, the grunts evolving, getting more and more articulate as they need to be for purposes at hand. Absolute clarity and precision await messianic times. In the real world we have natural language, and the thought actually expressed by that language, however great the distance to some idealized conception of thought.

I fear that this way of putting the matter makes it sound as if natural language were deficient, the way the real world might be thought sorely lacking vis-à-vis some messianic future. Idealizations, though, have their own limitations. It is no longer clear that we are speaking of humans when we so idealize their virtues that they no longer have characteristic struggles with the world and with themselves, when there is no competition, when a godly love is altogether easy. What would the lives of such creatures be like?[7] Similarly, one may wonder whether the Fregean third realm of concepts and a logically perfect language to match would be such a good thing. What Frege took to be deficiencies may turn out to be virtues.

How so? One example is furnished by a commonplace observation about the vagueness of so many ordinary terms. Consider

---

Almog. This is presumably a difference between properties and concepts, the latter being representational.

[6] Quoted from Walker Percy, "The Delta Factor," collected in Walker Percy, *The Message in the Bottle: How Queer Man Is, How Queer Language Is, and What One Has to Do with the Other* (New York: Farrar, Straus, and Giroux, 1984), p. 17.

[7] In his wonderful science-fiction novel, *Star Maker* (1937; New York: Dover, 1968), philosopher Olaf Stapledon tells of coming across humanoid creatures who had reached a point in their evolution that they were ideally suited to their world. A consequence was that intelligence quickly deteriorated as vestigial. Also see Thomas Nagel's story, almost a parable, in *The View From Nowhere* (New York: Oxford University Press, 1989), of the spider in the urinal. Nagel tells of saving a spider from the Sisyphean fate of climbing up the urinal walls only to wash down

"rain." The utility of much of our ordinary talk of rain depends upon the fact that the concept is hardly sharply bounded. A quantitatively precise term for precipitation would be much less useful than our mushy term "rain." Vagueness is in this sense hardly an aberration.

Here we can begin to see the problem for propositions. How do we understand the proposition expressed by a sentence that contains a vague term? Frege presumably would have denied that there is a straightforward route from such a sentence to a propositional content. Perhaps the speaker is gesturing in the direction of several *thoughts*, each of them quite precise.

No doubt there will be responses to the problem just posed. One might maintain, for example, that propositions, just like the natural language sentences that express them, can be vague. Perhaps, but the idea of a proposition that is itself vague has the aroma of a fall-back position. In this way the suggestion is similar to one concerning the metaphysics of properties: That in the face of vagueness, we should suppose that properties can be vague.

Let's press on to another linguistic phenomenon that Frege— had he recognized it at all—would have taken to be a foible of natural language. At issue here is another important virtue of actual linguistic practice, one that creates a severe problem for propositions.

The phenomenon in question concerns general terms, an underexplored domain in the anti-Fregean literature.[8] How might one informed by the anti-Fregean approach to singular terms begin to approach general terms? What lessons might one carry forward? Mill is apparently quite traditionalist about general terms, seeing them as connoting properties that determine the terms' denotations. This might suggest that competence with a general term involves a grasp of the relevant properties. And this is something about which our experience with singular terms should make us wary. Competence, we should instead suppose, is a matter of practical know-how, the mastery of a practice. One is introduced to some examples and gets

---

with the next flush. Nagel rescued the spider, placing in on the dry land of the bathroom floor, only to find it the next day dried up there.

[8] There is, of course, a literature inspired by Putnam and Kripke on natural kinds. But the Kripke/Putnam position on natural kind terms has always seemed to me less well articulated and argued than anti-Fregean positions on names and indexicals. Moreover, the extension of the views of Kripke and Putnam to general terms more broadly considered—that is, beyond natural kinds—is relatively unexplored.

a feel for how to proceed, a sense of what counts as included in the category and what as not included. No doubt this sense is built upon more primitive or general competences, a feel, for example, for the ways we categorize.

I want to take issue with another aspect of Mill's approach to general terms. Mill's talk, and philosophical talk generally, of the denotation of a general term makes it sound as if there were associated with a term a determinate class, one determined by a property or set of properties. However, general considerations about the origins and development of language (like the bodies-bumping picture of origins I presented earlier in this section) as well as arguments by Wittgenstein and others make a powerful case for a very different way of thinking about general terms, and about our actual practices of categorization.

The idea is that our categorizations are often rough and ready—think of Wittgenstein's family resemblance examples—and hardly involve the sort of exact similarity that property-talk suggests in philosophy, a numerical identity underlying the instances. Accordingly, talk of properties determining the denotation of general terms will turn out to be mythological, potentially as misleading as talk, in the context of proper names, of senses determining reference. One might still find property-talk, which is after all not limited to philosophy, helpful. Such talk capitalizes on the fact that in many contexts it's not important how exact the relevant similarity is between the "instantiations" of the property, the members of the category. Talk of the property of being a game is thus harmless and sometimes useful.

What are the implications for propositions? A singular proposition is supposed to be an ordered pair of an object and a property. As I say, I don't mind property-talk, until one needs a property-entity to do a philosophical job, like that of filling a slot in a proposition. If much of our categorization is rough and ready, then for many of our assertions, we will fail to have a property to put in the predicate position of the singular proposition. This looks to be a serious problem.

Direct reference advocates, certainly me included, have been so focused on *reference*—on the singular term slot of a singular proposition—that the predicate slot was almost an afterthought. The properties would somehow take care of themselves. Indeed, Kaplan has suggested that perhaps the Fregean sense of a predicate might constitute the predicate constituent of a singular proposition. Given Kaplan's aversion to senses, I suppose this was an off-the-cuff remark; it perhaps reveals how focused Kaplan was upon the subject position.[9] My view, then, is that the concept of propositional content, specifically the Kaplan/Russell explication, is hardly a natural adjunct to the sort of picture I have been developing.

3. Local Utility

3.1. Propositions as Objects of the Attitudes

Classically, the two main functions of propositions are as primary or proper bearers of truth and falsity, and as objects of propositional attitudes. I'll begin with the latter function.

I've argued in the last two chapters against Frege's two core ideas, one semantic, one in the philosophy of mind. On the side of semantics, I argued for a non-relational reading of attitude sentences. A reporter uses a *that p* clause not in reference to a proposition but rather as a way of speaking for the agent whose thought, belief, speech is being reported. On the side of the philosophy of mind as well, propositions had no role. The sort of account I sketched was far removed from the traditional conception of believing as mental assent to an apprehended proposition.

It's not that I've avoided propositions, found ways to work around them. It's rather that they didn't find a natural place in the emerging account. And it's not that their abstractness made them problematic. If the received view of attitude sentences was correct—attitude reports as formulating a relation between an agent and a propositional content—then ordinary attitude reports would involve reference to propositional abstracta. The abstraction, according to me, would be unobjectionable. But ordinary talk does not involve any such abstraction.

I have been focused on attitude reports, but there is a linguistic phenomenon that might be thought to lend support to propositions, to the idea that we indeed speak in the abstract way in question, abstracting, for example, across utterances with respect to their semantic contents. Perhaps I wish to identify a remark you just made with one made by someone else. Clearly the utterances were distinct, one yours, one his. But, as we would say, you made the same point he made, you said the same thing, even . . . you and he said *that p*. We also speak this way about belief or thought: You and he

---

[9] In a conversation with John Perry some years ago about such passages, he told me he thought Kaplan was joking.

agree, you both think (believe) the same thing, namely *that p.* In such cases, isn't it propositional content that is at issue? Aren't we abstracting across utterances, for example, in just the way I have been denying? Moreover, isn't doing so counter to my view about the semantics of attitude sentences, according to which *that p* is not a referring phrase? In the sort of example just cited, we speak of two people saying the same thing and then seem to specify that thing with the expression *that p.*

Let me being with the semantics of *that p* in such contexts. We should remember that the contexts we are discussing are contexts of indirect discourse and attitude reports. Accordingly, if one takes *that p* to designate a content-entity, one invites many of the same puzzles and problems of substitutivity and the rest that I noted in chapter 8. Instead we can proceed along the lines of my discussion in chapter 9. If in reporting what you say or believe, I put words in your mouth, then in reporting what they both say or believe, I put words in their mouths; I speak for them. If "S believes that *p*" works as I suggest in chapter 9, then so does "S and T both believe that *p.*" And so does "S and T believe the same thing, namely that *p*"; this is to say that both of them believe that *p.* Perhaps the reader will think that I am pushing matters here, that "the same thing" ought to mean "the single entity which is identical in both cases." I'm not sure; but it's far from clear to me that the sort of idiomatic reading I'm suggesting is unnatural.

In the commonly cited examples of the same-saying, same-believing phenomenon two people utter very simple sentences like "It's raining," and its relatively exact equivalent, for example the French "Il pleut." Or ones in which there is a switch in indexicals: I say "I am tired" and you say to me "You are tired." If we focus on such examples, it can appear that what is in question is semantic content. But actual judgments that the same thing was said typically involve a much looser relation between the remarks. Two people express a political opinion with sentences that are hardly exact equivalents; if what their utterances "come to" is not much different with respect to what's at issue in the context, we count them as having said, or as believing, the same thing. "Same content" judgments—the imagery of content seems apt—are thus highly context relative. Two utterances may or may not count as saying the same thing; it depends upon what's at stake in the context.

Our colloquial "said the same thing" is thus hardly the philosopher's idea of propositional identity. Indeed the phenomenon in question—actual practice with expressions like "said (thought, believe) the same thing"—illustrates the point I was making in the previous chapter. With "same-saying," just as with the substitutivity patterns, it is something more like paraphrase than propositional identity that informs our judgments. Two people say or believe the same just in case their remarks are good enough paraphrases—relative to context, purposes, and so on—of one another.

I agree then that to talk of saying—thinking, believing—the same thing is to abstract across, say, utterances. But on the analogy of property-talk, this doesn't mean that we have laid our hands on a single semantic content. It means instead that we are identifying two different speech acts—perhaps utterances of very different sentences—finding enough similarity to count them as the same for a certain purpose.

3.2. Propositions as Truth Bearers

Let's turn to the role of propositions with which I started in chapter 1, propositions as truth bearers. There is an intuition—I quoted it there in the name of Cohen and Nagel (but I could have mentioned Strawson in "On Referring"[10] and lots of others as well)—that there is something awkward, if not worse, about taking sentences to be the things that are in the first instance true or false. Why is that so? Sentences, so the intuition goes, are mere symbolic devices. It's not the constellation of words that are right or wrong in the primary sense but rather what they say.

This is an intuition that had sway with me for a long time. In chapter 1 I laid out the appealing picture of propositional content in which it is grounded, Frege's. But Frege's picture was in the end unacceptable. The current candidate is Kaplan's, an ordered pair (in simple cases) of object and property. Do Kaplan's propositions fit the bill?

One immediate problem for singular propositions as truth bearers is this: An ordered pair is certainly no more intuitive a candidate for truth bearer than is a sentence. Indeed, much less so. Why would one suppose that an abstract entity such as a pair (in the mathematical sense), with or without ordering, would be the sort of thing that is either true or false, right or wrong? It's just a pair, after all; hardly a claim about how things stand. By contrast, a sen-

---

[10] P. F. Strawson, "On Referring" *Mind* (59) 1950: 320–44.

tence is in some sense indeed a claim about how things stand. And the contrast makes sentences look much better as bearers of truth value.

It begins to seem as if the Kaplan explication is too abstract. That is, it abstracts away from the proposition—a claim about things, after all—to yield a pair that consists of the items under discussion in the proposition. Although Kaplan often writes as if singular propositions were ordered pairs, he might nevertheless agree with what I just said, that ordered pairs are abstractions from propositions. He has often commented that ordered pairs merely *represent* singular propositions. This side of Kaplan's thought identifies propositions with ordered pairs in the way that one might identify the natural numbers with different set-theoretical constructions for different purposes. As Benacerraf argues in his classic article, "What Numbers Could Not Be,"[11] identification in this sense does not settle questions of identity, the real identity of the numbers.

On the reading of Kaplan that I am now entertaining (and in fact favor), his extensive discussion of singular propositions does not settle questions of their real identity. Kaplan is clear, of course, that they are not Fregean thoughts and that they have objects and properties "in them." In the Introduction to this book I suggested that Kaplan's conception was, by contrast with my dissertation's intuitive remarks on propositions, theoretically refined. Perhaps I was wrong; perhaps Kaplan does not tell us much about the propositions themselves.

That Kaplan's ordered pairs are merely representations of propositions can be seen in another way. Consider Kaplan's use of ordering. Why order the items paired; what does doing this accomplish? I believe it is Kaplan's attempt to model predication. In the proposition itself, a property is affirmed of the object. Ordering, I'm suggesting, is Kaplan's representation of this affirming. But it is hardly the same idea, or a clarified version thereof.[12] Russell, in his talk of

---

[11] *Philosophical Review* 74 (1965): 47–73. I discuss this and related matters in "Can What Is Asserted Be a Sentence?" in *Has Semantics Rested on a Mistake? and Other Essays* (Palo Alto, Cal.: Stanford University Press, 1995).

[12] Another possibility is that Kaplan is offering a reductive philosophical analysis or explication, *reducing* predication to ordering, and similarly reducing the proposition to an ordered pair. I don't doubt that such a reductive account is what some direct reference advocates wish to provide here, but I doubt that it's Kaplan's way. My sense—I don't have textual proof—is a matter of discussion with him over the years.

propositions, does not speak of ordered pairs but of complexes or facts. While this is also hardly an explication of the propositional (or affirmational) tie between object and property, it at least incorporates such a tie. Kaplan's ordered pair construction represents propositional contents in a way that points to some of their crucial features.

To return to the intuition with which I began this subsection, it's supposed to be the singular propositions and not their linguistic expressions that primarily bear truth values. What of this intuition? Does it survive the radical change of perspective that has been my project here?

My early rejection of Frege's sense-reference approach—like that of other direct reference people—by no means called into question Frege's broader outlook. So propositions were very much on my mind—as truth bearers and objects of the attitudes. The big question was how to make sense of propositions in the absence of Frege's senses. What seemed like a major step forward in my dissertation was the idea that the references of names, indexicals, referential descriptions could "figure in" what was asserted; references could thus play the role that Frege reserved for senses. The Fregean intuition that propositions rather than sentences were the primary truth bearers was very much alive.

Notice that the initial intuitive objection to sentences as truth bearers was not absolute. The Fregean intuition is best not understood as supposing that "true sentence" is somehow fundamentally incoherent, as if this description involved a category mistake. For one thing, it was perfectly acceptable to take sentences to be derivatively true-or-false. The intuition was more pro-proposition than it was anti-sentence. Its center of gravity was the idea that sentences derive their semantic life from propositions. Sentences symbolize propositions. The real action concerns the latter.

Now step with me outside this traditional framework. The project of this book has not been one of finding a way to think about propositional content. Indeed, I'm calling into question the utility of propositions. Propositions no longer play their key role as objects of the attitudes. Moreover, the idea of propositions as representational intermediaries seems out of sync with the direct reference antirepresentationalist tendency. Propositions have lost appeal from another direction as well: The Fregean intuition that "what is said" is the primary truth bearer has less immediate relevance than we would have previously supposed, for the colloquial "what is said" is not a proposition.[13] With ingenuity, one could probably find a way to still hold onto propositions as truth bearers. The idea seems less and less motivated, however, a little like holding onto anthropocentrism in modern times, when its supporting structures have crumbled.

It might seem that I have been trying to prepare the way for sentences as the truth bearers. But my doubts about the broader Fregean framework go so deep as to make even this avenue problematic.

Michael Dummett, in his Dewey Lectures,[14] says that the question of whether it is propositions or sentences that are the primary bearers of truth is not, in his view, a deep question. I'm not sure what he means, but I love the comment. In chapter 1, on the other hand, I say that it's a kind of paradigm philosophical question. So much has changed since then. Let me explain.

Here's how Richard Cartwright begins his classic essay "Propositions":[15]

"Botwinnik uses the French Defense"
"That's true."

To what precisely is the second referring with his demonstrative? That, says Cartwright, is the fundamental question. The bearer of truth, presumably, will be whatever it is to which he is referring. Perhaps it's the other's sentence, or his utterance, or the sense of his sentence, or a singular proposition, or . . . .

Nowadays I wonder whether Cartwright's question admits of a definite answer. I don't mean to advocate agnosticism; my issue is whether there is really some one thing that counts as the right answer, from God's point of view so to speak. My worry is conditioned by the two thoughts.

---

[13] Still there is something to the original intuition. Perhaps this is it: To say that it's the propositions, not sentences, that are primarily right or wrong is a bit like saying that what is important is not the particular words you use, but rather the point you are making. Such remarks simply emphasize the inessentiality of particular formulations. They do not concern the philosophic issue that is our concern, that of the "proper objects" of truth and falsity.

As I argued in the last sub-section, talk of "what is said" is abstract talk, but not talk that makes reference to propositional content.

[14] Michael Dummett, "The Dewey Lectures 2002: Truth and the Past," *The Journal of Philosophy* 100, no. 1 (2003): 5–53.

[15] In *Analytical Philosophy*, R. Butler (ed.), First Series (Oxford: Blackwell, 1962), pp. 82–103.

First, consulting speakers' intentions would do no good here. To suppose that there are determinate intentions that would discriminate these answers is a bit like supposing that when I look at my wife wearing something new and respond, "Beautiful!" I have a determinate intention that will discriminate whether I mean the dress, or how it suits her, or whether I mean it's really her in this dress, and so on.

Second, leaving aside speakers' intentions, there is nothing about what we are after in predicating truth or falsity that would favor one of these answers over the others, nothing that would make it intuitive that only this sort of thing and not the others bears truth. Frege (and many others including me) thought that there were intuitions about thought contents that would resolve the matter. But, as I have explained, I'm now skeptical.

I am inclined then to suppose that it doesn't much matter which of the candidate truth bearers one chooses; that the purposes for which we make truth-value ascriptions would be satisfied by any of these, modulo the adjustments. It is not built into the practice of ascribing truth that one and only one of these is the actual truth bearer.

I fear that what I'm suggesting will seem to be a form of relativism or antirealism about truth, something that denies the definiteness, stubbornness of reality. Antirealism I'm not sure about, since I'm never quite sure what it is. But my position is not relativistic. I'm not suggesting any sort of mushiness about reality, about the world. But the concept of *truth* pertains not to the world directly but to our representations of reality. And among a number of choices for privileged representation, our practice with the term 'truth' is indifferent, egalitarian. That's my suggestion.

I maintained in chapter 1 that the problem of the proper bearers of truth was a paradigm philosophical issue, since something very much like common sense leads in divergent directions. Although much has changed for me since then—Wittgenstein has become one of my teachers—my emphasis on something like common sense, on naturalness as fundamental in philosophy, remains. Naturalness is dynamic, however; what seems natural changes as one grows. Philosophers don't always like this idea. They want a criterion of truth to which any rational being might appeal. By my lights, the entire enterprise is more human, for better or worse mired in our ways.

Wittgenstein liked the analogy between his project and psycho-therapy. His point was not—except in his dark moments—that philosophical problems are pathological. It was rather that there are more or less large pictures that underlie the things we say and think about the world, pictures that are not altogether available to us—at least not without great and sustained effort. A good therapist spots the maladaptive picture much earlier than it would be wise to com-municate it to the patient. The patient, confronted too early with what he may really be thinking or feeling, is not likely to recognize it. Much of what we think in philosophy is similarly a matter of the underlying pictures. Pictures, as Rorty says, and not propositions, determine much of what we think.[16]

I, and my direct reference colleagues, rejected early what we saw as Fregean excesses. What we failed to grasp was the underlying outlook that informs Frege's philosophy, the antecedents of which stretch backward from him a couple of thousand years. My long-term project has thus been one of uncovering the deeper roots of Fregean thinking. In this book I have tried to come to terms with this underlying picture—or to begin to do so. I thus find myself looking at all sorts of things in very different ways. Cure was never the aim of psychotherapy; neither is it Wittgenstein's. Both aspire to encourage increasingly natural, unconstrained relations with the world—in one's behavior or in one's reflection.

---

[16] Cf. 166, n. 30.

Index

235